socialist
alternative

This work was published by Red Flag Books, an imprint of
Socialist Alternative, Australia's largest revolutionary socialist group.

Find out more about Socialist Alternative, read our fortnightly
newspaper, and browse our bookstore at *redflag.org.au*

First published in 1989

This edition published by Red Flag Books, Melbourne
July 2025

Red Flag Books is an imprint of Socialist Alternative
redflag.org.au

Cover design by Jeremy Laycock
Interior Layout by Luka Kiernan
Proof Reading by Tess Lee Ack

Printed by IngramSpark

Sex, Class, and Socialism

LINDSEY GERMAN

RED FLAG
BOOKS

Contents

1989 Introduction

Women's lives today would be virtually unrecognisable to the eyes of previous generations.

Nowhere is this more obvious than where women work outside the home. Here there has been a major, permanent transformation. More than nine million women in Britain now work in some form of paid employment. Many of them are married. Alongside this change in women's work have gone corresponding changes in other aspects of their lives: in marriage, motherhood and the family.

These changes have given rise to the demand for women's liberation. More than at any other time in human history, the demand that women should have a degree of equality is widely accepted throughout society.

But the situation is paradoxical. Many of those most vociferous in demanding full legal and political equality for women are also those who have failed to come to terms with the changes in women's lives over the past few decades.

So we are presented with a series of myths about women which—if they were ever true—bear little connection with present-day reality. In particular, many feminists stress the home-centredness of women's lives. This coincides with the common image of women as housewives—a view subscribed to by Tory and Labour politicians, advertising agencies and the media. Women are still regarded first and foremost as housewives, who may occasionally work in part-time jobs. Men, on the other hand, are almost universally assumed to be the breadwinners.

In recent years these ideas have led some feminists to adopt a view based on the traditional image of women as wives and mothers, to such an extent that it becomes positively reactionary. Germaine Greer, the militant feminist who wrote *The Female Eunuch* 20 years ago, now appears on television chat shows and stresses the fulfilment of motherhood. Betty Friedan, author of *The Feminine Mystique*, recently stressed that traditional "women's values" had to be taken into account as well as the desire to work outside the home:

> Feminism is not just about women having opportunities in a man's world, but having real choices. Traditional values of women, and new integration of family, home and work, should both be important.[1]

Even most feminists who are committed to socialist ideas have accepted that for women work outside the home is secondary. Studies of women at work have tended to concentrate on the difference between men's and women's jobs and therefore the divisions inside the workforce,[2] or to stress the problems women face in organising[3] alongside men at work and in the unions, rather than looking at any possibilities for unity. Some feminists subscribe to the erroneous view that women are at best reluctant participants in the labour market, to be disposed of at the whim of the employers or even of male workers.

This view was particularly fashionable in the early years of Margaret Thatcher's government, when it was argued that the recession, combined with public spending cuts, would result in mass unemployment for women. Beatrix Campbell put it forcefully in 1982 when she asserted that "the great post-war boom in female employment has been abruptly halted and thrown into reverse".[4]

Yet women increasingly live their lives in the world of paid work, not in the home. By the turn of the century, the estimated economic activity rate of women workers will be only 13 per cent below that of men, and women will make up 44 per cent of the labour force compared with 40 per cent in 1980.[5]

To anyone with an idea of what the working class actually looks like, these figures should not come as a great surprise. Women are more likely to be permanent workers, to work for more years of their lives, and to join unions than they ever were. All future projections point to married women workers being the single biggest expanding group of workers. Predicted skill shortages in the 1990s indicate an even larger proportion of married women will enter the workforce.

This book therefore attempts to look at the position of women from a very different perspective from that of most feminists. It looks at the real position of women workers today and the attitudes that follow from that. These vast changes in women's lives as workers would be impossible without a corresponding change in their ideas about themselves and in the view society holds of them.

Here the change has been as deep, if not deeper, than in the arena of work. Women have much greater freedom to control their lives and their sexuality than ever before. Traditional values and norms have much less effect than previously. Divorce is now extremely common. There has been a real increase in pre-marital cohabitation since the early 1970s.[6] The number of first marriages is a third below the 1971 figure.[7]

---

1. Betty Friedan, quoted in "Careering off the Mummy Track", in *The Guardian* (London) 6 April 1989.
2. See for example Dex; Abbott and Sapsford, chapter 1; Campbell and Coote, chapter 2.
3. Campbell (1984), pp.150–2.
4. Campbell and Coote, p.74.
5. Labour Force Survey in *Employment Gazette* (Department of Employment: London), April 1989.
6. *General Household Survey 1983* (Office of Populations, Censuses and Surveys: London).
7. *Social Trends 1986* (Central Statistical Office: London).

Illegitimate births in England and Wales more than doubled between 1961 and 1984 (despite the much wider availability of abortion and contraception during those years than before) and the number of illegitimate births registered in the name of both parents rose from 38 per cent to 63 per cent.[8] This demonstrates a much greater willingness for both parents to decide to have a child outside marriage—and a much more relaxed attitude to illegitimacy than a generation ago.

A major trend throughout the advanced capitalist countries in the years since 1945 and the end of the Second World War has been for women to decide to have fewer children and to have them later in life. The annual birthrate per 1,000 of the population is 12.8 today, compared with 15.5 in 1951.[9] The average number of children per family today is 1.8.[10] The figures demonstrate an obvious fact: that women no longer see their role as staying at home after marriage to care for children while the man goes out to work.

This also explains the figures for abortion and contraception. Three-quarters of all women aged between 18 and 44 use contraception. There are two favoured methods: the pill, used by 28 per cent of women in this age group—and by a majority of younger women, and sterilisation (of the woman or of her partner), which was chosen by 22 per cent of women in the age group but was favoured by older women.[11] Obviously the majority of sexually active women favour some form of contraception and the methods used indicate that most seek long-term solutions. Legal abortions, too, have risen dramatically, from 54,157 in 1969 to 171,873 in 1985.[12]

The changes in women's attitudes clearly have roots in their changed economic role. The state has also been important in legitimising certain reforms for women and so accelerating the speed with which ideas have changed. The Abortion Act of 1967, the Divorce Reform Act of 1971, the free and widespread availability of contraception, even the inadequate Equal Pay and Sex Discrimination Acts, all helped to change the attitudes of millions and to heighten awareness of at least a formal right to equality.

Even attitudes towards work have changed. An American study shows that while in 1957 a quarter of employed wives questioned wanted to be in the home full-time, the percentage preferring full-time housework by 1976 had dropped to only 3 per cent.[13] A more recent British study showed that nearly half of all women who worked full-time said that they shared the housework equally with their husbands.[14]

One further feature of economic development since the Second World War has dramatically affected the position of women: the expansion of higher education. This should not be exaggerated: for most, the prospects for advancement through education and "career" jobs are still small. Only 1 per cent of the children of unskilled manual workers,

---

8. *Social Trends 1986.*
9. *Equal Opportunities Commission Report 1984* (London).
10. *General Household Survey 1983.*
11. *General Household Survey 1983.*
12. *Abortion Statistics 1985* (Office of Populations, Censuses and Surveys: London).
13. Iglehart, p.27.
14. Martin and Roberts.

for example, get to university.[15] But for a thin layer of the working class (especially those with white-collar jobs) and of the lower middle class, this expansion of education opened up new prospects. A hitherto undreamt-of number of women, hundreds of thousands, have been able to gain qualifications and entry into more skilled jobs, such as teaching or social work. These jobs tend to command higher status and often better rates of pay than traditional women's work.

The period of educational expansion coincided with the growth in the number of women entering the workforce. So whereas in 1953–54 there were 17,300 women at university, by 1968–69 this had risen to 50,200.[16]

All these factors have contributed to an awareness about social and political issues concerning women. At one end of the spectrum this is reflected in a numerically fairly small but extremely influential feminist movement, at the other by the acceptance of general ideas of equality on a mass scale (inside education, in women's magazines and so on).

How then do we explain the continuing oppression of women? All the changes, all the advances, and entry into the workforce have not been the key to unlock real liberation for working-class women. Women's oppression is still clearly a major feature of capitalist society.

At the heart of that oppression lies the institution of the family. It is the family which shapes women's role in the workforce. It ensures that women's wages remain substantially lower than those of men, that jobs are often segregated on gender lines, that child care is not socialised but remains the responsibility of the individual family, that the idea of the family wage is dominant, with all that means for women's low pay. In all these cases the hidden assumption is there: that women have two roles—one social in the world of work, the other privatised inside the home. It is this contradiction which explains women's oppression today.

The contradiction also explains the many false images of women. The family's existence is ensured precisely because society regards what women do outside the home as abnormal or additional to their main role as wives and mothers. Hence the attitude that women are inferior remains widespread. Yet false images and sexist attitudes are only manifestations of women's oppression. They cannot explain why it exists. This is precisely the trap that many feminists fall into. By confusing symptoms with causes they conclude that sexist behaviour can be eradicated through heightened awareness; unequal pay can be changed by legislation; violence can be dealt with by women's refuges. As recent years have shown, despite the limited advances that all these reforms can bring, they leave the basic structures of oppression untouched.

Most people on the left explain this failure of reform by the existence of patriarchy—seen as an unchanging structure of male domination acting independently of class relations. Yet there is no need to look outside class society in order to explain oppression.

15. *Social Trends 1986.*
16. *Social Trends 1970.*

The explanation lies crucially in the role that the family plays in the reproduction of labour power. This has been true for all class societies where the freedom of women has been subordinated to the needs of production. Despite the changes between various modes of production the oppression of women has remained a feature of all class societies, and it is true of the capitalist mode of production today.

Marx and Engels thought the proletarian family—and consequently the oppression of working-class women—would disappear as capitalism advanced. To understand why this did not happen, we need to understand what happened to the working-class family under the impact of the Industrial Revolution and the untrammelled advance of capitalism. We also need to look at why the family continues to exist today.

The first part of this book attempts to deal with these questions. It attempts to show that the family is not defined by a static relationship known as "patriarchy" but, rather, by the changing demands of the mode of production. The family cannot therefore be understood apart from classes and social production. The second part of the book looks at the role of women in the British working-class movement, and at the impact of oppression on women as workers. It considers the Labour Party and the modern women's movement. Why have working-class women never found a real voice through these organisations? Have these ever really represented working women's interests?

Finally I try to examine the potential working-class women have for changing the world, alongside the male half of the working class. What are the barriers to this change? If such change comes, will women be liberated alongside men? In short, what is the revolutionary answer to women's oppression?

Part I: The changing family

CHAPTER ONE

The family under capitalism

The past 200 years have seen greater changes in women's lives than in the whole of previous human history. The development of capitalism has brought with it massive technological advances which have totally altered every aspect of work, home life, education and even sexuality. But while the lives of individual women have improved, women's oppression still remains a central feature of capitalism. That oppression has meant that even fundamental social changes have not always given women equal access to work, education or the vote. These have all been granted grudgingly, if at all.

The reasons for women's continuing oppression are complex. They lie most fundamentally in the nature of the family under capitalism. Yet the family is not unchanging. Exactly the opposite is true. The family itself is a product of the division of society into classes, but its particular form depends on the type of class society—the particular mode of production—in which it exists. The way men and women work to produce their subsistence determines the nature of reproduction in that society.

Any transition from one mode of production to another—for example from feudalism to capitalism—leads to, and requires, an upheaval in the family. The development of capitalism—and the huge impetus given to its spread by the Industrial Revolution—led to massive changes in the nature of the family. Women's oppression today can only be understood by reference to these changes brought about by the capitalist mode of production. The capitalist production process threw up such new and different ways of working that contemporary commentators were led to extreme conclusions. Some bemoaned the passing of the old society while others—including the young Marx and Engels and the utopian socialists—believed they were witnessing a new dawn for women. Capitalism's rapid development led to a massive expansion of the world's economic resources and thus to the possibility of greater freedom for women.

Early capitalist society both fulfilled and denied its promise. Women's lives did indeed change radically. They moved from domestic industry to the factory or the mill. In the process the old patriarchal family—based on production around the home and organised through the usually male head of the household—was broken down. As wage labourers, women acquired a degree of social and financial independence not often found in the old agricultural society.

At times in the first half of the nineteenth century it appeared the family of the new industrial working class was weakening, if not disappearing altogether. But it did not disappear. Instead it maintained and eventually reasserted itself. The second half of the nineteenth century saw a certain heightening and even celebration of family life—with the development of "family values" which remain with us today.

Perhaps the most common explanation for this is that the change in the mode of production from feudalism to capitalism didn't change the family form or women's lives within the family. This is certainly the dominant "common-sense" view put forward in society today. The family is seen as something eternal and unchanging. Right-wing ideologues such as Ferdinand Mount, for example, subscribe to this view.[1] But it is totally erroneous.

The years at the end of the eighteenth century and the beginning of the nineteenth were ones of intense social upheaval. They saw a population moved—often forcibly—from the land and into the cities. They saw England change from a predominantly agricultural to a predominantly industrial society—and they saw capitalism transform the methods of both agriculture and industry. There was a population explosion, and mass migration. Some traditional types of work or occupations disappeared almost completely, while new ones sprang up. Work which traditionally had been done by women sometimes became the preserve of men; other men's jobs became women's. This was the case with spinning and weaving in the textile industry.

It would have been truly remarkable if the old form of family had survived such changes. It did not. The family underwent great change. Again, certain assumptions are usually made about these changes. It is commonly asserted, for example, that feudalism was characterised by a large "extended" family while capitalism ushered in the small nuclear family. The picture is not nearly so simple. In the more developed parts of western Europe, in later feudal society, the family was often quite small. Although the household might contain several generations, it tended not to spread horizontally across one generation. Large extended families of several generations, and of all the brothers of one generation, were much more common in eastern Europe.

Conflicting evidence exists on these questions and there were obviously big variations in the family, depending on a whole range of factors: geography, the stage of development and type of agricultural labour practised and other forms of production.[2] The family in early modern England, for example, was not greatly different in size and structure from the family which exists under capitalism.

The main difference between the capitalist and pre-capitalist family lies not in their size and composition but whether they were units of *production*.

In England in 1750 the primary means by which men and women earned their living was by working the land. The family in which they lived had at least some productive features, where goods were produced for consumption and sometimes for sale. This

---

1. Mount, chapter 2.
2. See for example Shorter; Stone; Aries.

production defined the woman's role within the family, ensuring that women remained dependent on the male head of the household for their immediate sustenance and, indeed, for their livelihood.

Work tended to be centred around the home. Both married and single women would be employed—although often at different tasks. Since married women's work was integral to the family, it was taken for granted that they would work, as long as they were healthy and able. There was no question of married women being unsuited to productive work, or that their role as wives and mothers disqualified them from production: "not till the home ceased to be the main centre of economic activity did the married woman worker become an object of pity or disapprobation".[3]

Women's work was considered central whether the family was agriculturally based or in one of the domestic industries, such us the putting-out system in textiles. Here too there was a strict division of labour: spinners of yarn were women, handloom weavers were men, while children were involved in production when old enough to perform basic tasks.

The transformation of the old family took different forms, depending on what form of production underpinned it. In agriculture, the revolution of the late eighteenth century was brutal. The development of large-scale capitalistic methods of farming involved the destruction of old methods and means of livelihood. Primarily this meant the development of arable farming at the expense of pasture and dairying and the enclosure of the common lands. The changes in dairying—now no longer geared to small-scale domestic production but to the needs of the burgeoning cities—tended to marginalise women from their traditional role. New methods of cheese-making, for example, employed men to turn the larger and heavier cheeses.

These changes in agricultural production transformed women's lives. For some, there was a change for the better. The wives and families of those farmers who benefited financially from the agricultural revolution dropped their productive role and accustomed themselves to a comfortable life of leisure. For other, poorer, farmers' wives, social mobility operated in a different direction. Deprived of their means of livelihood, many were thrown into poverty and sometimes destitution.[4]

Enclosure of the common land had even more severe consequences. It took the means of livelihood, and especially the source of fuel and of some food, from many poor farmers. Often forced to become day labourers, they were totally dependent on the wealthy landowners and farmers for their livelihood. All too often such dependence resulted in appalling poverty. By the start of the nineteenth century the wages of most agricultural labourers were so low that it had become "almost impossible for a married labourer ... to support his family without aid".[5]

---

3. Hewitt, p.3.
4. For a detailed description of this period see Pinchbeck, Section 1.
5. Pinchbeck, p.69.

Most labourers' families relied on poor relief to survive—but it was barely survival. The effects on family life were devastating. Wages were depressed, especially in the south of England, where labourers' families lived on a diet of bread, cheese and tea. Cooking was impossible for many, since fuel was not easily available. The high cost of wheat meant that even this basic diet was sometimes unobtainable. It is hardly surprising that these attacks on the rural workforce led to intense demoralisation and misery:

> Unable to give warmth, comfort and any variety of food to her family, the housewife lost interest and the condition of the home went from bad to worse. In despair the labourer sought comfort at the ale-house and his wife the solace of tea-drinking with her neighbours.[6]

Many families were forced onto poor relief, and often to vagrancy. A world which had seemed settled was changing with unbelievable speed. Fewer and fewer people owned the land and those denied access to it had either to work for the landowners at low wages, or look elsewhere. They formed the core of the emerging industrial working class in the cities. In the countryside they became the rural poor, dependent on relief to supplement their wages.

The development of wide-scale factory production had an equally devastating effect on the domestic textile industry. This had been based on the "putting-out" system, where employers supplied raw materials to be worked on by the family in the home. They then paid for the finished product. In the last decades of the eighteenth century a number of inventions transformed this industry. The spinning jenny, the mule and the water frame encouraged the transfer of textile production from the home to the factory. Textile production became the motor of the Industrial Revolution.

At first women were adversely affected by these changes. Mule spinning in the factory was performed by men, whereas women had been spinners in domestic industry. But with further technological advances at the beginning of the nineteenth century, the traditional male domain of handloom weaving came under severe attack. This radically affected the traditional division of labour within the family. The factory owners favoured women and children as employees, rather than men.

These workers were at first drawn not from families traditionally employed in textiles but from "agriculturalists unsettled by the agrarian revolution, from domestic servants, the unskilled of all trades and parish paupers".[7] The handloom weavers and their families put up bitter resistance, refusing enter to the factories and mills. Within a generation, however, the wives and daughters of weavers were also working there:

> The majority of girls who attended the power looms in the 'thirties and 'forties were the daughters of distressed handloom weavers who entered the factory to better their prospects; and the married women, more often than not, were wives of weavers, forced by bitter necessity to leave their homes.[8]

---

6. Pinchbeck, p.51.
7. Pinchbeck, p.184.
8. Pinchbeck, p.185.

At first, the process of change for the family itself did not seem too severe. Its structure was often reflected in the early factories, with the head of the household hiring his own children to work for him. But as the textile industry grew—especially following the coming of the power loom in the 1820s—so the men became increasingly marginalised economically.

In the 1820s and 1830s, even when whole families were employed, the man often earned less than his wife or children and sometimes found employment at the mill only as a porter.[9] These years also heralded a major change in the economic relationship between the father and his children. Not only were women and children more in demand than men, they were now recruited to work "by the masters, not the operatives".[10] Now every member of the family was thrown onto the labour market to earn a wage, dependent on his or her wage in order to live. So the family, instead of forming a productive domestic unit, now comprised a collection of individual wage labourers: "The special contribution which capitalist production relations made to the family was its atomisation. Each member of the family stood separately and alone in the labour market".[11]

This broke many of the ties of the old patriarchal family. Where it was common for the woman or even the older children in a family to be the sole or main breadwinner, all sorts of accepted norms and values were turned on their heads. Friedrich Engels pointed out that for the Manchester working class in the 1840s "the employment of the wife dissolves the family utterly and of necessity". He goes on:

> In many cases the family is not wholly dissolved by the employment of the wife, but turned upside down. The wife supports the family, the husband sits at home, tends the children, sweeps the room and cooks.[12]

To many observers, it appeared that the working-class family was collapsing or, at least, slowly disintegrating. The wife and children no longer depended on old patriarchal authority. Their wages and working lives gave them a degree of independence which they had never had previously. The woman's labour was no longer characterised predominantly by what she did in the home. Not only had the established sexual division of labour broken down, but some of the traditional domestic tasks were now transferred onto the market to be bought and sold as commodities. A contemporary report noted in 1862 that "a very large class of women derive their maintenance entirely by providing for the wants of the mill hands".[13] Recent studies have reinforced the point:

> In textile districts ... the high level of women's employment and aggregate family income meant that practices like eating shop-made pies and puddings, and having the day-care of infants, the washing and basic cleaning done by women who specialised in these jobs were common among the working class.[14]

9. See Smelser, p.202.
10. Smelser, p.200.
11. Ramelson, p.24.
12. Engels (1973), p.182. See also Hall.
13. Ellen Barlee on her visit to Lancashire, quoted in Hewitt, pp.63-4.
14. Barrett and McIntosh, "The family wage", in Whitelegg, p.74.

Marx and Engels on the family

The working-class family appeared in a precarious state by the 1840s. Certainly Marx and Engels at this time doubted its survival. But from the very beginning they made a crucial class distinction when considering the family. In the *Communist Manifesto*, published in 1848, they described this:

> On what foundation is the present family, the bourgeois family, based? On capital, on private gain. In its completely developed form this family exists only among the bourgeoisie. But this state of things finds its complement in the practical absence of the family among the proletarians.[15]

Their analysis was based partly on empirical observation, especially the study by Engels of Manchester workers in his book *The Condition of the Working Class in England*. The horrendous lives of most factory workers made any talk of family life laughable. However the starting point for Marx and Engels' analysis was the connection between the family and private property. That the working class had no property meant there was no real material basis for the working-class family. This lack of property they saw as the basis for the family's abolition. Engels, writing nearly 40 years later, linked the rise of class society with the rise of the family and therefore of women's oppression:

> The first class antagonism that appears in history coincides with the development of the antagonism between men and women in monogamous marriage, and the first class oppression coincides with that of the female sex by the male.[16]

Both Marx and Engels stressed where inequality lay: in the division of labour in class society, of which the sexual division of labour is a major part. This therefore gives rise to the unequal possession of property within society as a whole. The first form of that property lies within the family itself, "where wife and children are the slaves of the husband. This latent slavery in the family, though still very crude, is the first property".[17]

The existence of a new sort of family, one not based on property, was therefore a breakthrough in the liberation of women, or at least for working-class women. Marx and Engels did not, however, believe that the family would disappear just like that, despite what is sometimes imputed to them. For the bourgeoisie the family became, if anything, a stronger economic tie. Work outside the home was the prerogative of bourgeois men. Their wives and daughters were expected to live totally in the sphere of the private, leading leisurely and privileged but stultifying and narrow lives. Monogamy was vital to ensure inheritance. This was the material basis for the bourgeois family—ensuring that the capitalist's wealth passed to his legal heirs. It therefore continued to exist and flourish.

But even for the working class, there was a difference between the collapse of the old patriarchal family, with its values and norms, and its total abolition under capitalism. In

---

15. Marx and Engels, (1968), pp.49–50.
16. Engels (1978), p.75.
17. Marx and Engels (1964), p.44.

particular, reversing the sex roles so the woman became the breadwinner and the man the homemaker did little to remedy the problems. It merely highlighted the artificial position of the old family:

> So total a reversal of the position of the sexes can have come to pass only because the sexes have been placed in a false position from the beginning. If the reign of the wife over the husband, as inevitably brought about by the factory system, is inhuman, the pristine role of the husband over the wife must have been inhuman too ... If the family of our present society is being thus dissolved, this dissolution merely shows that, at bottom, the binding tie of this family was not family affection, but private interest lurking under the cloak of a pretended community of possessions.[18]

So the dissolution of the family did not mean the creation of a free and equal union between individuals, but the disappearance of old property bonds. The great indictment of capitalism is that this process leads not to happiness and genuine freedom, but to the horrendous conditions under which the working class of early industrial England lived. According to Engels, the full flowering of relationships can only come with a classless society: "Full freedom of marriage can therefore only be generally established when the abolition of capitalist production and of the property relations created by it has removed all the accompanying economic considerations".[19]

But what if the classless society did not materialise? What would happen to the family then? The growth of capitalism as a world system had major implications for the development of the working-class family. Far from the family disappearing, both the capitalist class and the working class acted in order to stabilise and shore it up. This development characterised the second half of the nineteenth century—and ensured that women's oppression remained a reality.

The re-establishment of the family

In the 1830s and 1840s the whole family worked where possible as wage labourers. Relatively large numbers of married women worked; so did young children, and sometimes very young children.[20] The hours that the women worked left them little enough time to sleep, let alone attend to domestic work. It was common to spend over 12 hours a day at work. With travelling time and meal breaks this stretched to 14 or 15 hours.[21]

Childbirth was dangerous—and the danger was exacerbated by factory work. Women were expected back at their machines very soon after confinement. Young babies were suckled with pap, not with mother's milk. The minders of older children who were still too young to work drugged their charges with laudanum-based patent medicines to keep them quiet.

---

18. Engels (1973), p.184.
19. Engels (1978), p.94.
20. See Anderson, p.115; Burr Litchfield, p.182; and Hewitt, chapter 8.
21. Hewitt, pp.21–2.

Children worked in the mills from the age of four or five. Marx's *Capital* describes the horrors of the early factory system: the high infant mortality, the maiming of children and the incredible injuries which befell so many of the early factory workers. He pointed to the connection between women working outside the home and infant mortality. So in Manchester more than a quarter of all infants died before the age of one in the early 1860s. Such death rates were not unique to the big cities. Wisbech in the Fens, a centre of capitalist agriculture where women worked as day labourers in the notorious gang system, had an infant death rate virtually as high as Manchester. The common factor was "the employment of the mothers away from their homes, and the neglect and maltreatment arising from their absence, which consists in such things as insufficient nourishment, unsuitable food and dosing with opiates".[22]

Such conditions—which extended to housing, adulterated food, factory accidents, poor physical welfare and every area of working-class life—caused social upheaval among the working class. The great Chartist movement was in part a protest at such conditions in the 1830s and 1840s. Such was the scale of misery and deprivation that even many bourgeois commentators and philanthropists were moved to protest. Increasingly there were calls for young children, and then women, either not to work at all or to have their hours and conditions legally controlled.

The structural changes to the workforce brought about in part by the protective legislation of these decades had a major impact on the developing working class and its family. In addition the idea of a family wage—a wage which could be paid to the head of the household to cover the costs of reproduction of the whole family—gained resonance among both workers and employers. Finally the new and hated Poor Law of 1834 had a profound effect on the ideology of the family.

Protective legislation

Early legislation was concerned with two aspects of work: the reduction of hours and the removal of certain sections of workers from some industries, predominantly mining. In both cases the concern of the legislators was firstly with the conditions of children. Only later were women included in legislation to reduce working hours.

So the Factory Act of 1833 was applied to children and young persons. No child under nine could work at all; those between nine and 13 could work no more than eight hours; those between 13 and 18 could work no more than 12 hours; and no one under 18 could work nights. The Act was prone to large-scale evasion by the employers. Where they could not evade it directly, they established an oppressive double shift system for the children.

Eleven years later, with the Factory Act of 1844, women were placed in the same category as young people and forbidden to work nights or for longer than 12 hours. In reality this tended to reduce the hours of men to around 12 hours as well. In. 1847

22.   Marx (1976), p.521.

a further Act called for a 10-hour day for all women and young persons, to take effect from 1 May 1848.

Every attempt to shorten the day was met by bitter resistance from the employers. The Acts were not enforceable in some parts of the country because the magistrates, often factory owners themselves, refused to convict other factory owners. Where they failed to prevent the restriction in hours, they instead responded by cutting wages. Nonetheless, despite these rearguard battles, the Acts became law and eventually succeeded in reducing the length of the working day.

It would seem that the major reasons for this reduction lay in the horrific conditions of the working class at the time, and in the conflict of interests among the employing class. While those factory owners most directly affected raised an outcry, other more far-seeing members of the bourgeoisie understood that they could benefit from slightly better conditions for working people: this could have rapid political results and would ultimately result in a healthier and more productive workforce.

Marx gave some weight to these considerations when writing on the passage of the 1844 Act:

> However much the individual manufacturer might like to give free rein to his old lust for gain, the spokesmen and political leaders of the manufacturing class ordered a change in attitude and language towards the workers. They had started their campaign to repeal the Corn Laws, and they needed the workers to help them to victory![23]

If the capitalist class was to maintain its extraction of surplus value from the working class, then its interests lay in a certain restructuring of the working class in order to create a more skilled and more educated workforce, which was better cared for and healthier. This could help to increase the rate of exploitation. These interests coincided with the demands of men and women workers who, understandably, were constantly struggling to reduce the hours they had to work. Protective legislation meant that fewer family members would have to work the lengthy hours which were then the norm. A reduction of hours also brought benefits for the working-class family. Margaret Hewitt describes this improvement following the 1847 Act: "The extra hour's freedom from the mill ... seems to have been almost exclusively devoted to the better care of their homes and families".[24]

However the reduction in hours didn't in itself alter the structure of the working-class family.[25] What it did do was encourage the view that women should not have to work. This in turn strengthened the idea that women should be in the home—even if most women still worked outside it.

A similar situation occurred with the 1842 legislation which prevented women from working underground in coal mines. This was the result of the Mines Commission

---

23. Marx (1976), p.393.
24. Hewitt, p.25.
25. Smelser (p.241) argues that the 1833 Act, by reducing the hours worked by children under 13 to eight, broke the relationship between the father—whose hours were not similarly reduced—and the child. Thus the child broke with the traditional family division of labour.

investigation of abuses of child labour underground. Women were added to its brief only in 1841, apparently as a result of the "numerous petitions on the subject [which] were addressed to parliament from Lancashire and Yorkshire towns".[26] The Commission's Report in 1842 revealed the shocking conditions of employment in many of the mines. Women and children crawled like animals along wet tunnels. Apart from the physical consequences to women themselves, the damage to pregnancy and childbirth was immense. Many women had miscarriages or stillbirths. Those who overcame the obstacles and successfully delivered were back at work in a few days.

There was an outcry among middle- and upper-class society in London due to the publicity the report received. There was much feeling—especially among the middle classes—that the law should prohibit women's work in the mines. Again, however, there were attempts by the mine-owners and their allies to block the legislation in parliament. They failed, but in certain areas women continued to work in the pits for some years afterwards—even dressing as men to do so. And in Wigan the pitbrow lasses continued working until well into the twentieth century. These instances would suggest that some women workers resisted exclusion from the mines quite strongly.

A common argument today is that women were forced out of this employment by an alliance of capitalists and male workers. The capitalists stood to gain, it is argued, from the improved reproduction of labour power. The male workers stood to gain directly from taking women's jobs; and from better personal services in the home. However, even the Report of 1842 points towards other conclusions.

The employment of women in coal-mining was, even in the 1840s, by no means universal. It was confined to the West Riding of Yorkshire, Lancashire and Cheshire, East Scotland and South Wales.[27] This was partly due to the nature of the industry in different areas and partly due to the fact that where there were other jobs available women tended to take them. There was also a disparity between the numbers of women employed in mining in these areas. There were only 22 adult women per thousand men in Yorkshire, while there were 338 per thousand in east Scotland.[28] In addition the division of labour was such that men and women did different work within the pits—in the hewing system, women and children transported coal while men did the hewing (cutting) of coal,[29] and employment tended to be based on a family system—the hewer being responsible for those working on the cutting and transport of coal.[30]

It is therefore simply not true that men and women workers were in *direct competition* for jobs in the coalfields. It is not even clear that men benefited financially from women's exclusion in the short term. Ivy Pinchbeck argues, for example, that they did not gain financially, since they "depended on the support of women and children to make up for

---

26. Pinchbeck, p.244.
27. Royal Commission Report 1842, quoted in Pinchbeck, p.244.
28. See Humphries (1981), p.7; also Pinchbeck, p.247.
29. Humphries (1981), pp.8–9.
30. Humphries (1981), p.8.

their own irregular labour. But apart from the financial loss, miners stood to benefit by improvements in their own conditions".[31]

She goes on to say that some male miners wanted women out of the pits to prevent their cheap labour from undercutting wages and conditions. However Jane Humphries, in her excellent article on the 1842 Act and its consequences, goes so far as to say that it was in the men's interest to oppose protective legislation, because they lost income which otherwise their wives and daughters would have earned, and therefore the overall income of the family fell.[32] In addition, the fact that men earned higher wages and often worked fewer hours than women meant they had no real material interest in supplanting women.[33]

Yet there was no real opposition from male workers to women leaving the pits. The fact that men, however reluctantly, went along with this exclusion has led many to see the workings of "patriarchal privilege" in this piece of protective legislation. In reality, like the reduction in hours, the acceptance of mines legislation by the working class was an attempt to improve the living standards of the working class and its family in the face of a hostile world.

There is little doubt that much of the impetus for protective legislation came from the employing class. Some of the employers were genuinely shocked by the conditions reported in 1842. The "immorality" of the coal mines was stressed time and again. Victorian morality was offended by the fact that women worked underground naked from the waist up. However the attacks on immorality did not stem from a concern with working-class living standards. Rather they were attempts to impose discipline and control over a new and young industrial workforce. The growth of Chartism in the 1830s and 1840s increased the ruling-class fear of workers, and therefore increased their willingness to look for new forms of control.

Representatives of management felt that a prohibition on female and child labour, by making colliers responsible for the whole of family maintenance, would force them to change their irresponsible habits.[34]

Thus what was involved was not simply a restructuring of the coal mining industry by the capitalist class, but also an attempt to impose cohesion, discipline and a more effective "work ethic" on an increasingly important workforce. Parallels can be drawn with the imposition of stricter timekeeping and greater management control around the same period.[35]

Protective legislation helped to shape the sexual division of labour in industry. But its impact should not be overestimated. No aspect of the legislation was central in restructuring the female working class. Only a small minority of women worked in mining, or in the other industries such as glassblowing, where protective laws were applied. The

---

31. Pinchbeck, p.264.
32. Humphries(1981), p.15.
33. Humphries (1977), p.36.
34. Humphries (1981), p.23.
35. Humphries (1981), p.23.

largest groups of women by far were employed either in textiles or in domestic service. Restrictions on hours did not seriously affect their employment.

But the legacy of both sets of laws was to leave its mark on future patterns of employment. Women in coal-mining areas—often isolated from other work opportunities—faced unemployment, early marriage or migration to other areas.[36] This reinforced a strict division of labour inside the coal-mining family. It was increasingly argued that there was work which women could not or should not do. This in turn reinforced rigidity and division inside the labour market. Ideologically, of course, protective legislation—even though it only seriously affected a minority—gave a great boost to the family and the notion of woman as wife and mother rather than worker.

The Poor Law

A second body of legislation which was to have a devastating effect on working-class life was the Poor Law Amendment Act of 1834. Poor or parish relief had existed since Elizabethan times. In 1834 it was withdrawn, in an attempt to force poor labourers into even lower-paid work. Prior to 1834, most agricultural labourers were dependent on the parish to supplement their wages. But after the new Poor Law those who could not work, or could not find work, were dragooned into workhouses. The conditions of these "Poor Law Bastilles" were exactly those described by Dickens and other contemporary writers. Engels called them "the most repulsive residence".[37]

The purpose of the law was to ensure sufficient cheap wage labour for the new industries and for capitalist agriculture. Workers would accept abysmal wages because the alternatives were so dire. This was indeed what happened, at least partially. So there was an increase in women working the land in East Anglia after 1834, with consequently lowered agricultural wages: "after 1834 the earnings of women and children allowed married men to be employed for wages on which they could not otherwise have lived".[38]

A further consequence of the workhouse was the systematic breaking up of families unfortunate enough to fall within its jurisdiction. Engels graphically described what that meant:

> To prevent the "superfluous" from multiplying, and "demoralised" parents from influencing their children, families are broken up; the husband is placed in one wing, the wife in another, the children in a third, and they are permitted to see one another only at stated times after long intervals, and then only when they have, in the opinion of the officials, behaved well.[39]

Workers did everything they could to stay out of the workhouses, and nurtured a hatred for them which lingered even up to their abolition a century later. The system contributed greatly to the breaking up of the working-class family. Anyone who lost their livelihood

---

36. See Gittins (1982), p.39.
37. Engels (1973), p.323.
38. Pinchbeck, p.102.
39. Engels (1973), p.324.

or fell into destitution was likely to lose their family as well as everything else. It was the forcible separation of the members of the family which was most hated.

But although in the short term the law worked to break up families, in the longer term it also posed the question of what was the alternative to the family. The capitalist class saw two major ways of otherwise supporting those members of the working class who could not support themselves: the workhouse or private charity. Workers, on the other hand, felt there had to be a better way than this of caring for the old, the sick and the orphaned: state institutions manifestly could not be relied on to do so.

It is hardly surprising that the family appeared as a more attractive proposition. A family which had adequate time and resources to care for all its members, where not all its members had to sell themselves on the labour market, where there was time for basic education, and which provided a decent home and safer childbirth for women, became part of working-class aspirations.

And it appeared there was a way of achieving these improved living conditions: the demand for a single wage high enough to keep the male worker and his wife and children in reasonable conditions, the family wage.

The family wage

The idea of the family wage appealed, for different reasons, to both employers and workers. For the working class, its attraction was that the woman in particular would not have to work outside the home. This would end some of the unpalatable aspects of industrial life. Above all, it would both enable the mother to care adequately for the children, and protect children themselves from the worst aspects of waged work. All the horrors of children's injuries and premature deaths would theoretically become a thing of the past.

If, in addition to this, married women could be removed from the labour market, then many considered that there would be a radical increase in the living standards of the working class. Nursing or pregnant mothers would be much less likely to suffer illness, maiming or deformity, as too would their babies. A secondary but no doubt important factor was that labour performed in the home—a near-impossible task when the woman too worked more than 12 hours a day away from the home—would improve the living conditions of all workers.

There is much evidence to suggest that such ideas provided an impetus for the demand for the family wage. After all, the very existence of the working-class family was at stake.[40] But it is unlikely that these factors alone were responsible. If the working class simply wanted more time, leisure and so on, the traditional demands for shorter hours and higher wages could have achieved much the same results.

---

40. See Brenner, who argues that in a sense the reproduction of the working class was endangered by industrial capitalism. See also Humphries (1977).

In fact the call for the family wage reflected the overall wages situation in the early nineteenth century. The development of capitalism had firstly cheapened the value of labour power by drawing all members of the family into wage labour; then women workers were often used to undercut the wages of men. The cheapening of labour-power, explained Marx, was the result of the large-scale machinery constantly being introduced by the factory owners:

> The value of labour-power was determined, not only by labour the time necessary to maintain the individual adult worker, but also by that necessary to maintain his family. Machinery, by throwing every member of that family onto the labour market, spreads the value of the man's labour-power over his whole family. It thus depreciates it. To purchase the labour-power of a family of four workers may perhaps cost more than it formerly did to purchase the labour-power of the head of the family, but, in return, four days' labour takes the place of one day's, and the price falls in proportion to the excess of the surplus labour of four over the surplus labour of one. In order that the family may live, four people must now provide not only labour for the capitalist, but also surplus labour.[41]

This cheapening of the value of labour-power meant that in order for the working-class family to survive, more members of that family had to work, and for lower wages. The capitalist class was quick to take advantage of this situation by paying lower wages to women and children and using this to undercut the wages of men. The constant competition between different capitalists accelerated this process. Often the consequences were severe for the workers concerned, as this example (taken from a contemporary article) of the demise of a skilled printworker in the 1830s shows:

> Unemployment followed the introduction of new print machinery into his workshop; children weeping with hunger; days looking fruitlessly for work and nights of drunken despair in the pub; followed at last by eviction and homelessness.[42]

This process was common. The introduction of new machinery and technological changes transformed many trades: former craftsmen were displaced by unskilled machine operatives, often women and children at much lower wages. There is no question that the employment of this cheap labour caused antagonism between the sexes. Sometimes women aroused the anger of men by working for only half their rate of pay.[43]

Sometimes whole industries were restructured to incorporate women workers, as in the Staffordshire pottery industry.[44] Women became an ever larger proportion of the workforce—and the men correctly feared such competition. In some industries female undercutting of wages led to strike action by the men against the women. This was true of the London tailors in 1834.[45] However it is also true, as Ivy Pinchbeck points out,

41. Marx (1976), p.518.
42. Quoted in Taylor, p.203.
43. Drake, p.6.
44. Hewitt, p.18.
45. Taylor, p.114.

that the threat to men by women was greater in terms of lowering wages than actually through taking their jobs.[46]

Against this background the demand for the family wage became inextricably bound up with the defence of working-class living standards. Many workers harked back to a world where their old skills and occupations had brought them a decent living. If the future was to be an improvement, then it should be through a higher wage for men which could cover the cost of the family's reproduction.

The issue was also, to a certain degree, one of control. Even in early manufacturing, there had been a degree of subcontracting in wage labour. Hewers and buttymen were responsible for recruiting certain sorts of labour in the pits.[47] Parts of the cotton industry operated similarly: in Preston in 1816, more than half those under 18 in the mills were paid by the spinners and rovers, not the millowners.[48] This meant control of the children's (and sometimes the women's) labour was in the hands of the family head—who received a wage to cover the cost of reproduction of the whole family. He was able to regulate the labour done, so the level of naked exploitation was to a limited extent mediated by parental control.

This idea of family control involved all sorts of reactionary notions. It enforced unequal relations between individual family members. But it was also double-edged, as Jane Humphries has argued: "One of the few sources of working-class control over the supply of labour lay in the levers that could be brought to bear on the labour supplied by married women". The tragedy of this situation was that "action could not be controlled on a class basis but had to be regulated systematically on the basis of female labour, so reinforcing sex-based regulations of dominance and subordination".[49]

The family wage came to be viewed as a means by which the competition of cheap labour could be diminished, and the supply of labour regulated.

However the attraction of the family wage was not simply for the working class. It increasingly fitted with many of the ideas of the bourgeoisie. The early capitalists had been content and even eager to employ women and children as cheap flexible labour and so maximise their profits. This phase of capitalism did not last. As the accumulation of capital continued, so the pre-eminent position of textiles within British industry declined. Industry dominated by much heavier machinery developed and a different workforce was required. Operation of machinery required more training, and in turn this required a better educated and healthier workforce—since the capitalist wanted returns from the investment in workers' training. There was no point in treating skilled workers as though they were completely expendable and could be replaced by five-year-olds. Social control of the working class also became increasingly important to the ruling class.

In short, more financial and ideological investment had to be put into the workforce. This took a number of forms. One was an increased ideological commitment to

46. Pinchbeck, p.101.
47. See Humphries (1981), pp.11–13.
48. Anderson, p.114.
49. Humphries (1977), p.36.

a working-class version of the bourgeois family, involving at least a token support for the idea of the family wage.

So there was a coincidence of interests between the capitalist class and the working class. But this did not flow from a patriarchal convergence, as some feminists argue; as we have seen, motives differed across the class divide. For working-class men and women it came from the wholehearted desire for a better life. The family wage was not necessarily seen as oppressive by either men or women inside the family. Indeed the fact that women worked hard for low wages outside the home was seen as the most oppressive factor in the situation:

> The fact that women had for so long worked as assistants to their husbands and fathers was largely responsible for their bad economic position ... So long as they were contributors to, and participants in, a family wage, however, this system was not necessarily oppressive; but as soon as women became dependent on their own exertions the hardship of their position was at once apparent. By tradition their wages tended to remain at a supplementary level and they found themselves excluded by lack of training from skilled and better paid work.[50]

The demand for the family wage both arose from particular historical circumstances, and was seen as a means of improving working-class living standards. It was not in any sense seen as a betrayal of women workers. However as a solution to the problems of the working-class family it was an extremely narrow and backward-looking approach. It implied that women had to be dependent on men for their livelihood, and that men had a greater right to work than women. It was therefore a step backward for women. As with protective legislation, the ideology of women's place being in the home was strengthened.

It is important at this point to understand one thing: while the *ideology* was strengthened, the reality was rather different. Throughout the nineteenth century, only a fairly small minority of male workers earned anything approaching a "family wage":

> The proportion of working-class families who could survive on the basis of a man's wage alone was very small. Nevertheless, the objective of a single male breadwinner per family was one of the most radical changes in family ideology of the modern era.[51]

Charles Booth's survey of a section of the London poor in 1889 showed that 30 per cent of the population could not rely on the men's wage alone.[52] But there was one overriding indication that men's wage levels could not cover the costs of reproduction of the whole family: the number of married women who continued to work outside the home. In the textile industry, for instance, women continued to make up a substantial proportion of the workforce. By the 1860s, 65 per cent of all power loom weavers in the cotton industry were women and over half of all mule spinners.[53] A fairly large number of these

---

50. Pinchbeck, p.2.
51. Gittins (1985), p.29.
52. For this and other examples see Lewis (1984), pp.47–8.
53. Burr Litchfield, p.185.

were married women: "the proportion of married women among female mill workers increased from 18 per cent in 1841 to 28 per cent in 1851 and to 33 per cent in 1861".[54]

A pamphlet calling for day nurseries in Manchester and Salford in 1850 said that 27.31 per cent of women who worked outside the home were married.[55] In 1851 37.15 per cent of women in the Staffordshire pottery industry—where women were more than half the workforce—were married or widowed.[56] These levels were either maintained or increased until the end of the nineteenth century.

> In the half century from 1841 to 1891 the number of women in the textile factories of England increased [by] 221 per cent, whereas the increase in the number of men during this period was only 53 per cent.[57]

Initially at least, this increase in married women working was connected with the fact that far fewer children could work at all, especially since the passing of protective legislation in the 1840s.[58] The married women substituted for their children's labour while the children were too young to work, and tended to give up paid work when the children were old enough themselves to contribute to the family's income. A study of the nineteenth century hosiery industry in Leicester, for example, shows that

> in 1851, 30 per cent of wives with children under the age of seven were employed, but only 20 per cent of those whose children were all over seven were. The pattern was even clearer in 1871. Over 20 per cent of those with children under seven were employed, but only 10 per cent of those with older children worked for pay.[59]

Clementina Black's study of married women's work around the turn of the nineteenth century points to a wide array of industries and trades where married women made up important components of the workforce.[60]

These women needed to work to supplement the man's wage, which in most cases fell below the level of a "family wage". The necessity of waged work by more than one member of the family is shown by the fact that older children were substituted for female labour where possible.

The consolidation of the working-class family

But why, when the family wage and legislation did not succeed in bringing about women's withdrawal from waged work and the labour market, did the family grow in importance for the working class from the middle of the nineteenth century to the present day? And there is little doubt that it did. The historian Dorothy Thompson

54. Burr Litchfield, p.182.
55. Hewitt, p.13.
56. Hewitt, p.19.
57. Goodsell, p.424.
58. Tilly and Scott, pp.134–5.
59. Osterud, p.59.
60. Black (1983).

describes well the process whereby women "withdrew" to an extent from society and took refuge in home and children:

> A change seems to have occurred in women's expectations, and in their idea of their place in society. In the light of the hideous stories of unskilled child-care and the overworking of women and children in the factory areas of the earlier part of the century the positive gains from the increasing tendency for married women with children to stay at home and care for their children do not need to be stressed. But in return for these gains, working-class women seem to have accepted an image of themselves which involved both home-centredness and inferiority. They could not, in the nature of their way of life, assume the decorative and useless role which wealthier classes imposed on women in this period, but they do seem to have accepted some of its implications.[61]

The reasons why this change took place are obviously complex. But there are a number of factors which at least contributed to it. Dorothy Thompson herself points to changes within the working-class movement. The first of these was the decline of the Chartist movement. This was the first major political movement of the working class, which in its heyday fully involved women as active participants.[62] Its decline had a bad effect on women's political involvement. This was particularly marked since the political structures which eventually emerged inside the working class to replace Chartism were quite different:

> In moving forward into mature industrial capitalist society, important sections of the working class developed relatively sophisticated organisations, trade unions, political pressure groups, co-operative societies and educational institutions ... In a variety of ways they were able to find means of protecting their position within an increasingly stable system. They left behind the mass politics of the earlier part of the century, which represented more of a direct challenge to the whole system of industrial capitalism at a stage in which it was far less secure and established. In doing so, the skilled workers also left behind the unskilled workers and the women, whose way of life did not allow their participation in the more structured political forms.[63]

The changes inside the working-class movement were marked in the 1850s and 1860s. The consolidation of the skilled trade unions (which refused to organise the unskilled, immigrants or women), the development of societies such as the Orange Lodge in areas like Lancashire and central Scotland, and the deep political conservatism of the working class—all were features of this period, and indeed of much of the second half of the century.

The relative weight of textiles declined in relation to new and developing industries such as shipbuilding and heavy engineering. These industries, with their lengthy apprenticeships and skill structures, were almost exclusively male. A third industry which grew in relative importance was coal mining. By this time, this too was largely male. Thus

---

61. Thompson, p.137.
62. Thompson, pp.123–6.
63. Thompson, p.137.

in relative terms, women became a less centrally important part of the workforce than when textiles were predominant.

By the years prior to 1914 "approximately 75 per cent of all Britain's exports consisted of coal, cotton, iron and steel, and machinery; they accounted for half of the national product and employed almost a quarter of the working population".[64] Only cotton employed large numbers of women. The ideology of the stable family fitted well with these changes. Men were seen as the providers outside the home, working in heavy industry, in hard and often dangerous conditions. Their respite from work, so the argument went, lay in a comfortable, well-ordered home, presided over by a wife who could give all her attention to her husband and children. This rosy picture bore little relationship to reality for the mass of the working class. In some ways, it was not meant to. Instead it was modelled on the reality of those middle- and upper-class families where the wife could live in leisure because of her shared participation in the exploitation of the working class. The working class was expected to look up to and imitate its "betters" in the area of the family as in all others.

But the dream was powerful. It could become reality for a layer of skilled workers, and it was the aspiration of many more. As capitalism developed and became more all-embracing, so the strength of the dream grew.

A study of middle-class Chicago families in the latter half of the nineteenth century shows how the family became centred on the wife and children, a "focus of a new kind of intense family life, a life that was private and isolated".[65] These homes became "little islands in the midst of an enormous city".[66] This was true of middle-class families; there is evidence of a similar phenomenon among working-class families at the time.[67]

But if the "intensification" of the family grew, there were other, material factors at play. The first was the intervention of the capitalist state in the running of the working-class family. This had been in evidence throughout the century, but increasingly the state intervened to regulate welfare, education, health and other aspects of family life. If individuals inside the working-class family could not provide these things adequately, then the state would have to step in. The state has always preserved—and only rarely challenged—gender roles within the family through its interventions.

A second major change in the family came through the increased "childhood" of its children. Childhood itself was a relatively new phenomenon as a distinct period in life. It arose in all its essentials as part of capitalist social relations. The emphasis on childhood in the nineteenth century was connected with the expansion of education, which was seen as a means of increasing the general level of skill and of instilling order and discipline into the next generation of workers. By 1870, the Education Act provided for board education up to the age of 13.

---

64. Gittins (1982), p.38.
65. Sennett, p.50.
66. Sennett, p.53.
67. See also Cliff, p.205.

The effect of extending education through all the classes increased the financial burden on the family: "the eventual consequence to the family is a steady and unremitting rise in the cost of reproducing children".[68] This was no doubt one reason why the birthrate fell throughout the late nineteenth century among the working class.

Either the costs of reproduction are offset by the labour of both the man and the woman outside the home; or the man earns sufficient that labour and emotion can be invested by the woman in care for the child in the home. This was the choice for the working class. In many cases the family became the centre for the child, with the woman increasingly servicing her offspring. This further tended to extend childhood. The children were thrown onto the labour market much later in life. It also served to cement the family as the central institution in the reproduction of labour power.

The final material reason for the maintenance and strengthening of the working-class family lay in the needs of the working class itself. The family exists for the reproduction of labour power for the capitalist class, which consequently has a great stake in the family even though the reproduction of labour power is privatised. But there were also reasons for the working class to protect and maintain the family. It was (and is) the main, and sometimes the only, area of life where those members of the family who are not working can be protected and cared for. In the nineteenth century, when the workhouse with all its horrors was the only real alternative to the family, this became a particularly pertinent reason. The family remained the best option for caring for the old, the sick and young children. In any case, it was the only one on offer.

The strength of the family has been explained in this way by one historian, Jane Humphries: "the endurance of the family reflects a struggle by the working class for popular ways of meeting the needs of non-labouring comrades within a capitalist environment". In addition, "kinship ties provided a major source of non-bureaucratic support in conditions of chronic uncertainty."[69]

The family is the only source of support for those of its members who could not sell their labour.

According to this view, the working-class family is at least partially a defence mechanism against the capitalist system. It provides a haven from the worst of exploitation, a resting place for those who can no longer be exploited—or for those who have yet to experience exploitation; it therefore gives workers a degree of control over their lives. This is surely a much more credible explanation for what took place in the latter part of the nineteenth century than the idea that there was a male "patriarchal" conspiracy between male workers and the capitalist class. In addition, it helps to explain why women were willing participants in the move towards re-establishing the family. The patriarchal conspiracy theory assigns to them the role of dupes or passive victims—a view that is particularly insulting to women, since it sees them only as the objects of history and not its subjects.

---

68. Minge, p.20.
69. Humphries (1980), pp.154 and 151.

Various other developments in the late nineteenth century helped to cement the family to the working class. Perhaps the major change was the increased prosperity of at least a section of workers. This prosperity made a home as we would understand it today (with several rooms, a kitchen, decent furniture) a possibility for increasing numbers. Education at elementary level became universal. This coincided with a decline in the number of children born to each mother.

Although the declining birthrate might seem to point to a lessening of the importance of the family, in fact it did not. By early in the twentieth century the proportion of married women working appears to have declined[70] as the respectable notion of the wife at home spread through wider sections of the working class. Fewer children per family meant that greater economic resources could be devoted to the home. In 1851, one married woman in four was employed; by 1911 the figure was one in ten.[71] Many of these women still worked for payment—taking in lodgers, doing dressmaking or laundry. And often the older children worked to supplement family income. But the separation of women from work outside the home not only increased, it even became something which was idealised and aspired to.

The dominant ideas in society continued to stress the sanctity of the family. But the capitalist system itself was increasingly unable to deliver a stable society in which the family could flourish. The family was never free of economic, social and psychological tensions:

> The glorification of private life and the family represented the other side of the bourgeois perception of society as something alien, impersonal, remote and abstract—a world from which pity and tenderness had ed in horror. Deprivations experienced in the public world had to be compensated in the realm of privacy. Yet the very conditions that gave rise to the need to view privacy and the family as a refuge from the larger world made it more and more difficult for the family to serve in that capacity.[72]

This statement remains true for the family today. The means by which the family was shored up—the ideological stress on it, the increased intervention of the state, the myth of the woman as a passive ornament in the home—have left their imprint on the family form. Today it has to cope with even more: the destruction of old industries, the wiping out of communities, the increased pressure on each individual to deliver, all have left huge marks on the family. Yet the institution endures, despite the most important change of all—the drawing into the workforce of married women workers. Today women have fewer children and work for a far greater period of time outside the home. In doing so, they partially negate the traditional picture of woman as wife and mother. To understand why people today live in families we have to understand what keeps the family going.

---

70. Although even here figures are contradictory. See figures for the 1901 and 1911 censuses in Klein, pp.27–8. In general, however, the number of married women workers overall was around 10 per cent. According to a recent article, the figure for the US was even lower: "In the United States in 1887, well before any significant legislation, only 4 percent of all women factory workers were married" (Brenner and Ramas).
71. Oakley, p.44.
72. Lasch, p.8.

CHAPTER TWO

The family today

The modern family is the subject of endless study and debate. Sometimes it is assumed that the family is disappearing, wrecked by divorce, lower childbirth rates or the atomisation which is one of its major features. On the other hand, it is regarded as an eternal and unchanging citadel: a source of strength in an uncertain world. Yet the family in late capitalism contains elements of both. The capitalist system itself both sustains and undermines the family.

The family is a mass of contradictions, some of which result from the fact that it is a universal institution. Families may vary considerably from class to class, but nearly all of us are born into, live and die in families. Attempts to create alternatives to the family, such as communes, tend to founder on the fact that family-type relationships and attitudes reproduce themselves within these alternatives.

Those who try to break from the family norm, as gays do, suffer prejudice and discrimination as a result. Indeed, many gay relationships end up reproducing traditional sex roles. Some sociologists point to groups within society who do not live in the family as it usually understood: students, young flatsharers, soldiers in barracks and even travelling salesmen. But the situation of all these is transient and relatively temporary and most of these individuals will end up in some form of the family after at most a few years. The dominance and importance of the family can also be seen by society's attitudes to those who live outside one. Children in care, old people in institutions and the homeless are regarded with pity. The very use of the name "home" to describe these institutions shows the value placed upon the privatised family. And all too often individuals in institutions see their ideal as living in a "normal" family.

One of the most surprising features of the family today is the astonishing tenacity with which workers cling to it. This again is despite many appearances to the contrary. Adolescents may rebel against their families. For the upper and middle classes this may be quite a lengthy process, with higher education prolonging adolescence often into the mid-twenties. But marriage and childbirth are still seen as the ideal for most working-class women—and as an inevitability for most working-class men. This is despite the experience of individuals' own families, where reality rarely approaches the ideal. Daughters of unhappy homes often see marriage as their main source of escape from the family. Lillian Rubin's study of US white working-class families bears this out:

> Being grown up *means* being married. Thus, despite the fact that the models of marriage they see before them don't look like their cherished myths, their alternatives often are so slim and so terrible—a job they hate, more years under the oppressive parental roof—that working-class girls tend to blind themselves to the realities and cling to the fantasies with extraordinary tenacity.[1]

To understand why this is, we need to comprehend the differing tendencies inside the family.

Capitalism operates at one level to break down the family, especially by creating and demanding greater mobility of labour power. So the years since 1945 have seen migration on an unprecedented scale: of Caribbean and Asian workers to Britain; of Turks, North Africans and Yugoslavs to northern Europe; of workers from the Middle East, Far East and central America to the US. All this has had a major effect in breaking down the old family, often with heart-rending results. Immigration controls consciously exclude or put stringent tests on workers' dependents. European immigrants, denied citizenship, are separated from their dependents forced to stay in the home country. So the costs of reproduction of this section of the labour force are not even carried by the "host" country.

Alongside the growth of immigrant labour has been the massive entry of women into the workforce. Married women working also means major changes in the lives of most working-class families.

But while these changes have fundamentally altered the families of millions of workers, there is a countervailing tendency for workers to cling to the family, and to attempt to reinforce its supposed traditional values. This is shown by the increased ideological importance of the family and the centrality of the home under late capitalism.

The development of home-centredness was a feature of the late nineteenth-century family, as we have seen. This has become even more marked under modern capitalism. Home "improvement" is a major industry. Warehouses on the edge of every town sell the basics for a "dream home" and one of the most common features of leisure activity is shopping for commodities to fill the home. Home ownership is the aspiration of many workers.

If any further evidence were needed, it can be found in the attitude of both major parties to the question of the family. Labour prime minister James Callaghan proposed a Ministry for Marriage in 1978. Margaret Thatcher equates free market Toryism with traditional family values. Recent appeals to stronger moral values are based on the most traditional ideas of the family, with both parties supporting the maintenance of established family life as a potential vote-winner.

The family, however, fails to live up to expectations. Firstly, the majority of people, at any one time, do not live in the conventional "nuclear" family of two heterosexual

---

1. Rubin, p.41.

parents and dependent children. Nearly a quarter of all households consist of a single person—compared to one-tenth of all households in 1951. By 1985, the proportion of children living in single-parent families stood at 13 per cent. Illegitimacy is at record levels, at over one-fifth of all births.[2] Divorce is becoming more commonplace, with 11 per cent of women aged 18–49 having experienced divorce; a third of all marriages in 1983 involved at least one partner who had been divorced.[3] Although the total number of marriages has risen, a lot of these are remarriages; the number of first time marriages is actually falling.[4]

For millions the family is a very poor place. Key periods of poverty within the family are old age, or when there are young children in the family. Nearly eight million people are dependent, at least partly, on some sort of benefit—including a quarter of all pensioners and half of all single parents.[5] The crucial factor connecting children to poverty is the inability of the woman, because of the tasks of child care, to earn a decent wage in the child's early years. Heather Joshi recently estimated that mothers earned on average 30 per cent less than women without children.[6] For those on state benefit the situation is even worse. The average family spends "50 per cent more on food, four times more on alcohol, five times more on clothing and footwear, six times more on services and durable household goods and seven times more on transport" than those on benefit.[7]

Happiness inside the family is constantly equated with material resources. So advertisers paint a never-never world of spacious houses, massive kitchens filled with sparkling modern equipment such as dishwashers and tumble dryers, or new "family" cars which cost the equivalent of a year's wages for most workers. These families are always white, healthy and good-looking. Parents never lose their tempers and mothers smile happily as they pile dirty clothes into the machine or mop the floor yet again. Violence, battering, debts or unemployment do not impinge on any of these families. This rosy picture approximates to nothing real—it portrays a carefree, affluent middle-class lifestyle which only exists for a tiny number of people. It is a million miles from the cramped physical conditions and the narrow emotional lives of most workers. Insofar as workers do afford any of these things, they do so by putting themselves into debt which they can ill afford to repay.[8]

Unemployment, sickness or injury can in these circumstances become the trigger to real poverty. The Tories may uphold the dream of a property-owning democracy, but between 1982 and 1986 the number of repossessions by building societies rose from

---

2. *Social Trends 1988.*
3. *General Household Survey* 1983.
4. *Social Trends 1988.*
5. See Bradshaw and Morgan.
6. Quoted in Milne.
7. Bradshaw and Morgan.
8. Credit cards have boomed in recent years, with 12.1 million Visa cards and 9.8 million Access cards on issue at the end of 1986. This compares to about 3 million each at the end of 1975. Total outstanding consumer credit debt at March 1987 stood at £31 billion (*Social Trends 1988*).

6,000 to 21,000; 14 per cent of all cases of homelessness were a result of defaulting on mortgage repayments.[9]

The family is also a very violent place. A horrific catalogue of beatings and worse take place within the four walls of the home. As well as wife battering and child abuse—both physical and sexual—Jean Renvoize's book *Web of Violence* also points to the phenomenon of "granny bashing"—the physical abuse of old people by their children or grandchildren.[10]

Violence tends to increase at Christmas and New Year, when individuals spend most of their time with their families and tensions come to the fore.[11] Certainly the family is more dangerous than the streets. Jean Renvoize quotes a study of America's most violent city, Detroit, in 1973. It showed that four out of five homicides were committed by friends, relatives or neighbours of the victim.[12]

Perhaps most at risk in the home are young children—both from physical and sexual abuse. Parents often use their children as pawns in disputes between themselves. A relatively high proportion of parents who abuse are having some sort of psychiatric treatment.[13] Child battering is often connected to acts of caretaking such as changing or feeding, which probably explains why a high proportion of women batter children.[14] Figures from the National Society for the Prevention of Cruelty to Children show that abuse of children was more common among women housewives or unemployed than among men, either in work or unemployed.[15]

The family may exist for all classes, but there are major differences in family life between the classes. The greatest differences are related to poverty. Lillian Rubin's study found that even in the affluent United States "at least intermittent poverty was the common experience of the children growing up in most of these working-class families".[16]

Asked what they would do if they got some money, many working-class people said they would pay off their bills. Middle-class families tended not to respond like this, having far fewer economic worries. And 34 per cent of working-class families said they would help their own parents and families "so they wouldn't have to worry any more". Only one middle-class man gave a similar reply.[17] Poverty exists not just for those who are unemployed or living on benefits. The level of wages for most workers is such that it rarely covers the costs of reproduction of the whole family—poverty is a fact of life for most workers, at least for large parts of their lives. Recent figures for Britain show that the gap between rich and poor is widening.[18]

9. *Social Trends 1988.*
10. Renvoize, pp.113–24.
11. Renvoize, p.50.
12. Renvoize, p.40.
13. Renvoize, p.32.
14. Renvoize, p.171.
15. Quoted in German.
16. Rubin, p.30.
17. Rubin, chapter 9.
18. *Social Trends 1988.* The trend is similar in the US where, according to the US Bureau of Census, in 1985 dollars, those earning below $20,000 a year increased from 30.7 per cent in 1973 to 34 per cent in 1985; while those earning over $50,000 increased from 16.5 to 18.3 per cent (*Democratic Left*, volume xv, number 4, September–October 1987).

Divorce rates among the manual working class are nearly twice as high as those in the professional and managerial classes. In addition, "less than one in ten brides in social classes 1 and 2 were pregnant at marriage compared with one in four of those in classes 4 and 5".[19] Jean Renvoize makes a similar point about child battering: "The majority of severe physical battering takes place in lower socio-economic groups ... few of the mothers do full-time work and the perpetual presence of young children irritates them considerably".[20]

Another study carried out in the 1960s shows that physical battering played a part in the break-up of 40 per cent of working-class marriages compared with 20 per cent of middle-class ones.[21]

There are many other—sometimes less quantifiable—differences between the families of the different classes. Lillian Rubin's study is particularly valuable here. She points to the narrowness of working-class lives, and how manual labour in particular destroys any social side to the family. Inside the working class, couples rarely socialise with each other outside the home; they rarely invite non-family members into their home; they often hardly communicate verbally. "Again and again, the men and women I met recall parents, especially fathers, who were taciturn and unresponsive."[22]

Stuck in dead-end jobs, the parents often did not value themselves. Although they wanted better for their children, they often did not expect much. Emotionally, the families tended to be repressed, and sometimes treated their children in a harsh and disciplinarian manner. The narrowness of their horizons can be seen by the three attributes repeatedly quoted when asked what these women valued in their husbands: "he's a steady worker, he doesn't drink, he doesn't hit me".[23]

Middle-class families tended to be much more open; matters affecting individual family members were much more likely to be discussed and there was a much more liberal atmosphere. Money did not surface as a major problem—while middle-class fathers might be preoccupied with work problems, they did not suffer the same withdrawal as working-class men. Whereas working-class women talked about their husbands "letting" them do things, there was much more equality, at least on the surface, inside the middle-class family—not because it was necessarily more egalitarian, but because "the *ideology* of equality is more strongly *asserted* there".[24]

All these features add up to a working-class family which is often a nightmare for its individual members. Despite all the attempts to portray the family as an oasis of calm in a violent, dangerous and hostile world, it is often the very centre of misery. Yet the incontrovertible fact remains that despite all this, working-class people continue to live in families. The institution is central both to their lives and to the capitalist system. Why does it assume this centrality and dominance?

19. Brayshaw, p.23.
20. Renvoize, p.171.
21. A study by Levinger, quoted in Renvoize, p.23.
22. Rubin, p.36.
23. Rubin, p.93.
24. Rubin, p.97.

The answer is not simple or even obvious. The capitalist family is a unique institution. It differs from all previous family forms in one central respect: it is not a productive family. For most of human history, a non-productive family would have been an impossibility: the family was the arena of both production and reproduction. It was also the centre of whatever social intercourse took place, and all members of the family tended to engage in production in and around the home. This was the case in the predominantly agricultural society of Britain up to the time of the Industrial Revolution.

The nuclear family which exists under capitalism could not stand in greater contrast to this. Men and women no longer marry each other on the basis of the skills each one possesses: on whether the man can plough a field or whether the woman can sew. All the items which workers need to live—food, housing, clothes—can be, and usually are, bought as commodities. So the family, far from being a unit where commodities are produced, has become increasingly a unit of consumption. The family home will be ready-built (although constantly "improved" through decorating, do-it-yourself and so on). Supermarket shopping means meat trimmed and wrapped, fish filleted and coated in batter, ready-to-cook prepared vegetables and sliced bread. Ready meals which simply need heating in a microwave.

A small minority of families will be exceptions to this: the woman may bake her own bread for example. But the pressures of two adults working makes this increasingly difficult. Labour-saving food becomes much more convenient. Often it is cheaper because of mass production techniques and inferior ingredients.[25] Similarly, the vast majority of women do not make most of their own or their children's clothes. Many will knit or possess a sewing machine, some will work in the home being paid for sewing for neighbours, but their labour is unlikely to be central either to the family's income or to the clothing of the family. It is still far cheaper and more convenient to buy clothes produced in Portugal or Taiwan than to make them at home. Yet only 200 years ago the spinning wheel or distaff was part of the furniture in every English farmhouse and many of the cottages.[26] The development of commodity production has totally altered the nature of work performed in the home.

Today the family has, at least on the surface, little obvious or apparent economic role; above all it is regarded as the escape from the world of work. Marriage and the family are not about work, but about individual romantic love. Finding "Mr Right" and having children are seen by women as the fulfilment of their lives. The social world—work, mass-produced leisure, education—all lie outside the home. The family is the domain of the private—supposedly of private love and happiness, but all too often the scene of private pain, of violence, or of failed expectations.

A further contradiction is found when the family does not live up to its image. It is the haven in a heartless world, but also a hell for many of its participants. The outward

25. Decent food becomes increasingly the prerogative of the middle classes, with the working class often trapped into bad diet through its relative cheapness; for example the price of white sliced bread is sometimes nearly half that of brown unsliced.
26. Pinchbeck, p.133.

appearance of the family and its reality are very different. An understanding of this is essential if we are to come to terms with why the family continues.

Its economic role, although different from the economic role of the family in previous class societies, is central to the workings of the capitalist system. And there is little that is voluntary about the family as an institution. It is not about individual men and women falling in love, getting married and having children. That is of course the process whereby most men and women do set up their own individual families. But every pressure to do so—whether from friends, parents or the state itself—stems from the central economic role which the family plays.

This central economic role is the reproduction of labour power for the capitalist class. Reproduction of the next generation of workers is crucial to all societies throughout history. The family form (of reproduction) is therefore always linked to the form of production. Engels, writing on the family in his book *The Origin of the Family, Private Property and the State* spells out this connection:

> On the one side, the production of the means of subsistence, of food, clothing and shelter and the tools necessary for that production; on the other side, the production of human beings themselves, the propagation of the species.[27]

The "production of human beings" is more important today than ever. The bulk of housework and child care in the home is concerned with precisely this. The existing generation of workers is cared for, fed, clothed and receives personal and sexual services inside the family. Even more important, the next generation of workers is brought up, cared for, taught to look after itself and is subject to usually massive amounts of attention from its parents—especially from the mother. So the labour market is constantly replenished with young, healthy workers who are socialised to accept dominant ideological values in a number of different ways.

This is of real economic benefit to the capitalist class. For it is a combination of the unpaid labour of the woman (and to a lesser extent the man) in the home, with the wage labour of both men and women outside the home which reproduces the commodity of labour power. Kath Ennis made this point in the early 1970s. She, however, argued that: "the surplus (profit) extracted by the boss is a surplus not simply from the man at work, but from the combined labour of the man at work and the woman in the home".[28]

Today it is even clearer that capitalism *also* relies on the paid labour of the woman outside the home, as well as her unpaid labour inside it. But the basic argument is correct: women's domestic labour contributes to the reproduction of labour power and therefore indirectly to the surplus produced for the capitalist class by lowering the value of labour power.

This also enables the capitalist class to pay wages which are based on the assumption that this domestic labour exists. There can be little doubt that this is the case. In

27. Engels (1978), preface to the first edition.
28. Ennis, p.26.

fact the whole capitalist wage system is based upon the assumption that all individuals in society live in family units. This has major implications. It means those not in family units are among the poorest—for example pensioners or single parents. It also means that the capitalist class can get away with paying both men and women lower wages than would otherwise be the case.

Men's low wages are rooted in the existence of the privatised family. Male workers do not have to pay for the costs of their reproduction directly as commodities. Food is prepared, clothes washed, housework and child care performed as part of the family unit. This makes the costs of reproduction lower, since these services do not need to be bought directly out of the wage on the market.[29] Women working for wages, para-doxically, tend to lower wages even more, as women's wages (in addition to men's) are necessary in order to buy commodities used in the home.

Women's wages are also affected .by the existence of the family. On average women earn only between two-thirds and three-quarters of the average male wage.[30] There are different ways in which this is brought about—part-time work, grading, the sexual division of labour, among others. But the overwhelming reason for women's unequal pay lies in the tacit assumption of the existence of the family, and therefore that women have other means of support than their own wages. That many women do not have this support, their wages being vital to maintaining the family economically, does not enter into these calculations. The capitalist class is more than content to pay women's wages at the lowest possible cost of reproduction.

The structuring of women's work by the family extends to more than wages. Women make up the vast majority of part-time workers. Even when they work full-time, they tend to work fewer hours than men outside the home.[31] Their hours and conditions at work have to take into account their unpaid labour at home, especially child care. This probably accounts for the fact that women take more time off work sick than men.[32]

Although the family's central economic role lies in the reproduction of labour power, obviously this is not its only role. It has other economic roles, and a major ideological one as well. It still acts as a support system for those members of the family who cannot sell their labour power: many of the sick, the disabled, the old and increasingly of the young. Youth unemployment, the cutting of benefits and the raising of the school leav-ing age tend to mean that many adolescents are dependent on the family for material support. Although many try to find alternatives to the family, there are few available: this is evidenced by the increasing numbers of young homeless.

---

29. The true economic worth of women's unpaid labour can be shown by the various insurance company assess-ments of what a "wife" would cost on the open market if all her functions had to be bought as commodities. The weekly amount is around double the average weekly male wage.
30. *New Earnings Survey 1986* (Department of Employment: London).
31. *New Earnings Survey 1986.* However this isn't as simple as it looks: 49 per cent of all men and 59.7 per cent of all women employees work an average of between 36 and 40 hours. But whereas 23.6 per cent and 15.6 per cent of men worked 40–48 hours and over 48 hours respectively, only 8.3 per cent and 1.8 per cent of women did so. Another survey points to the view that men whose wives work full-time work shorter hours than those whose wives work part-time. (Martin and Roberts, chapter 4)
32. *Social Trends 1988.*

The euphemistically named "community care" means ever larger numbers of sick, old, mentally ill or disabled people are thrust back into the privatised family. The nineteenth-century workhouses have gone and there are now a massive number of institutions—prisons, hospitals, mental hospitals, children's homes, schools, colleges—but today there is also constant pressure to reduce state spending on these institutions. This is done at the expense of the working-class family. Especially in times of crisis, the capitalist class places more and more burdens on privatised reproduction.

The market has also increasingly encroached on the tasks traditionally performed by the family—a gradual process, starting with the development of capitalism itself. The factory production of textiles was capitalism's first major industry. Gradually commodity production has entered into every area of life, including social life. It is now almost a truism to regard the sex act as a commodity: bought and sold on videos, in porn magazines, through prostitution.

This relationship with the market spreads into all areas of life, affecting every individual member of the family:

> The population no longer relies upon social organisation in the form of family, friends, neighbours, community, elders, children, but with few exceptions must go to market and only to market, not only for food, clothing and shelter, but also for recreation, amusement, security, for the care of the young, the old, the sick, the handicapped. In time not only the material and service needs but even the emotional patterns of life are channelled through the market.[33]

So the family, as it loses its productive functions, increasingly becomes a unit of consumption. Every area of family life comes onto the cash nexus.

As a unit of consumption, the family is important for capitalism in a number of ways. The atomisation of family life means the multiplication of commodities. Electrical machinery in the home lies unused for the majority of the time: washing machines are used for at most an hour a day, cookers for perhaps two hours, videos for a few hours a day. Cars are often only driven one or two hours a day, spending most of their time in car parks or garages. Yet 82 per cent of homes have a washing machine, 34 per cent a tumble dryer, 32 per cent a video and two-thirds of all households have regular use of a car or van.[34] There is no rational justification for this state of affairs. It results from the drive by the capitalist class to accumulate.

The development of the family as a unit of consumption and its destruction as a productive unit therefore has a number of effects. Firstly it *increases* the level of commodity production. More and more areas of life are brought into production. Even areas once considered part of the family are transformed into "service industry": catering, caring for the sick, teaching, social work. As this happens, more and more people are drawn onto the labour market. This is especially true of women. The transformation of the family through women working develops

33. Braverman, p.276.
34. *Social Trends 1988.*

the powerful urge in each family member toward an independent income, which is one of the strongest feelings instilled by the transformation of society into a giant market for labour and goods, since the source of status is no longer the ability to make many things but simply the ability to purchase them.[35]

This process in turn leads to atomisation and isolation for various members of the family. But this in itself is contradictory: as each individual becomes atomised, so the family as an institution becomes increasingly important to the working class. We can only explain this by looking at the nature of work under capitalism. Harry Braverman describes the way in which the worker's life is regarded as only beginning when work ends:

> In a society where labor power is purchased and sold, working time becomes sharply and antagonistically divided from non-working time, and the worker places an extraordinary value upon this "free" time, while on-the-job time is regarded as lost or wasted. Work ceases to be a natural function.[36]

The worker becomes completely separated from the product of his or her labour. In this process, described by Marx as "alienation", work is seen as "a sacrifice of his life ... life begins for him where this activity ceases, at table, in the public house, in bed".[37]

There is no escape for the working-class family from this alienation: it can be abolished only with the abolition of wage labour and exploitation itself. So the family cannot provide a genuine haven. On the contrary, the family is where some of the worst tensions of working-class life take place. But it is more complex than that.

With the spread of commodity production into all areas of life, the separation of work and home is accentuated. At work the worker feels least in control of circumstances: there is no choice over which work to do, there are rigid hours of work, there is strict supervision, and the product of the day's labour does not belong to the worker but to the capitalist. Sometimes it is possible to rebel against this—to organise a strike or other form of protest which wrests some control and decision-making into the hands of the worker. But most of the time that is the exception, not the rule.

So the world outside work takes on an importance where it appears as the realm of freedom and choice. We can choose what we spend our wages on: the cinema, alcohol, clothes or football matches. We can decide whether we want to marry or have children. In reality this choice is almost totally illusory. There are so many economic constraints inside society that the only real choices become totally trivial ones. But the *illusion* of choice, of freedom to decide the way to run one's life is very powerful.

Under such circumstances the family increases its ideological importance. With inequality built into the system, everyone gets something different from the family. The children depend on their parents for financial and emotional support; the wife will often depend on the husband at least partly for financial support; the man depends on the wife and children for emotional support. In addition both man and woman depend

---

35. Braverman, p.276.
36. Braverman, p.278.
37. Marx (1968), p.74.

on the family for status: the man as "head of the family", the woman in her supposedly most important role as "wife and mother".

The family thus becomes an important goal for the worker, but it provides no real release. Some feminists argue that it does; that the family is the source of male power under capitalism. But although the situation of the individual man may be better than that of the woman, his position is one of powerlessness. Male workers are denied any real control over their lives. To misunderstand this is to deny the reality of the working-class family. Far from being the repository of power, the family becomes a defence mechanism for the protection of all its members. This is vital in explaining the survival of the family. As Jane Humphries has correctly pointed out, the strength and resilience of the family is partly a result of its ability to protect workers and their living standards.[38]

The economic role of the family explains its survival from the point of view of the capitalist class; but other aspects of the family explain the positive attitude to it of many workers. Here again, however, the dual nature of the family means that it can never truly measure up to the expectations placed upon it. As the outside world encroaches more and more into family life, so the family becomes more of a hell and less of a haven. Tensions within the family increase. Any blow may reduce the family to a social services statistic.

This is why, despite the talk of freedom and choice, the history of capitalism has been one of outside intervention in personal and family life—often through the agencies of the capitalist state itself: compulsory education, health and welfare provision, housing regulation, laws governing the relationship of individual family members.

State intervention is not new. The eighteenth and nineteenth centuries saw a whole series of legislative incursions into family life. Lord Hardwicke's Act of 1753 required marriage to be solemnised through the Church of England. The Poor Law Bastardy Act of 1832 attempted to cut illegitimacy (which grew partly as a result of Hardwicke's Act).[39] Abortion was made a statutory offence—as opposed to one in common law—in 1803.[40] The 1830s, 1840s and 1850s saw a rash of state regulation concerning the family, the Poor Law and protective factory legislation being only the most important. The nineteenth century also saw laws introduced which attempted to control sexuality by penalising prostitution and homosexuality.

State intervention emerged as a central plank of capitalist policy on the question of the family around the turn of the century, when the family's importance to capitalism was underlined through the expansion of state welfare provision. Child rearing was taken out of the sole control of the parents through the advent of universal compulsory education, and of institutions such as juvenile courts. Various professionals employed by the state played an increased role in directing the family. This development was most marked in the United States, but it was also noticeable elsewhere. In Britain, elementary education was introduced in 1870. The Liberal government's budget of 1906 provided

---

38. Humphries (1980), p.140.
39. Gittins (1985), pp.82–3.
40. Gittins (1985), p.101.

for a relatively large amount of state spending on welfare for the old, the sick and the young—the non-wage earners. A degree of unemployment benefit was also introduced. This was the first major implementation of a welfare "safety net" which would catch those not provided for within the confines of the family or directly through the wage.

Since then, increasing amounts of money have been spent on what is loosely described as "welfare" or "social services". In 1986, total government spending was 45 per cent of gross domestic product—10 per cent more of GDP than in 1961.[41] Although significant amounts of this go on non-welfare spending such as policing or defence, there has been a massive expansion of certain areas of welfare. For example, 47 per cent of all three- and four-year-olds were in education in 1985, compared with only 15 per cent in 1966. And whereas there were 51,000 day care places for under-fives in 1951, there were 609,000 in 1985.[42]

Today the state is a major employer and provider of services once performed within the family or not at all. State education is a major feature of late capitalism: all children between five and 16 have to attend full-time education; increasing numbers study beyond those years. This higher education is generally encouraged; and statutory penalties are placed on those who do not send their children to school for the statutory minimum period.

But state intervention in child care starts well before formal education. Even before the child is born, the state welfare system intervenes in the shape of social workers and health visitors who ensure that neither parent is damaging the mother or the child. Contraception is distributed free; abortions are performed by the state in certain circumstances; forced sterilisations and the use of the injected contraceptive Depo Provera are used on a class basis to limit the pregnancies of those considered "unsuitable" mothers. After the birth, the mother continues to receive health visits and state benefits in order to help bring up the child. All sorts of interventions can be backed up by the force of law; even some inoculations are compulsory.

Indeed the work of the health and social services is deeply enmeshed. Old people are admitted to hospitals if they cannot cope on their own; children can be placed in council care on evidence of ill-treatment or if their parents cannot care for them properly; laws exist to enforce minimal health standards in public institutions, at work and in shops and restaurants.

Social services intervene directly to top up the incomes of large numbers of the very poor in capitalist society—the unemployed, pensioners and the low-paid. Various state benefits stop millions from literally starving or falling into total destitution, though these fall far short of an adequate income. A study which attempted to use Supplementary Benefit levels to feed, house and clothe a family of four found the task virtually impossible. Diet was nutritionally deficient, and consumer durables impossible to replace.[43]

41. *Social Trends 1987*.
42. *Social Trends 1987*.
43. Bradshaw and Morgan.

State intervention is the modern equivalent of the Poor Law or charity; it enables the very poor to survive, but only barely.

State intervention extends to women's role at work. Legislation now provides for maternity leave, equal pay and an end to sex discrimination. These legislative provisions are woefully inadequate, but they are nonetheless a recognition that special provision has to be made to integrate women into the capitalist workforce. The same can be said of the whole body of "family law", that concerning divorce, child welfare and battered women.

In every area of family life the state now intervenes to ensure that certain things are performed or that others are prohibited. This intervention is the subject of some controversy. Right-wingers who believe in free market forces—and who are committed to cutting public spending—are inclined to call for a drastic reduction in state spending on the family. Ferdinand Mount sees the family as a celebration of privacy and resents any outside interference: "public busybodies do not have the right to enforce their personal scale of priorities on the rest of us", he writes.[44]

For him, the role of the state is tied up with lack of freedom, a form of state "socialism" and middle-class social work attitudes. The working class, according to Mount, is against such things, and jealously guards its privacy. Of course his views are not shared by all right-wingers. Many of his co-thinkers prefer a degree of social engineering: providing abortion and sterilisation for the poor and "feckless"; forcing through intervention into the family. This view bemoans the higher divorce and illegitimacy rates in the "lower" working classes, and wants social training to correct them. One such writer deplores a situation where

> far too many young working-class girls, in particular, want the status of being a married woman, with the achievement of a double bed and a pram, and find in some willing and convenient young man a means to this end.[45]

In practice successive government policies have charted a course somewhere between heavy intervention to regulate the poor and no regulation at all. But since state intervention is now so crucial and central to the whole success of capitalism the reality is that they have had little room for manoeuvre. Postwar history demonstrates this.

The Second World War and the long boom which followed shortly after its end were periods of virtual full employment. In the 1950s there were consequently severe labour shortages, drawing immigrant labour and married women onto the labour market. State intervention sought to regulate this supply of labour: in the case of women by ensuring that the family still remained a priority—that future workers were not neglected. Much of the cost of this could be placed on the shoulders of individual parents, for example where they were able to buy commodities such as vacuum cleaners or washing machines. Where this was not achievable the state would subsidise directly, although never willingly:

---

44. Mount, p.172.
45. Brayshaw, p.16.

poor nursery provision for under-fives reflects the high labour intensity and therefore high wage costs of the work involved.

In addition to drawing new layers of workers onto the labour market, capital's needs dictated an increase in the level of skills of at least a minority. This was done through the expansion of education provision—and especially of higher education.[46] A layer of highly skilled workers could be trained at the expense of the estate, thus increasing the productivity of labour. Health expenditure was similarly designed to ensure a workforce relatively free from sickness and so more productive.

As we have seen, both these areas of expenditure had far-reaching implications for the family. They have also become permanent fixtures, despite the cuts of recent years. State spending on these areas continues at a high level, and the sheer amount involved makes it difficult for the state to disentangle itself from the family. The direct interests of the capitalist class, too, ensure a high level of investment.

State social expenditure fulfils two major functions:

> For a long period capital felt that welfare expenditures could satisfy simultaneously two different needs—to buy the acquiescence of the working class, but at the same time to raise productivity so that the cost of doing so was not a burden on accumulation. Just as wages both reproduce labour power *and* are seen by workers as justifying the toil of work, so the "social wage" element in public expenditure both increased the productivity of labour power and made workers believe society cared for them.[47]

Both these aspects are crucial. They explain the constraints successive governments have been under in seriously cutting back the social wage—and the strong feelings of workers in defence of institutions such as the National Health Service. They also show how central is state intervention to the maintenance of the family. Any theories of women's oppression and of why the family continues to exist have to take account of the system's positive aid in maintaining the family. Quite simply, the capitalist system has a stake in keeping the privatised family as the means of reproduction of labour power.

---

46. See Harman (1984), p.105.
47. Harman (1984), p.106.

CHAPTER THREE
Theories of the family

Feminist theory has become established in society over the past 20 years. Feminism in university courses is now an accepted area of study. This is demonstrated both by the substantial number of women's studies courses which now exist and by feminist approaches to history, sociology, economics and media studies which are now widespread. It is argued that due to women's oppression, the women's dimension in academic study has been ignored. The common response is for feminism to be integrated into academic study.

There are, of course, many different theories of women's oppression. But increasingly one theory has become hegemonic, not just among radical feminists but among socialists and Marxist feminists too. That is the theory of patriarchy. It is now almost universally accepted by feminists and among the left that patriarchy, the patriarchal family or even patriarchal capitalism is responsible for the oppression of women. Sometimes it is even said that patriarchy *is* women's oppression.

There is obviously a conceptual problem: what does the term mean? "Patriarchy" literally means "rule of the father". Marx used it in this sense to describe the domestic household system of production. He applied it to a historically specific form of the family, not as a general phrase meaning women's oppression, and certainly not in any transhistorical sense.

Clearly most feminist theorists do not use the term in this manner; their application is much less rigorous. What most of their theories have in common, however, is an insistence that male domination exists over and above the particular economic mode of production in which it features—and that it therefore cannot be explained either in class terms or by reference to Marx's economic theory. According to many feminist theorists, although the forces of production advance, and although revolutionary social change takes place, male domination still remains—something constant and given for all time. Women's oppression has always existed, we are told, and will continue to exist, even after a socialist revolution.

Such ideas are often put forward by those who consider themselves Marxists. But Marx and Engels approached the question quite differently and came to different conclusions. They started from the assumption that women's oppression arose alongside the division of society into classes and the development of private property. Alongside this went, in Engels' phrase, "the world-historic defeat of the female sex"[1]—the defeat of mother right and the establishment of the family.

As society developed, oppression took on different aspects. The development of the forces of production gave rise to different forms of society; and as society changed so the family form changed. All forms of consciousness are rooted in social being. So both the ideas and material reality of women's oppression changed along with the change from one mode of production to another.

A famous passage from Marx's writing makes the point that it is the way in which workers are exploited which determines their oppression:

> Morality, religion, metaphysics, all the rest of ideology and their corresponding forms of consciousness, thus no longer retain the semblance of independence. They have no history, no development: but men, developing their material production and their material intercourse, alter, along with their real existence, their thinking and the products of their thinking. Life is not determined by consciousness, but consciousness by life.[2]

Ideas, then, are rooted in material reality. However, when we talk of women's oppression and capitalism, there are other features to consider. In particular, Marx saw capitalism as a totality: an economic system which encroached into every area of life, throughout every part of the world; which changed all previous production; which altered all the social relations of production. It involved constant processes of change, and this in itself set the capitalist mode of production apart from all previous modes. Whereas in all previous modes of production the ruling classes attempted to conserve the old ways of producing, the capitalist ruling class—the bourgeoisie—behaves in exactly the opposite way:

> Constant revolutionising of production, uninterrupted disturbance of all social conditions, everlasting uncertainty and agitation distinguish the bourgeois epoch from all earlier ones. All fixed, fast-frozen relations, with their train of ancient and venerable prejudices and opinions, are swept away, all new-formed ones become antiquated before they can ossify.[3]

Every area of life—including the family and women's oppression—is rooted in social production. The implication in Marx's theory is that socialist revolution will dissolve the old family, end the legal restraints on women's equality and lay the basis for genuine women's liberation. Such a view cuts across the views of the patriarchy theorists.

From the Marxist point of view there are two major flaws with patriarchy theory. It is idealist—there is no conception of ideas being rooted in material reality; and it does not consider the capitalist system as a whole.

The early patriarchy theorists are clear examples of both propositions. Their assumption is that patriarchy exists, is all-embracing and ahistorical, and they are overtly opposed to any class analysis. Kate Millett argues in her book *Sexual Politics* that no

---

1. Engels (1978), preface to the first edition.
2. Marx and Engels (1964), p.35.
3. Marx and Engels (1968), pp.30–1.

major differences of class exist between women,[4] while Shulamith Firestone subverts Marxist categories to argue that sexual struggles, not class struggles, have been the real dynamic of history—so she argues for a separate revolution.[5] Women's oppression is explained either by biological difference (which cannot be overcome until women wrest control of their reproductive functions) or simply in terms of male chauvinist ideas.

Such arguments have provided the basis of radical or separatist feminism throughout the existence of the women's movement. They have recently been more widely adopted by socialist feminists of all descriptions. In the process they have been much embellished. But crucially they have retained the idea of separateness: of ideology as autonomous from economic struggle; of patriarchy as separate from capitalism. Class antagonisms are therefore overlaid, it is argued, by the antagonisms between men and women.

The theoretical basis for the theory of patriarchy is that there are two areas of production, or modes of production, not one. Hence there are two separate struggles—economic struggle and ideological struggle. Juliet Mitchell puts it succinctly: "we are dealing with two autonomous areas, the economic mode of capitalism and the ideological mode of patriarchy".[6] Others find this formulation too idealist, and try to develop a Marxist interpretation. Descriptions of patriarchy as an "ideological mode" tend to abandon any idea of a materialist analysis.

Attempts to couple the two theories are common: they too express themselves in the formulation of two modes—the capitalist mode of production and the family mode of reproduction. This is widespread among separatist feminists. So the French feminist Christine Delphy argues:

> There are two modes of production in our society. Most goods are produced in the industrial mode. Domestic services, childrearing and certain other goods are produced in the family mode. The first mode of production gives rise to capitalist exploitation. The second gives rise to familial, or more precisely, patriarchal exploitation.[7]

Delphy considers both spheres to be completely separate—what goes on at work is totally divorced from what takes place in the family. Whereas the male worker has to depend on the employer for his sustenance, the wife has to depend on the man. Her relationship to him is *totally* subordinate; she is dependent on him for her well-being in every sense. "Her standard of living does not depend on her class relationship to the proletariat; but on her serf relations of production with her husband."[8] Again, for Delphy, class is not key: she argues that wives of the bourgeoisie are not themselves bourgeois, and that women who see themselves in class terms suffer from false consciousness and an identification with "enemy patriarchal classes".[9]

---

4. Millett, p.36.
5. Firestone, p.11.
6. Mitchell, p.412.
7. Delphy, p.69.
8. Delphy, p.71.
9. Delphy, p.76.

From a Marxist point of view there are fundamental problems with this analysis. It totally abandons any analysis of class differences. It also misunderstands the nature of capitalism by arguing that feudal relations of production can exist within the capitalist family. That a radical feminist like Delphy takes such a view is no surprise. But many socialist feminists who would agree with few of her conclusions have accepted similar arguments. Even Sheila Rowbotham in one of her earlier books, *Woman's Consciousness, Man's World*, argued that women's subordinate role within the family could only be explained with reference to pre-capitalist modes of production. While not explicitly developing a patriarchy theory (and indeed later attacking the whole concept) she put forward similar arguments: "in the relation of husband and wife there is an exchange of services which resembles the bond between man and man in feudalism".[10]

Sheila Rowbotham draws back from arguing that the relationship is *actually* feudal. However she then refers to women's labour as maintaining "a subordinate mode of production within capitalism" which "retains elements of earlier forms of production".[11] Such formulations are used to justify the separation of struggles—against capitalism and against men. Endorsement of this position is taken from Engels' famous passage on the production and reproduction of human life, part of which was quoted above, where he talks of the production of everyday life on the one hand, and of the family on the other:

> According to the materialistic conception, the determining factor in history is, in the final instance, the production and reproduction of immediate life. This, again, is of a twofold character. On the one side, the production of the means of subsistence, of food, clothing and shelter and the tools necessary for that production; on the other side, the production of human beings themselves, the propagation of the species. The social institutions under which people of a particular historical epoch and a particular country live are conditioned by both kinds of production; by the stage of development of labour on the one hand and of the family on the other.[12]

Any feminist theorist who wants to retain some commitment to socialist theory (and some who don't) will use this passage in an attempt to argue that even Engels acknowledged a separation and therefore at least some degree of autonomy between the two modes. But their argument is flawed and stems from a misunderstanding or wrong interpretation of what Engels actually wrote. For he goes on to argue that as human beings developed production, so the family became relatively less important: "the less the development of labour and the more limited the amount of its products ... the more the social order is found to be dominated by ties of lineage".[13]

The development of the forces of production bring about changes in how people live. In particular, the rise of the state and the establishment of groups based on geographical

10. Rowbotham (1973), p.62.
11. Rowbotham (1973), pp.64–5.
12. Engels (1978), p.4.
13. Engels (1978), p.4.

connection rather than lineage leads to a "society in which the family structure is completely dominated by the property structure".[14]

On this construction, the more developed a society, the more the family form is subordinated to production. However there is always of necessity a connection between the two; the family and the form it takes arises from the particular mode of production. It is not autonomous, separate or distinct from that mode of production. Reproduction is tied up with production.

Most feminist theorists would disagree. Annette Kuhn argues for example that:

> Patriarchal structures have their operation within history, but not within modes of production: they are overdetermined in particular modes of production by more immediate characteristics of the social formation.[15]

Many argue from this that Marxism can only be used to explain the *economic* development of society; the *ideas* which arise in any particular society cannot be explained in these terms. Accordingly Marxism is supposedly inadequate to explain the ideological or the unconscious. This approach involves abandoning some basic ideas of Marxism: that social being determines consciousness, and that there is a distinction between base and superstructure. The "relations of production" do not arise from any separate mode of *reproduction*. They are a product of the particular mode of production in which they exist.

This is clear if we start from an understanding of how societies change and develop. Marx's description went like this:

> At a certain stage of their development the material forces of production in society come in conflict with the existing relations of production or—what is but a legal expression of the same thing—with the property relations within which they had been at work before. From forms of development of the forces of production these relations turn into their fetters. Then comes the period of social revolution. With the change of the economic foundation the entire immense superstructure is more or less rapidly transformed.[16]

Marx's analysis differs from feminist ones in that it talks about change and contradiction. For Marx there is nothing static or eternal about society, and the change from one mode of production to another brings about a transformation in every area of life. The description exactly fits the changes which took place in the transition from feudalism to capitalism. The old forms of family became obstacles to new methods of production. For the new methods to succeed, among other things the old family has to be smashed and so this obstacle removed.

Production then moves from the family to the factory—the separation of work from home—and is transformed completely in the course of the ensuing social upheaval. The family becomes, for Marx, part of the immense superstructure of society which is changed as society itself changes.

14. Engels (1978), p.5.
15. Kuhn, p.65.
16. Marx (1971), preface.

The distinction between base and superstructure attempts to show the relationship between economic production and ideas: that the forces of production themselves give rise to particular ideas, cultural and social formations. Many feminists try to ditch any such connection, talking instead of the "relative autonomy" of patriarchy from the capitalist mode of production, so it can be seen as "a relatively autonomous structure whose operation is overdetermined conjuncturally by precisely such structures as class".[17]

This leads to the kind of distinction made by Roisin McDonough and Rachel Harrison: .

> Although as Marxists it is essential for us to give analytic primacy to the sphere of production, as feminists it is equally essential to hold on to a concept such as the relation of human reproduction in order to understand the specific nature of women's oppression.[18]

In doing so, they are unable to explain either the development of society or the connection of ideas to economic change. Concepts such as patriarchy become free-floating, transcending modes of production. Any relationship between the two—as when class "overdetermines" patriarchy—is seen as purely accidental. So these feminists abandon any Marxist theory of change and resort to a combination of economic determinism and complete idealism.

The theories are only sustained by maintaining them at the highest level of abstraction. Any connection with changes in the family or with the real lives of women today would point to too many inconsistencies.

The basic flaw in the argument is a failure to see the link between production and reproduction. This link exists for all class societies, both in the narrow biological sense of the reproduction of the species, and in the wider sense of the reproduction of the labour force. Capitalist production gives rise to the capitalist form of family. This last point is clearly accepted by Joan Smith in her article "Women and the Family".[19] However she makes the opposite error from the patriarchy theorists by arguing that the capitalist family is not superstructural at all, but is part of the economic base of capitalism.

Like many patriarchy theorists, Joan Smith misinterprets Engels' formulation and adopts the two-modes theory, claiming that the family constitutes the mode of reproduction; capitalism could not abolish the family without abolishing the very basis of capitalism itself. For her, the family is as central to the capitalist system as wage labour or accumulation.

But her thesis is not tenable. Even within capitalism there have been *major* changes in the way in which labour power is reproduced. Capitalism does not depend for its existence on privatised domestic labour. In theory the family could be abolished without that spelling the end of capitalist society. The interests of the capitalist class are not necessarily served by maintaining women as unpaid labourers in the home, rather than as wage labourers in social production directly producing value for the capitalist class. What evidence there is seems to suggest the reverse is true. It is at least arguable

---

17. Kuhn, p.53.
18. McDonough and Harrison, p.28.
19. Joan Smith (1977).

that massive investment in the socialisation of aspects of the family, thus releasing more women workers to produce surplus value for the capitalist class, would be of greater economic benefit to the capitalist system than the existing method of reproduction of labour power.[20]

It is important to stress this, because to view the family as being as central to the capitalist system as the process of exploitation itself leads to serious political problems: in particular, into equating the fight against oppression with that against exploitation. But while the privatised family is not essential to the survival of capitalism, its abolition is not at all likely while capitalism exists. There are a number of reasons for this. Centrally, the level of investment in the socialisation of the family which each capitalist state would have to undertake would be massive. Any individual state undertaking this task would be at a disadvantage, at least in the short term, with regard to its main rivals internationally. In periods of prosperity and expansion socialisation might be considered, but the crisis-ridden nature of the system is such that it becomes far too daunting for any single capitalist class. It is worth remembering that even in the record postwar boom, the level of spending on public child care provision by the advanced capitalist countries remained appallingly low.

Despite all the inefficiencies and inconsistencies of the privatised family in terms of the reproduction of labour power, any alternatives to it in a crisis-ridden, profit-oriented system are highly unlikely. The present combination of increased state intervention, a growing level of public child care (though often through private capitalist investment) and women's jobs "fitting in" with the care of young children, is therefore likely to continue.

Joan Smith's analysis fails to take into account the contradictions present in the family, and so slips into an almost mystical faith in the family's centrality to capitalism. By sticking rigidly to the-two-modes theory, she ends up moving back towards patriarchy analysis with its transhistorical features, rather than breaking with it.

One of the problems in developing a theory of the family has been the abandonment by so much of the academic left of any notion of base and superstructure. This abandonment developed at least in part from a rejection of rigid Stalinist notions of a deterministic relationship between the two. Today, however, it is widely but erroneously accepted that there is *no* real connection between the economic base of a particular society and the ideas which develop within it.

Some of the confusion over the base and superstructure distinction arises from the belief that by allocating the family to the superstructure, its economic role is thereby diminished, as is its importance as a unit of women's oppression. This is not the case. As Chris Harman has put it:

> the distinction between base and superstructure is a distinction between social relations which are subject to immediate changes with changes in the productive forces, and those which

---

20. Bruegel (1978).

are relatively static and resistant to change. The capitalist family belongs to the latter rather than the former category, even in its "economic" function of reproducing the labour force.[21]

The family has a very important economic role. This is equally true of other superstructural formations such as the capitalist state. But it does not form its own dynamic, nor is it part of the dynamic of capitalist production. Indeed as we have seen, it can act as a conservative force, a defence mechanism for the protection of its members against the ravages of class society. And its economic role is subordinate to the process of accumulation. This was the point made by Engels, and Marx gave a similar description of the family. The development of social production brought with it a corresponding decline of the family form of production: "The family, which to begin with is the only social relationship, becomes later, when increased needs create new social relations and the increased population new needs, a subordinate one".[22]

The domestic labour debate

Recognition of the centrality of the family to capitalism was one feature of attempts by Marxists in the late 1960s and early 1970s to theorise women's oppression. The domestic labour debate was about the economic contribution of women's labour in the home to the capitalist system of production. It was characterised by academicism and a level of abstraction. While it was a serious attempt to locate women's oppression in capitalist society and to use Marxist terminology to explain oppression, it was also a concession to feminist ideas. It was a response to the criticism that Marxism only concerned itself with production, and that Marxists always regarded housework as a totally separate sphere.

So while some of the writing on domestic labour produced some valuable insights, there were a number of major flaws in the arguments.

The early domestic labour theorists tended to emphasise the two modes of production and reproduction, and so accepted that housework formed a separate mode of production.[23] Many fell into the functionalist trap of believing that capitalism could not under any circumstances manage to survive without the privatised family. Others argued that the labour of women in the home was productive of surplus value through the commodity of labour power. So women constituted a separate class which had an interest in fighting for wages for housework.[24]

The problem with these theories was that both, in their different ways, separated housework off from social production. They first put domestic labour on a par with wage labour performed for the employer, equating it with socialised commodity production. Secondly, they implicitly assumed the continued existence of privatised domestic labour, by claiming that it constituted a separate mode of production.

---

21. Harman (1986), p.22.
22. Marx and Engels (1964), p.49.
23. See for example Harrison; and Seccombe.
24. DallaCosta and James.

Several critics of these various positions pointed out that housework could not be equated with wage labour in this way:

> To compare domestic labour with wage labour in a quantitative way is not comparing like with like. However unevenly it operates, the process of value creation within commodity production enables one to talk about quantities of abstract labour in the case of wage labour in a way that is not valid for domestic labour. It is therefore not possible to add together domestic labour-time and wage labour-time in order to calculate the wife's surplus labour because the two are not commensurate.[25]

The housewife has no rigid distinction between work and leisure; she is not directly controlled or supervised; and she is not producing for a market. She is atomised rather than part of a collective. Because market forces do not directly govern her work, the tasks connected with the reproduction of labour power are performed whether that labour power is in immediate demand or whether it is not (due to old age, unemployment and so on).

Nor is the housewife *directly* productive of surplus value. It is often argued that what the housewife produces are simply use values:

> Domestic labour is the production of use-values, the physical inputs for the production being commodities bought with part of the husband's wage. The housewife produces directly consumable use-values with them ... Child-care is the most time-consuming part of the work of full-time housewives ... it is the most essential task performed by the housewife for the continuance of capitalism.[26]

To say simply that the housewife is concerned with the production of use-values implies that she is merely a servant to her husband and children. However, domestic labour has a social role. The reason that child care is the most essential task performed for capitalism within the home is that there is a connection between this work and the production of surplus value. Put succinctly, "the relation of domestic labour to the production of surplus value is simply that the former makes the latter possible".[27]

Domestic labour can be seen to be *indirectly productive* of surplus value, through being directly productive of labour power. This feature is important in order to retain what is central to the domestic labour debate, and to draw the correct conclusions from it. The two dominant strands of the debate in fact lead to wrong conclusions: either to the wages-for-housework campaign espoused by Selma James, or to the idea that the use-values produced by the housewife have little to do with commodity production or indeed capitalism. This analysis leads to the view that the reproduction of labour power takes place outside the capitalist mode of production.[28] Either theory leads yet again to complete separatism in terms of struggle and the embracing of patriarchy theory.

---

25. "Women's domestic labour", in Political Economy of Women Group, p.10.
26. Political Economy of Women Group, p.9.
27. Political Economy of Women Group, p.13.
28. See for example Paul Smith, p.214.

The connection of domestic labour with capitalism lies not in the production of values but in the reproduction of labour power. The housewife produces only use-values; but these in turn affect the value of labour-power.

Separatist conclusions may not have been the intention of many of the domestic labour theorists. They saw their work as a serious attempt to theorise Marxism and women's oppression. But their attempt to put unpaid work in the home on a par with the categories of Marx's *Capital* led to a major weakness: the lack of an understanding of the connection between family and work. This may appear a contradiction, for after all, one of the central aspects of the reproduction of labour power under capitalism is the separation of home and work. But the two complement and reflect one another as well. Domestic labour exists in the form it does precisely because of wage labour and commodity production.

The domestic labour theorists instead saw the family as a separate sphere. They therefore set out to prove that women's domestic labour was central not just to the family but to the capitalist system as well. This led away from attempts to synthesise the two. It similarly failed to take sufficiently into account the fact that women's labour was increasingly social—outside the home, in the workplace. Consequently, the theory was only able to give a partial view of women's oppression.

Male benefits

By the late 1970s, the domestic labour theory was being usurped by more overtly patriarchal theory: in particular the view that men gained some material benefit from women's oppression in the home. Woman's oppression was seen as maintained through men's control of every aspect of her life, including work. So it has been argued that: "at marriage, the wife gives into the control of her husband both her labour power and her capacity to procreate in exchange for subsistence for a definite period, for life".[29]

Heidi Hartmann, who describes Marxism as "sex-blind", has attempted a similar materialist, rather than purely idealist, analysis of patriarchy, by arguing that "the material base upon which patriarchy rests lies most fundamentally in men's control over women's labour power".[30]

For Hartmann, control does not merely lie within the family but throughout the structures of capitalist society. She too bases her ideas on the two-modes-of-production analysis, and states quite categorically that fledgling capital and men of all classes went into alliance in order to maintain this control over women. Working-class men achieved this through ensuring protective legislation and a family wage. This kept women in the home and gave men a "higher standard of living than women in terms of luxury consumption, leisure time and personalised services".[31]

29. McDonough and Harrison, p.34.
30. Hartmann (1979), p.11.
31. Hartmann (1979), p.6.

Similar arguments are put by Zillah Eisenstein, who explicitly refers to "capitalist patriarchy" in her attempt to dene women's oppression.[32] The substance of this argument has been dealt with already, but it is worth pointing to a couple of its weaknesses. Firstly it stems from a total misunderstanding of women workers' relationship to the labour market. The woman worker sells her labour power on the market in exactly the same way that a male worker does. No mediating structure exists between female wage labourers and the capitalist class, preventing her from being able to sell her labour power. She is employed directly, without reference to her husband.

To pretend that women are somehow in a servile or bond relationship to their husbands with relation to the labour market is simply denying the facts. More important, it leaves patriarchy theorists with no understanding or explanation of the continued preference of the capitalist class for employing cheap female labour.[33]

Protective legislation and the family wage were, as we have seen, the result of class interests and part of a class response to the worst ravages of the system, when there seemed little alternative to the awful conditions the working class lived under. Nor were male workers in a powerful position over female ones: only a minority were even in unions; and protective legislation was nowhere near as devastating to women's work as some feminists imply. For example, hardly any such legislation existed in the US until well into the twentieth century, yet the structure of the working-class family in the US was similar to that in Britain. Johanna Brenner and Maria Ramas make this point in their article "Rethinking Women's Oppression":

> It is very difficult to make a convincing case that so precarious a socio-political edifice could have played a major role in conditioning the sexual division of labour or the family household system, either in England or the United States.[34]

In Britain, reductions in hours for women and children were often seen as beneficial for the whole working class, since they tended to shorten the working day. Where the unions did act to exclude women from work, they often did so for the most class-conscious reasons: to prevent the undercutting of wages and conditions.

> It is entirely unnecessary to resort to ideology to explain why trade unions were particularly adamant in their opposition to female entry into their trades. It is quite clear that when unions were unable to exclude women, a rapid depression of wages and general degradation of work resulted.[35]

Although it may be relatively easy to point to the inconsistencies of Hartmann's historical analysis, it is much harder to defeat the *thrust* of her argument, which does not depend on historical accuracy for its appeal. The idea that men do gain substantial benefits from women's labour in the family is widespread. Most feminists argue that men receive these

32. "Developing a theory of capitalist patriarchy", in Eisenstein, pp.5–40.
33. They cannot comprehend the fact that married women workers have been the "strongest area of employment growth, both full and part-time ... Between March 1983 and September 1987, the male employed labour force rose by 394,000 and the female by 1.116 million". (*Financial Times* (London), 17 February 1988).
34. Brenner and Ramas, p.40.
35. Brenner and Ramas, p.45.

real benefits—more leisure, more food, more power—and it is this which leads them to support the status quo.

These ideas are powerful precisely because they reflect the appearance of the society in which we live. After all, the "common sense" of society points to the fact that men get their meals cooked, that they have control over family finances, that they retain control over their wives and children. This is certainly how things would appear and, most feminists would argue, how they actually are.[36]

Yet again, the argument centres on the role of the family under capitalism. Is it for the reproduction of labour power or is it additionally for the benefit of individual men? If the latter proposition is true, then does this mean that working-class men have a *material* interest in defending the capitalist system?

To argue that men do have such an interest leads away from a class analysis of women's oppression. It is in the overwhelming interest of the working class to fight for the overthrow of the society which exploits them and therefore to fight for—among other things—the liberation of women. It is in the interests of the capitalist class, on the other hand, for labour power to be reproduced privately as it is at present: for women to labour inside and outside the home, being paid low wages for work outside and nothing for domestic labour; and for the man to see his responsibility in society as providing, however inadequately, for his wife and family.

This situation leads to unequal relationships between the sexes, and within the family. But it does not lead to a situation where the man benefits. On the contrary, all members of the family would benefit from being able to live in a society where relationships were not straitjacketed as they are at present.

Often the question of male benefits is reduced simply to one of power. The argument, put at its most basic, is that whereas the male worker is exploited, alienated and downtrodden through his relationship to the capitalist at work, at least in the home he is boss. He can bully and sometimes physically assault his offspring and wife. Even where he does not do so, he controls the home, both financially and ideologically.

But the working class as a whole is characterised not by its power, but its *powerlessness*. The worker is denied access to the product of his or her labour, and through this is denied access to property or to any real standing inside capitalist society. The only worth of the worker to capitalism is his or her ability to sell labour power. Once this ability no longer exists—through age, sickness or there being a surplus of labour power—then workers are denied even the few crumbs granted to them while in work.

Some feminists talk about patriarchy as a hierarchical pyramid, with old, white men at the pinnacle. The picture could not be more misleading, for inside capitalist society it is only *rich* old white men who have any real power. Once workers are too old to sell

---

36. This argument has been extensively debated in *International Socialism*. See Chris Harman, "Women's Liberation and Revolutionary Socialism", in 2:23 (Spring 1984); John Molyneux, "Do working-class men benefit from women's oppression?" in 2:25 (Autumn 1984); Sheila McGregor, "A reply to John Molyneux on women's oppression", in 2:30; and John Molyneux and Lindsey German, "Debate on Marxism and Male Benefits", in 2:32 (Summer 1986). See also Lindsey German, "Theories of Patriarchy", in 2:12 (Spring 1981); Lin James and Anna Paczuska, "Socialism needs feminism", in 2:14 (Autumn 1981).

their labour power, they are hardly valued at all by capitalist society, since they no longer possess the ability to earn and therefore to spend money. This contrasts strongly with feudal society, where old men (heads of the patriarchal family) often have the monopoly of power within the family. But a crucial feature of capitalism is the lack of power of the working class.

Images of the man as an all-powerful and dominant figure inside the family are in reality a capitulation to the stereotypical "Andy Capp" view of what the working class looks like. They degrade the role of working-class women within the family, and suggest that women and children are totally passive and submissive. There are, of course, families which fit the mythical stereotype; many more do not. In some families the women have control of finance within the family. In some men and women co-exist happily; in others the family becomes an arena of struggle between different family members.

The idea that the family is a patriarchal plot can be rapidly dispelled when considering the often quite backward role of the woman in socialisation within the family. It is simply not true that sex roles and gender definition are always forced on women. Often women are some of the strictest enforcers of oppressive sex roles, as for example when mothers force their daughters to conform to these roles.

The argument about male benefits clearly reinforces patriarchy theory, and predicates two separate and autonomous spheres of struggle. It also leads to another argument quite dominant among the left: that the unequal situation in the home can be solved by either reversing the roles of men and women or by evening up the amount of housework done by both sexes. The argument is put, for example, by Beatrix Campbell and Arma Coote in *Sweet Freedom*: "If women are to share domestic labour equally with men; then men will have to increase their time spent on unpaid work".[37]

Few could argue with the sentiments of equal work-sharing in the home. But the political argument often takes the form of utopianism. Although the strategy can improve the lot of individual women, it does not raise the question of why *anyone* should have to engage in boring repetitive drudgery around the home. In addition, because work-sharing does not challenge the fundamental structure of society, it is likely to remain a utopian dream. Given that society is structured so that men tend to work longer hours for more money, altering women's role in the household will require more far-reaching changes than work-sharing.

The division of labour in the home today is reinforced by the patterns of work in the workplace—the fact that men work far more overtime than women (especially when they have young children, because women are least able to work at this time) and that they tend to travel further to work. That is why it is much easier for middle-class men—who are more likely to earn a reasonable income without overtime—to share child care.

Failure to understand this leads to the sort of narrow reformism expressed by Michele Barrett and Mary McIntosh in *The Anti-Social Family*. They argue that feminists should avoid oppressive relationships and live pure feminist lives, avoiding coquettish behaviour

37. Campbell and Coote, p.247.

and marriage—even avoiding going to other people's weddings. Their real concerns are revealed in one of the most telling statements of modern feminism:

> For those who can afford it, paying someone to clean the house or cook meals is preferable to making it the duty of one household member. Many socialists have qualms about this, without being very clear why ... It should be more like engaging a plumber and less like having a skivvy.[38]

Most women, of course, are likely to be the ones doing the paid cleaning rather than employing the cleaner; even if such an option were desirable, which it is not, it is simply not available for most women workers. Role reversals do not begin to challenge the privatised family and its role in the reproduction of labour power.

Yet the reason many feminists put forward such arguments is not simply to do with their feminism. Their politics rests on the reform of the existing system, rather than its revolutionary overthrow. Patriarchy theory fits exactly with such an outlook.

Ideas of patriarchy allow the continuation of the existing privatised family regardless of the social conditions under which it exists. Patriarchy theory can coexist with the gradual reforms of the Labour Party. It is a welcome alibi for Communist Party feminists such as Beatrix Campbell. She and others influenced by Stalinist ideas played a major role in popularising these theories throughout much of the 1970s. They provided a justification for continuing support for the oppressive and exploitative regimes in Eastern Europe by giving a feminist veneer to explanations for the various inequalities there. How else, after all, could one explain the oppression of women in the "socialist countries" or the discrimination against gays in Cuba or East Germany? One can either conclude that these countries have nothing to do with socialism, or that socialism cannot bring women's liberation—and a separate fight against patriarchy is needed.

The extent to which patriarchy theory has been adopted shows the dominance of reformist ideas within the socialist and women's movements. Most feminists are happy to concur with Heidi Hartmann when she argues:

> I do not agree with those who argue that the USSR, China, and Cuba are not socialist—they may not have the socialism we would like, but they regard themselves as socialist and so do most other folks.[39]

This may not be the most scientific analysis, but it has the virtue of encapsulating the dominant view in the women's movement. It is also typical of an anti-intellectual approach common among many patriarchy theorists. This leads them to attack any serious or rigorous attempt to theorise women's oppression. So Jane Humphries is described as "non-feminist"[40] while the domestic labour debate is derided as "functionalist".[41]

Perhaps the greatest weakness of patriarchy theory, however, is that it parallels the separation of home from work which is a feature of capitalist society. Feminists as a whole

38. Barrett and McIntosh (1982), pp.144–5.
39. Hartmann, in Sargent, p.364.
40. Campbell and Charlton.
41. See for example Bruegel; and Barrett, pp.172–5.

were slow to recognise or acknowledge that women were no longer simply housewives but played a crucial role in the workforce; many have still not come to terms with this fact. The separation is convenient for those who pretend that economic struggle goes on at work, whereas political or ideological struggle takes place elsewhere. Some of these people even try to deny that women workers really are part of the working class—relegating only manual workers to the proletariat. So men are seen stereotypically as manual workers, while women are seen equally stereotypically as oppressed housewives.

This is a major error in considering the working class today. Women are a major and permanent part of the working class. As we shall see, there are major divisions inside the working class, that between the sexes being one of the most fundamental. But that women are part of the working class is indisputable. To see them as separate means developing only a *partial* understanding of women's oppression.

To develop a total picture we need to look at the working class as a totality. We must also see the family as part of class society—a product of the capitalist mode of production. Viewed like this, the fate of the family is seen to be tied up with the fate of capitalism itself. The ending of women's oppression is inextricably linked to the self-emancipation of the working class.

Part II: Women at work

CHAPTER FOUR

The sexual division of labour

Women in Britain may be workers on almost as wide a scale as men, but they often do different work. Job segregation is widespread. Among full-time women workers, 58 per cent work in "women only" jobs; among part-time workers a full 70 per cent.[1] Women are also concentrated in fewer occupations than men. It is often assumed that because of this sexual division of labour, women do the jobs which are badly rewarded, easily disposable and undervalued in capitalist society. Men, it is argued, have all the industrially powerful jobs, while women are relegated to the periphery of work.

But it is only possible to draw such a conclusion by looking at a *minority* of women workers—and even then in a fairly simplistic way. Within the work done by women there are major differences, with distinct patterns of female employment for full-time and part-time workers. The work done by full-time women workers in particular gives the lie to the idea that women's work is marginal to the economy, and shows that many women are in work which is very important to the running of the system.

A full 42 per cent of full-time women workers are in clerical and related occupations—by far the biggest single occupation for women. This category includes work such as banking and insurance, local and national government, and major aspects of retailing and marketing. The vast majority of these workers are machine operators or routine clerical workers. The second largest occupation is professional and related in education, welfare and health: teachers, social workers, nurses and so on. At 19 per cent of full-time workers, these are less than half the number of clerical workers.[2]

The pattern of part-time work is very different. By far the largest occupation among part-time workers is catering, cleaning, hairdressing and other personal services: 39 per cent, compared with only 9 per cent of full-time workers in this sector. The other occupation with a higher proportion of part-time than full-time women workers is selling (12 per cent as opposed to 6 per cent). Analysis on the basis of industry rather than occupation shows similar patterns. Over half of all part-time workers are in either

---

1. Martin and Roberts, chapter 3. Figures for the United States show a similar pattern. In 1985, 70 per cent of full-time women workers were concentrated in occupations which were at least three-quarters female (see Rix, p.118).
2. *Equal Opportunities Commission Report 1986.*

professional and scientific services or retail distribution and repairs. Only a third of full-time women are in these same two industries.[3]

The typical woman worker is much more likely to be in a clerical or professional job (nursing, social work, teaching) than in catering or cleaning. In fact nearly as high a proportion of women work in engineering (4 per cent) as in hotels and catering (5 per cent).[4] Yet the popular image of the woman worker is much more commonly that of a cleaner or kitchen hand rather than an engineering worker.

Figures for particular industries bear this out. So women comprise 28 per cent of the workforce in the chemical industry, 28 per cent in instrument engineering, 30 per cent in electrical engineering, 35 per cent in food, drink and tobacco manufacture—as well as nearly half in textiles and 69 per cent in footwear and clothing.[5]

Women still comprise a sizeable proportion of the manufacturing workforce. However, it is in services that the expansion of jobs for women has been greatest. This is part of an overall trend. Jobs have declined overall in manufacturing in the past 20 years, and this has been true for women as well as men, although men are harder hit. Jobs in the service industries, meanwhile, have increased. But the new jobs have not only been women's jobs. Part-time jobs going to men in the service industries have increased at a faster rate than those for women during the 1980s (although from a smaller base).[6] And in one of the most expanding areas of services over this period, banking, finance and insurance, female employment has grown at about the same rate as male employment.[7]

Yet despite the real differences in women's employment prospects and opportunities, there clearly is a real sexual division of labour which ensures that certain jobs remain closed to one or other sex. This in turn implies that a whole set of values and assumptions are tied to certain jobs. How has this situation come about? Why do the expressions "men's work" and "women's work" form such a common part of our everyday vocabulary and experience? The answer is to be found in the particular way in which the capitalist mode of production has moulded and formed the sexual division of labour to suit its particular needs.

Certainly this division of labour preceded capitalism. Indeed the earliest divisions of labour, as Marx and Engels pointed out, were sexual.[8] The sexual division of labour itself arose from women's position in society. The fact that biologically women were the childbearers and childrearers meant that they were to an extent restricted geographically and physically. In some of the earliest forms of society there were certain tasks which were allotted to men while others were allotted to women. Inequality was not necessarily attached to this division. Indeed in some of these societies the sexual division of labour was minor: men and women did all the necessary tasks, including child care, interchangeably.

---

3. *Equal Opportunities Commission Report 1986.*
4. *Equal Opportunities Commission Report 1986.*
5. *Equal Opportunities Commission Report 1986.*
6. *Employment Gazette,* January 1989.
7. *Employment Gazette,* January 1989.
8. Marx and Engels (1964), pp.42–3.

But by the time the domestic household system had developed in the late middle ages, with its unequal and male-dominated family structure, the sexual division of labour was structured in such a way that women were put at a disadvantage. Their labour was not usually waged, and they depended for their livelihood, board and food on the head of the household, who was usually male. Production in and around the home tied them even more to the family.

There was no particular reason why this division should continue under capitalism. As we have seen, the old family was destroyed and with it the forms of production within the family. In the major arena of early factory production—the textile industry—the sexual division of labour was turned literally upside down. The division of tasks in the industry was reversed. Women—traditionally spinners when textile production was confined to the home—became weavers inside the mill. The job of mule spinning went to the men, who traditionally had worked at weaving in the home.

This alteration in the traditional division of labour came about as a result of the introduction of new technology, particularly the spinning jenny and the mule. Technology completely changed the production process, allowing people who had previously been unable to work at certain jobs—especially women and children—to do so. The impact of this change was contradictory. Initially at least it seemed to bring benefits to a wide range of workers. But the traditional male handloom weavers suffered terribly. Their incomes and conditions were undercut by the new methods. At the same time young women were able to work for reasonable wages. This was a step forward for them, but even so they worked long hours in bad conditions.

As the factory system developed, far from the sexual division of labour in the textile equalising out, it became more uneven. The real sharp change came in the years after the Napoleonic Wars, when further technological innovation pulled more and more women and young children into work. Increased productivity in larger mills brought about the kinds of conditions which Engels described so graphically in the 1840s.[9] The labour force in the cotton towns was overwhelmingly young and increasingly female by the middle decades of the nineteenth century. A study of Stockport in the 1840s to 1860s shows that:

> Women made up 44 per cent of cotton workers aged ten to 69 in the sample in 1841, 49 per cent in 1851 and 55 per cent in 1861, while the proportion of women under thirty increased from 36 per cent to 41 per cent and the proportion of women in their twenties increased from 14 per cent to 20 per cent.[10]

The same study indicates that women moved increasingly into the more skilled jobs. So by 1865, 56 per cent of mule spinners were women (compared with 30 per cent in 1841) and 65 per cent of power loom weavers were women (compared with 55 per cent in 1841).[11]

---

9. See Engels (1973), pp.112–3.
10. Burr Litchfield, p.182.
11. Burr Litchfield, p.185.

The breakdown of the sexual division of labour can be seen in other ways. The Poor Law Commissioners attempted to encourage the migration of families into manufacturing areas such as Lancashire after 1834. Between 1834 and the 1837 depression, 203 families (1,660 people) migrated under contract. But the men often earned less than their wives or children and were sometimes employed as carters or porters. The Commissioners' "concern with the size of migrants' families in this attempt reflects the great need for the labour of children and adolescents and the limited opportunities for adult males".[12] The wages of teenage workers were such that they "were able to free themselves from total economic dependence on the nuclear family".[13]

Other industries were transformed too by machinery or new methods of working. Again the traditional division of labour was turned upside down. For example, women were not central to the Staffordshire pottery industry until the introduction of machinery in 1845. After that date, the proportion of women working in the industry rose steadily.[14]

So it is hard to disagree with the view that the development of the factory system in textiles, and of factory production in other industries, dealt a blow to the traditional division of labour:

> The employment of women and children as weavers, to the exclusion of men, represented a decisive break with the traditional sexual division of labour in the family. A child could earn more in the factory than his/her father could earn at home on the loom.[15]

There was every reason, looking at the early development of capitalism, to believe that the pre-capitalist division of labour had broken down. And the textile industry in its heyday looked like the model of future industrial development. The capitalist class employed women workers and children to fulfil its constant thirst for the cheapest and most adaptable labour power. In the process the old family relationships, on which patriarchal authority had rested, were destroyed. Capitalism had no desire or particular need to favour men as wage labourers rather than women.

But the pattern established within the textile industry proved atypical. The development of factory production, and with it the revolutionising effect on the work process of new technology, was uneven. So in some industries the dominance of the man established in the pre-capitalist period remained largely unaffected.

In addition, women workers tended to be locked within the cotton industry, not to branch out into the newer developing industries. So throughout the whole of the nineteenth century the two major sectors which employed women remained textiles and domestic service. There were many regional variations, and many women worked in seasonal or casual trades, such as needlework, selling and agriculture, as well as in full-time permanent work. However, women tended to be excluded from a number

---

12. Smelser, p.202.
13. Anderson, pp.129–30.
14. Hewitt, p.18.
15. Hall, p.24.

of areas of work which were becoming increasingly important to the development of British capitalism as textiles lost their pre-eminent position.

There were, as we have seen, by the mid-nineteenth century few women in coal-mining (apart from a small number of pitbrow lasses). There were also none in shipbuilding and much of heavy engineering. Some of the reasons for this are easily accounted for: protective legislation, the insistence of groups of craft trade unions that women should be excluded from certain jobs.

However these features alone do not explain the phenomenon. Most industry was not directly affected either by protective legislation or by union protectionism (even in 1870 union membership only stood at 400,000—a small proportion of the working class).[16] The answer lies in the changing structure of capitalism, the different needs of the capitalist class from those of its workforce, and the disadvantage at which women found themselves in such circumstances.

There were two developments in particular which shaped the divisions in the working class. One was the increased investment in skilled labour power by the capitalist class. The other was the change inside the working-class family, the rising cost of the reproduction of labour power within the family and the role of women's fertility.

The changing nature of industry led to bigger plants and much greater investment by the capitalist class. Textiles lost their dominance, to be replaced by heavy industry. John Foster, in his study of the cotton town of Oldham, described the process:

> If the cotton industry can be said to have acted as the high-profit sector of the early industrial revolution (when engineering was still the preserve of the small master), the positions of the two industries were certainly reversed by mid-century—with the crucial differences that while cotton had been genuinely competitive, engineering was dominated by a mere handful of giants.[17]

Such giant industry depended on large concentrations of capital and massive investment; the capital owned by Platt's in Oldham in 1867 was £900,000—three times that of the whole local cotton industry.[18]

In order to work this machinery and to ensure the maximum return on investment, the ruling class wanted a much more highly trained and more permanent workforce. No longer was it felt sufficient to draw in masses of cheap child and female labour, which could be constantly replenished. What was needed instead was at least a substantial number of workers who had a degree of skill in operating the machinery—sometimes skill learned over a period of time. Restricted entry to certain sorts of work through apprenticeships became more common.

Women were at a major disadvantage in the labour market when it came to the question of training and apprenticeships. Their reproductive functions, and the fact that women's work was likely to be interrupted through childbirth, if not curtailed,

16. Rule, p.166.
17. Foster, p.229.
18. Foster, p.229.

meant they were considered much less likely to work permanently. Apprentice-based jobs became the preserve of men. Other work too, such as heavy labouring and dock work, was the prerogative of men. And the restructuring of the family both assumed and reinforced these trends.

Changes in patterns of employment were paralleled by developments in working-class life. In particular, the increase in public education towards the end of the nineteenth century changed the nature of the workforce. Children went to work later; more time and money was spent on their care and reproduction inside the home. It was the woman who bore the burden of this.

Therefore the family—and women's work within it—have remained central to the nature of the sexual division of labour in waged work. Yet it is over-simplistic to see the family as merely *conditioning* the nature of women's work. This is put crudely by a number of feminist historians, who see in women's waged work an exact duplication of their role inside the family. So Sally Alexander has argued that the division of labour is "a division sustained by ideology not biology, an ideology whose material manifestation is embodied and reproduced within the family and then transferred from the family into social production".[19]

This analysis does little to help us understand the division of labour in the past, and is of even less use in making sense of women's waged work today. Women's jobs do fit in with child care. But the part-time, casual or temporary jobs which are often taken by working mothers to fit in with childminders, school hours or holidays are not typical of the pattern of employment for the female workforce. These jobs were never the dominant "women's jobs" at any time throughout the nineteenth century. They have been typical only for those women at the margins of the labour market.

While it is true that domestic service overall was the largest single employer of women in the nineteenth century, its attraction as an employer was limited. It was especially the women of the rural areas who became domestic servants. For them there was often little choice. As Britain became more and more an industrial power, so a smaller proportion of the workforce worked the land. Whereas 12 per cent of women workers were in agriculture in the earlier nineteenth century, that proportion had dropped to only 2 per cent by 1881.[20]

Many rural women had to migrate to the towns and cities to work as domestic servants. "Only a quarter of London servants were London-born, and in Lincoln, Reading, Coventry and Bath over three-quarters of the servants came from rural districts, 45–55 per cent being born within a 20-mile radius."[21]

What these figures indicate is a division of labour not just along sexual lines but stratified through different generations of workers. The lowest-paid jobs were taken by the incoming rural labourers—since domestic service represented an advance in wages

19. Alexander, p.111.
20. Lewis (1984), p.156.
21. Lewis (1984), p.157.

and conditions on agricultural labour—but tended to be rejected by those women who could earn a living in other ways. There is further evidence that even those women who went to work in domestic service were quick to leave it when they got the chance, and they wanted something better for their children. So by 1911, census figures show a marked decline in the number of women in domestic service (and in the other major employer of women, the now rapidly declining textile industry).

Yet these women were not by and large absorbed into home-related work; instead they entered new and expanding industries:

> These women were reabsorbed primarily by the clerical and distributive services and to a lesser extent by the metals, paper, chemicals and food, drink and tobacco trades. The growth in these occupations were sufficient to absorb a particularly large increase in the numbers of women working between 1901 and 1911.[22]

So even by the beginning of the twentieth century, women's employment was adopting a familiar pattern. These trends were confirmed as the workforce and women's part in it steadily expanded. It would be untrue to say that *all* women were employed in such industries. There have always been a wide range of occupations which women, especially for married women, have entered to supplement family income. These include dress-making and other sewing trades, hatting, laundering, cleaning and selling (often on a casual basis). But these occupations have become increasingly less important as capitalist society has expanded, thus providing other large-scale employment for working women.

Fertility and the sexual division of labour

A major change in the sexual division of labour took place as the capitalist system developed. The rise and early expansion of capitalism was accompanied by a major growth of the population. This growth has continued, but has increasingly been the result of greater longevity. Medical advances, better sanitation and in the twentieth century increased welfare spending have all led to people living longer. Parallel to this has been a steady decline in the birthrate as women have chosen to have fewer children. Generally speaking, as women have entered the workforce more, so their fertility rate has declined.

It would be wrong to oversimplify the pattern of women's fertility within the working class. During the nineteenth and early twentieth centuries there were major differences in fertility rates between areas, and within different occupations. For example, the fertility rate among miners' families in the first half of this century was the highest of all occupations. This was followed closely by agricultural labourers and unskilled labourers. Textile labourers on the other hand, ranked almost as low in fertility as the professional and middle classes. Their fertility rate was substantially lower than that of skilled workers.[23]

---

22. Lewis (1984), p.157.
23. Gittins (1982), p.82.

Analysis on a regional basis establishes a similar picture, with the mining area of the Rhondda possessing one of the highest marital fertility rates, while the textile area of Burnley had one of the lowest.[24]

The explanation for these discrepancies lies at least partly in the nature of the sexual division of labour within different working-class families. Mining areas, especially largely rural ones like South Wales, provided little employment for women. They were prohibited from working in the pits and there was little other work to be found locally. So the pattern of employment was often women migrating from the mining areas to work elsewhere (often in domestic service) while men migrated into mining areas from agricultural work.

In textiles, there were always far more employment opportunities for women. Women were much more able to engage in full-time work outside the home. So in Burnley, both in the 1911 and 1931 censuses, over two-thirds of all women aged 15–64 were employed; nearly a quarter of these were also married, and all but 15 per cent were employed in textiles.[25]

The figures would seem to suggest that where women had the opportunity to work outside the home for adequate wages they did so, and that the availability of this work determined the level of fertility for married women, rather than—as is often thought—the other way round. So women would tend to have more children when paid work was not available. The area where work was most readily available to wo men—the Lancashire textile industry—had higher rates for abortion than elsewhere.[26]

Women also tended to have more children when they could easily combine paid work and work in the home. This conclusion is drawn by Diana Gittins in her interesting study of women's fertility, *The Fair Sex*:

> Agricultural work, outwork etc. are not connected with low fertility because they do not conflict with a woman's role as childbearer and childrearer. Only when work is distinctly separate from the home does it become associated with low fertility.[27]

So it is not surprising that areas of high fertility included not just mining, but the male-dominated shipbuilding and engineering area of Gateshead and the unskilled working-class area of Bethnal Green in London. Diana Gittins describes this area's characteristics:

> Most ... jobs were unskilled or semi-skilled, and insecurity and underemployment were common. Moreover, the majority of these jobs were very much male-dominated (unlike the textile industry) and, while wages were poor relative to other areas, they were a good deal higher than those which working-class women in the area could earn. Marriages were therefore likely to be characterised by segregated and unequal role-relationships, and the traditional values among local social groups were apt to deem large families and female responsibility for birth control normative.[28]

24. Gittins (1982), p.64.
25. Gittins (1982), p.101.
26. Knight, p.53.
27. Gittins (1982), p.187.
28. Gittins (1982), p.88.

The differences in fertility among different groups of workers also had implications for the sexual division of labour inside the home. In the mining areas couples married young, the wives did not work and there were numbers of children. A study of late nineteenth-century mining towns in northern France shows that

> the division of labour by sex in the coal miners' or metalworkers' families was especially sharp. Men and boys worked in heavy labour removed from the household. Married women generally stayed in the home and were responsible for housework, childbearing and child care.[29]

In these and other areas where women did not work outside the home, their major role was seen very much as that of dependent wife and mother, with all the inequality this implied. "The basic differences between women who worked and women who stayed at home after marriage was in their ideologies of the home, the family and children."[30]

Diana Gittins' various interviews with different working-class women show marked disparities between women who worked, especially those who worked alongside men in the textile industries, and those who did not. Women who worked had a much greater degree of equality in the home, and the husband and wife appeared to have much more in common. Conversely, the most unequal and bitter relationships were, she found, those which saw the man and woman in totally different roles. In such relationships, the men tended to do no housework at all. In contrast, textile women talked about the equal sharing of tasks by their husbands and children.[31]

Obviously no study of this sort can be conclusive, as it relies on subjective memory and so forth. But it is an important indication that the stereotypical view of the working-class family is at best only true for a minority of working-class people. And it further dents the notion that the sexual division of labour is the result of male patriarchal privilege. Instead it can clearly be seen to be based on material factors. Where opportunities to enter the labour market were available to women, it is clear that these were seized upon. Considerations on who performed the household tasks were then made in the light of the division of labour outside the home.

As the twentieth century advanced, there were signs of an evening up of fertility rates inside the working class. There was an overall decline in the number of live births and in the size of families, although even at the beginning of the century there were significant differences in infant mortality between different areas of London. So mortality was twice as high in Shoreditch, at over 18 per cent, as it was in Hampstead.[32] Clearly the difference can only be explained in terms of class.

By the 1930s, families were becoming much smaller. There were a number of reasons for this: the effects of unemployment on working-class families, which may have led to a reduction in size (as in the Rhondda, where fertility slumped dramatically between 1911 and 1931); the growth of education, which tended to raise the costs of reproduction and

29. Tilly, p.28.
30. Gittins (1982), p.155.
31. Gittins (1982), chapter 5.
32. Ross, p.81.

so limit the number of children in each family; the increasing importance of leisure time; and the easier availability of contraception. These factors combined to mean smaller families, less time spent in the functions of biological reproduction and an increase in women's general health and lifespan (which improved faster than those of men).[33] These changes in turn had a profound effect on the sexual division of labour at work, and began to shape the contours of the contemporary female working class.

The new industries

Modern industry and the present sexual division of labour is usually assumed to have its roots in the postwar boom which stretched from the late 1940s to the late 1960s. In fact, these patterns of employment date from the years between the two world wars. The number of women in paid work increased substantially, despite high levels of unemployment. The proportion of employed women grew by 16.7 per cent between 1923 and 1933.[34] In the United States, which suffered much more severe unemployment than Britain during the Depression, the female workforce grew by 22 per cent between 1930 and 1940.[35]

These dramatic increases in the numbers of working women began a trend which has continued until the present day. But the new women workers tended not to enter the old traditional industries. Instead they worked in new and expanding areas. The reason for this is easy to ascertain. The period between the wars was one of major re-structuring of industry. Traditional women's work of the nineteenth century—textiles and domestic service—was declining rapidly. So was much of traditional men's work, in the coal mines, in heavy engineering and in shipbuilding.

Young unmarried women in particular no longer wanted to work in domestic service. Figures there too fell steadily during the inter-war period. By the 1930s, women in indus-trial jobs outweighed those in domestic service.[36] At the same time, in various parts of the country (the Midlands, London, the South East) there grew up what became known as the "new industries": motor vehicles, aircraft, electrical goods and food-processing. A typical feature of these changes was the widespread employment of women—the female labour force doubled in certain industries, including food, drink and tobacco, chemicals, metalwork, engineering and electrical, and banking, insurance and finance.[37]

The case of electrical engineering is probably fairly typical. The industry expanded massively.[38] There was one overwhelming reason for this: the rapidly growing market for electricity and electrical goods. Eight million houses were connected to the national grid by 1938, compared with only half a million in 1919. This led to a huge expansion in

---

33. Lewis (1984), p.23.
34. Soldon, p.135.
35. Kolko, p.262.
36. Lewenhak (1980), p.208.
37. Lewenhak (1977), p.217.
38. Glucksmann, pp.22–3.

demand for electrical consumer goods and basic lighting equipment. Radio production expanded 378 per cent from 1930 to 1935. Morphy Richards was producing 5,000 electric irons a week through assembly line techniques by 1939. Women became key unskilled and semi-skilled workers in the manufacture of lamps, batteries, telephone and wireless equipment, valves, heaters and cookers.

By 1931 there were 68,000 women in electrical engineering—a rise of 123 per cent over ten years. There was a similar rise in women employed in other "new industries", and in the expanding clerical sector. The emphasis in these new rising industries was less on the old skills which had been common in heavy engineering (and which were entirely the province of a minority of male workers). Instead semi-skilled workers came into greater prominence. These were often women who learned sometimes intricate skills without a time-served apprenticeship—and who needless to say did not receive the rates of pay which skilled men received.

The expansion of these industries began the process which took ever larger numbers of single women from the home—and increasingly saw the employment of married women too. Referring to the vast expansion of women's work, which began in the inter-war years but really took off after 1945, Sheila Lewenhak describes it thus:

> Women became part of the cycle of production in which they themselves manufactured the canned and frozen foods, the labour-saving machines for homes; in which they provided the services that in turn eased their own domestic workload and enabled others to go out to make luxury articles.[39]

By the outbreak of the Second World War, this trend was well established. But why were women, employed in these industries? Why were men not taken on? After all, levels of unemployment were high throughout the inter-war years.

Part of the answer lies in the major restructuring of industry. Areas where heavy industry was concentrated saw massive lay-offs and closures. Many workers, especially young men and women, migrated from areas such as Central Scotland, the North East and South Wales. So the new industries, situated outside the depressed areas, often experienced labour shortages, amid an overall pattern of high unemployment. The employers therefore welcomed both migrants from the unemployed areas and women. The new women workers ideally fitted the need for young, hardworking and flexible labour (it is estimated that over half the workers in electrical engineering were under 21 in the 1930s).[40]

Women workers were also often amenable to the new production line techniques. From their point of view, these jobs had plenty of advantages. They provided better wages and conditions than most other work available, especially domestic service, and paid work was increasingly essential for many women during a period of recession. The

---

39. Lewenhak (1980), p.229.
40. From a 1937 survey by John Gollan, quoted in Glucksmann, p.27.

effect of unemployment appears to have been to throw more women onto the labour market in order to compensate for the loss of the male wage within many families.[41]

Although women welcomed this new employment, they were likely to start on the bosses' terms. The rates of pay they received were well below those paid to men. They were seen by many employers as a pliable, docile, "green" workforce, without the tradition of union involvement of many men. Hence they were often taken on *in preference* to men by employers.

The situation today

These developments are important if we are to understand why the sexual divisions inside the labour market continue to exist today. Obviously there is no one simple answer, especially not in terms of any theory of patriarchy.

Within the traditional industries sexual divisions have tended to remain more rigid: women in textiles, clothing, footwear; men in mining, shipbuilding and heavy engineering. But as all these industries have declined, so major changes have taken place.

If patriarchy is not the reason for the continued divisions, how then do we explain them? Firstly we should understand the employment of women in terms of the needs of the capitalist class. Employers have always attempted to find the cheapest, most pliable and least resistant workforce at any particular time. Because of the nature of the capitalist system itself, whose dynamic involves constant revolutionising of the means of production, it is constantly in search of new workforces.

In the past 50 years, therefore, new and traditionally inexperienced groups of workers—such as women and immigrants—have been constantly pulled into capitalist production. So the first and major reason for the continuing division of labour is to be found in the period when women entered the labour force in large numbers. Women provided cheap flexible labour which undercut that of men in the new industries. So there was no reluctance on the part of the employers to pull women into these industries.

This process was accelerated in the years after 1945. The long boom of the 1950s and early 1960s meant women were drawn into often part-time work both in manufacturing, and more commonly, in the growing clerical and services sectors. Women entered these jobs precisely because their entry into work coincided with the expansion of such jobs. At the same time, the nature of certain jobs changed as they became mass female occupations. Clerical work expanded into a mass, low grade and low-waged occupation. As it did so, it became more identified with women workers. Today women comprise roughly three-quarters of the clerical workforce. This has led to a concomitant downgrading of its status:

---

41. For an interesting study on women's employment in the US see Milkman (1976).

> In 1911 the proportion of women in clerical occupations, shop assistant and sales work was broadly comparable to their contribution to the labour force as a whole; by 1971 these occupations had become typically feminine.[42]

As clerical work expanded, so women increasingly entered the workforce and took the majority of clerical jobs.

However to describe such jobs as "feminine" is more than a little misleading. Yet it is an extremely common misconception to believe that men do the "real" jobs in society today while women perform jobs which are only a duplication of their role in the home.[43] According to this theory, women are engaged overwhelmingly in "caring work": they tend the sick as nurses, cook in canteens, clean offices, look after children; even their work in factories duplicates their home work—for example a major female employer in manufacturing is the food-processing industry.

The reality of women's work is very different from this picture. The majority of women workers are not in cooking or cleaning jobs but in clerical, professional, education and welfare or selling. Even when women do replicate their "traditional role" they require a skill qualification in order to do so. For example, just because you are a woman does not mean you can become a cook in a canteen; the job requires a level of training.

Crucial, however, is how the capitalist process of production transforms the labour performed in the factory or office. Production line food-processing has nothing to do with preparing food in the home; there is little in common between packing biscuits or canning peas, and cooking the Sunday roast. Even if a particular task performed in a factory is similar to one performed in the home (or originally performed in the home), such as working at a sewing machine, its nature is transformed by factory production. Work is performed under pressure of time and supervision, often on production line techniques, with a specific number of rigidly defined breaks allowed. The woman in the factory cannot combine her work with other tasks, such as looking after children or cooking, as she can in the home, and the end product is not something the worker produces for herself, either to use or to sell.

Indeed women's work has been subject to increased "proletarianisation" over the years. This is most obvious in clerical work. A minority and often male occupation until after the First World War, its expansion saw its downgrading socially with the development of mass production techniques and the introduction of women workers on a mass scale. The inter-war years saw the introduction of the typing pool. Since then women have formed the bulk of typists, comptometer operators, key punch operators and word processor operators, as well as clerks. These workers will often work in large and tightly supervised offices, with certain quotas to achieve. Often they will have to clock in. Their work is certainly cleaner than factory work, and still tends to enjoy a slightly higher status, but it is hardly less regimented.

---

42. Hakim (1978).
43. See for example Joan Smith (1977); Hartmann (1979); Hakim (1978).

The popular view of the mass of clerical workers as personal secretaries servicing the egos of their male bosses is inaccurate. Secretarial work, like the rest of clerical work, has become proletarianised. Secretaries who do play a servicing role for individual men (often not even typing much) are a tiny minority of clerical workers, usually only working for top executives. Today, most secretaries work for not one but several bosses, which has routinised secretarial work around typing and answering the phone. So if the role of women in work cannot be explained in terms of their "feminine" role in the home, how do we explain it? Many tend to resort to patriarchal ideology as an explanation. Men hold onto their jobs, so the argument goes, in order to maintain their power over women. There is a far simpler, materialist explanation. As we have seen, women supplied a need for cheap flexible labour at a time when particular industries were expanding at a rapid pace.

This was particularly true of the labour-intensive service sector. Women working part-time appealed to many service employers, since their hours could be organised round peaks and troughs in demand. The very cheapness of women's labour made them more attractive to the employing class. It also of course meant that wage levels in service industries have remained low. Indeed, traditional "women's work" has remained among the lowest paid, much lower paid than skilled or blue-collar manufacturing work.[44]

This creates a vicious circle. Certain work—routine clerical, low grade retail, hospital ancillary—becomes identified as "women's work". Male workers tend to gravitate towards work which is either better paid at an hourly rate or which offers the opportunity of substantial overtime (or both), for example the car industry, transport work, telecommunications engineering and so on. Attempts by women to break into many of these jobs have not been highly successful, although ratios have improved slightly.

Gender conditioning, ideology and therefore lowered expectations must all play a role here. Undoubtedly too there have been appalling cases of sexism—for example the "initiation rites" forced on women firefighters in London.[45] But sexual division at work is structured much more by a set-up which ensures that women's work and men's work remain carefully defined; and that women's work will in general be worse remunerated. For example, the employers' definition of "dexterity" in industries such as electrical engineering has fostered the idea of "women's work" as light, flexible and unskilled.[46]

This is not true for *all* women's work. There are certain signs of a breakdown in the division of labour, especially in white-collar work. But women's entry into new trades has often been at a cost for both men and women.

Typesetting is a case in point. This was traditionally the preserve of well-paid men, relying on highly effective craft organisation. The smashing of union organisation and the introduction of new technology has led to the end of apprenticeships, a much greater

---

44. Braverman shows this for the US in his *Labor and Monopoly Capital*, pp.297 and 367. He also points out there is massive intermarriage between white-collar and blue-collar; he gives figures for 1971 as 9 million men blue-collar workers and 4 million women, compared with 3.3 million men clerical workers and 10.1 million women.
45. See Waterson (1985).
46. For a detailed and valuable study on the US experience of this process, see Milkman (1987).

simplicity and flexibility in the work, and much lower wages and worse conditions. In such a situation, women have been able to enter the industry, but under unfavourable conditions. By 1985 they comprised 70.5 per cent of typesetters in the US, compared with only 16.8 per cent in 1970.[47]

Often such worsening of conditions has been the basis for women's entry into particular industries or trades. The problem here, therefore, lies not in the breaking down of the sexual division of labour, but the conditions under which it takes place. This is why socialists have always fought for women to have equal access to work, but on the basis of the existing rate for the job, and existing conditions. In these circumstances women and men working together can become crucial in helping to break down sexist divisions in general. If the changes are made on the employers' terms, however, exactly the opposite can happen.

There is another area, however, where the traditional division of labour appears to be breaking down: among a layer of the professional and managerial classes. Here women have made a real breakthrough in the past two decades. All the signs are that they will continue to do so. Women now make up 25 per cent of those in managerial grades compared with 18 per cent in 1977.[48] The number of women passing professional exams has similarly increased, with women making up 23 per cent of exam passes in the Institute of Chartered Accountants, 32 per cent in the exams for barristers and a massive 54 per cent for solicitors by the mid-1980s, compared with 7 per cent, 21 per cent and 19 per cent respectively in 1975.[49] An estimated 15 per cent of investment bankers in London earning more than £15,000 a year in 1987 were women.[50]

There are real barriers to women reaching the very top of these professions—primarily the fact that many women take time off to have children and this badly affects their promotion chances. But it is clear that for a substantial minority of women in the professional classes there is the opportunity to break down the sexual division of labour. As usual, this process has gone much further in the US than anywhere else: 44 per cent of accountants are women, and about a third of all management positions are held by women.[51]

These options are by definition only available to a minority. For the mass of working women there is no such choice. Instead women workers are locked into a labour market structured by low wages, the need for flexible hours and deskilled routine work. All these features are, in turn, a product of women's role in the family under capitalism.

---

47. US Bureau of Labor Statistics, quoted by Andrew Hacker in the *New York Review of Books*, 14 August 1986. See also Reskin and Hartmann.
48. *Labour Force Survey 1985* (Department of Employment: London).
49. "Turning Professional", in *The Economist*, 12 September 1987, p.34.
50. "Women make slow progress up the corporate ladder", in *The Economist*, 14 March 1987, p.67.
51. *The Economist*, 14 March 1987.

CHAPTER FIVE

Women and the reserve army of labour

The widespread assumption that women are peripheral to the labour force is, as we have seen, erroneous. Throughout the history of capitalism many women, including many married women, have taken paid work outside the home. Since the 1930s, however, the number doing so has expanded on a scale undreamt-of by their mothers or grandmothers. And the areas where they work have become increasingly central to the economy.

The numbers have been expanded both by mobilising the maximum number of single women into work, and, more importantly, by pulling increasing numbers of married women into the workforce. This process began in the 1930s, with the expansion of clerical work and of light manufacturing. But the trend was reinforced and made permanent by the advent of the exceptional conditions of the Second World War.

These special conditions showed the importance of the woman worker to capital, and the lengths which were gone to in order to ensure women were fully involved in production. Married women were encouraged to work—at first on a voluntary basis. There was for the first time state regulation of where and at what jobs women worked. The state provided substantial back-up in the form of child care, time off for shopping and health care in workplaces, with a Woman Power Advisory Committee established to deal with these issues.

Industrial and military conscription was rapidly introduced for women as well as men. The Essential Work (Registration for Employment) Order began this process in 1941. Women from industries such as woollens and the retail trade were released for more essential work, and women couldn't change jobs without permission. By 1942, stronger regulations were in force. Women aged between 20 and 30 could obtain work only through employment exchanges, and the only women exempt from paid work were those looking after at least one other person. By late 1943, all women between the ages of 18 and 50 were registered at employment offices—and nearly half of *all* women were either working or in the military services.[1]

---

1. Soldon, p.151.

By 1943, there were almost two million women working in the munitions industries, compared with half a million in 1939.[2] Women entered a number of heavy industries—such as shipbuilding, which had traditionally been virtually all male—and took over many of even the skilled jobs. This led to a whole number of demands for equal pay; workers struck over this issue at Rolls-Royce, in Hillington near Glasgow, in 1943 (strikes were illegal under wartime regulations). By and large equal pay was not granted, although women's rates in relation to men's rose, sometimes substantially.

Between 1939 and 1944, women's earnings in the metal, engineering and shipbuilding industries went up 6 per cent in proportion to men's, but still stayed at just over 50 per cent of the male wage. However women's time rates compared with those of male *labourers* in these industries rose over the same period from 62 per cent of men's to 74 per cent—nearly doubling from 32 shillings a week to 56 shillings.[3] These pay increases, although far from giving full equality with men, must have marked a real improvement for most women. They were in real contrast to the low wages of much pre-war "women's work"—especially domestic service.

The major upheaval in women's lives caused by the war had huge social implications as well. Women were encouraged to work long hours. The children of many married women were evacuated. Even where mother and children lived together, they might go for days or even weeks hardly seeing one another. One of the ironies of wartime was that mothers were encouraged by the authorities to leave their children, in order to benefit the war effort. One of the many government propaganda posters discouraged women workers from visiting their evacuated children too often. The official attitude to mothers devoting time to their children was the opposite of that in peacetime, when these same mothers would have been accused of neglect.

These women were not expected to put their major effort into homemaking during the war. Indeed, they were often discouraged from doing too much in the home. State-run restaurants provided hot food at cheap prices. Child care was available for at least some women workers. A few factories even employed shoppers to do the often time-consuming task of queuing for and buying food on behalf of war workers.

All these aids, and a whole range of propaganda weapons which encouraged women to work, helped to tap a major resource for capital: the married woman worker. Attitudes to women changed along with their role in the economy.

But there were many who believed that this state of affairs should only exist during the war—that women should only work while men were away fighting. A report from the National Women's Advisory Conference in 1942 called for married women to be encouraged to leave work and for a higher status to be given to domestic work. The TUC Women's Advisory Conference, meeting that year, voted to its credit to reject the plan.[4]

---

2. Royal Commission on Equal Pay 1944–46, from Statistics relating to the war effort, Cmnd 6564 (London 1946).
3. AEU memo to Royal Commission on Equal Pay 1944–46, appendix 8.
4. Lewenhak (1977), p.241.

But problems loomed for married—and indeed single—women. Well before the war ended it became clear that the postwar years might not be so rosy in terms of employment prospects. In the first place, men who had fought in the war were supposedly guaranteed their jobs back by law. This implied that a large number of women would be displaced. The reforms introduced to ease the problems of working women—from communal restaurants to nurseries—were not guaranteed after the war.

The aims of the capitalist class concerning women workers were made quite clear by Sir Stafford Cripps, who was to become chancellor of the exchequer in the postwar Labour government. Speaking in 1943, he argued that women would have to continue to play their traditional role in the home, *as well as* increasingly working outside the home:

> It is certain that we shall only be able to provide a decent standard [of living] for the people of this country if we can employ not only all the men, but a very large proportion of the women as well after the war. There is, of course, one essential difference which even the most fervent champions of equality will admit—women have an added responsibility which they would not wish to ignore—the responsibility of rearing and bringing up children. Woman is, and must remain, the home-maker.[5]

What Cripps spelled out happened. Women did maintain a major role in the workforce, but the functions of housework and child care remained very much their responsibility. And even their position in the workforce was very different from the one they occupied during the war.

The postwar boom

Between 1943 and 1948, one and a quarter million women left industry.[6] Many of these job losses were of course accounted for by the decline of munitions and other war-related industries. A high proportion were precisely those jobs which had been traditionally a male preserve, and now became so once again.

The women often did not want to accept this, and were sometimes reluctant to go. A survey by the engineering union, the AEU, of 1,000 women in the engineering industry near the end of the war, found that 663 women wanted to stay in the industry. Of these, all but 50 wanted to continue working full-time. A third of those wanting to continue working were married women.[7]

Women's departure from these industries was usually permanent. But their departure from paid work—if it happened at all—was usually short-lived. By 1947, the labour shortage was so acute that the government was appealing for 300,000 more women to work in hospitals and transport.[8] By 1948 there were 683,000 more women in industry

---

5. Speech by Sir Stafford Cripps, in *Women at Work*, journal of the British Federation of Business and Professional Women, March 1943.
6. Soldon, p.156.
7. AEU memo to Royal Commission on Equal Pay.
8. *Ministry of Labour Gazette* (London) June 1947.

than in 1939, and over three-quarters of a million more women trade unionists than before the war.[9]

Soon after, the war, a clear pattern of women's employment was established. The biggest and most sustained boom in the history of capitalism had begun, and was drawing women into the workforce at a rapid rate. In the process, it became obvious that these were not simply temporary or disposable workers who could be drawn into work in exceptional circumstances such as war, but a permanent part of the workforce. The trend towards married women working was accelerated in the postwar period by a number of features, including the growth in earlier marriages, the increase in the number of single women staying in higher education and of course the general expansion in the number of jobs available to women.

The number of married women working grew steadily throughout the 1950s. Whereas in 1950 married women were considerably outnumbered by single women workers, this situation had reversed only ten years later, when married women made up just over 4 million of a total female workforce of around 7.7 million.[10] Today there are twice as many married women working as there are single.[11]

Growth in married women working continued at a staggering rate after the war. By 1951 the proportion of married women who were employed stood at well over 20 per cent. This figure was nearly double what it had been 20 years earlier: it had stagnated at around 10 per cent for most of the earlier part of the twentieth century. Now it rose steadily over the next 30 years, so that by the 1980s the proportion of married women working was well over 50 per cent.[12]

In recent years women's jobs, as a proportion of all jobs, have increased to an even greater extent. Indeed, the total growth of the workforce from the early 1970s to the mid-1980s was "entirely attributable to the female labour force, which increased by 1.7 million".[13]

The number of young women (aged 20–24) who are working has risen steadily since the 1920s. But the most spectacular increase in employment has come among older married women, those between their mid-30s and mid-50s, whose rate of employment has increased much faster than that of young single women. The reason for this is not hard to see. It is inextricably connected with women's role as mothers and childcarers. This means that the break in women's employment is usually during their 20s and early 30s, when they have young children and have to care for those below school age. The pattern of women's work thus rests on their role in the family. This also determines a major feature of women's work, part-time working:

9. Soldon, p.157.
10. Klein, p.85.
11. *Labour Force Surveys 1983* and *1984*.
12. *Social Trends 1987*.
13. *Employment Gazette*, August 1986.

It is the age of the youngest child, and particularly the presence of a child under five, which is the main determinant of whether or not women work outside the home and whether or not they work full-time.[14]

Part-time work

Of the 9.3 million women working in 1985, nearly half were part-timers (4.3 million against 5 million full-time).[15] The trend towards part-time working has increased constantly, while the total of full-time women employees has taken a proportionate decline in recent years. Recent figures suggest that this is no longer the case, and that there is a slight resurgence of female full-time workers in proportion to part-time.[16] Certainly the projected skill shortages in the 1990s are likely to lead to an increase in the proportion of full-time women workers. But nonetheless, the number of part-time women workers, regardless of future trends, has expanded substantially and continues to be large.

Part-time work is so widespread because it holds advantages both for the employers and for women workers. The employers have used it to increase the productivity of labour by squeezing more work into shorter hours. Direct labour costs have traditionally been lower-for part-time workers (during the 1960s they did not require full National Insurance contributions, and they are less covered for benefit than full-time workers). Making some of the most monotonous jobs part-time may even help to diminish labour turnover. Part-time workers are also regarded as more flexible. There is evidence, however, that because of child care commitments, the need to work near home and so on, part-time women workers are often *less* flexible and less likely to move jobs than their full-time counterparts. For women, the jobs often fit conveniently with child care, with school hours or husbands' shift-working.

But the large-scale introduction of part-time work also creates major problems in considering women's role in the workforce. The most obvious is the connection between part-time work and motherhood: 70 per cent of working mothers work part-time compared with only 26 per cent of working women who do not have children.[17]

Part-time work is also associated with poor conditions, weak unionisation and lack of opportunities. The most comprehensive study on women working in recent years, Jean Martin and Ceridwen Roberts' *Women and Employment: a lifetime perspective*, bears out this view.[18] They show that whereas 58 per cent of full-time women workers were in "women only" jobs, 70 per cent of part-time women workers were. While 69 per cent of full-time women workers could join a union at work, this applied to only half of part-timers. Just over a half of all full-timers were likely to belong to a union, compared with just over a quarter of part-timers. Where part-timers worked fewer than 16 hours

14. Rimmer and Popay. See also *Equal Opportunities Commission Report 1986*.
15. *Equal Opportunities Commission Report 1985*.
16. *Labour Force Survey 1987*, quoted in *Employment Gazette*, March 1988.
17. Rimmer and Popay.
18. Martin and Roberts, chapter 5.

a week, only 17 per cent were likely to be in unions. Women working full-time, and those working alongside men, were both much more likely to belong to unions.[19]

Are women a reserve army of labour?

The differences between men's and women's work, and especially the existence of a large part-time female workforce, has led to the common assumption that women form a "reserve army" of labour: a disposable sector of the workforce which can be pulled into work in times of boom, and pushed out back into the home in times of recession.

This assumption underlay much feminist thinking in the late 1970s, and is still regarded as the "common sense" of much of the women's movement. The argument is important, because it concerns the whole nature of the working class, and indeed challenges the notion that there is any necessary unity of interest between men and women workers.

The term "reserve army" is taken from Marx. He described the way in which capital is constantly on the lookout for new workers. The revolutionising of the means of production means that old groups of workers are rejected from the workforce, while new groups of workers are brought in. This search for new workers brings larger and larger numbers into the workforce and these workers are drawn from various "reserves" available at any particular time to the capitalist class.

Marx talked about three sorts of labour reserve in his time: the latent, the floating and the stagnant.[20] The latent reserve he defined as a "once and for all" reserve army: workers who could be drawn into the capitalist production process, but, once in, would be highly unlikely to return to their previous occupations. His main model for this was the agricultural population, which in his own time was progressively being driven from the land and into manufacturing industry. The floating reserve he saw as those who might work seasonally, or in certain jobs which were only sometimes in demand, and so would move in and out of work. Perhaps the major proportion of the floating reserve in Marx's time were the Irish immigrant labourers working on the construction of roads, railways and buildings. The stagnant reserve was the pool of permanent unemployed.

It is obvious when we look at Marx's different categories that none applies particularly closely to the situation of women workers today. Nonetheless feminists use Marx's categories to argue that women are a disposable workforce—to be drawn into and thrown out of work at the whim of the employers. As we shall see, women's employment does not in fact fit this pattern. But there are two important aspects of the theory which need to be looked at more closely.

One is the question of wages, and whether women serve the role of reserve army in the sense that they undercut the wages of other workers. Clearly in some ways this is the case. Women's wages overall are slightly less than three-quarters those of men. A number of industries have been characterised by the undercutting of wages through the

19. Martin and Roberts, chapter 5.
20. Marx (1976), p.794.

introduction of women workers. Perhaps the most recent example is that of typesetters, where the introduction of new technology has opened up the industry to women, but has also meant an overall lowering of wages. Women's rates often undercut men's rates.

But even here the picture is not so simple. Although women's wages remain much lower than men's, the gap between the two has narrowed considerably since the introduction of the Equal Pay Act in the early 1970s.[21] There is also evidence that a number of better qualified women have been able to narrow or even close the wages gap with men, often in the industries where women are highly represented.

Nonetheless the picture has some truth. Even in the early 1970s, Harry Braverman's study of the labour process pointed out that the areas where women were most heavily concentrated in work in the US—services and clerical—also coincided with the lowest wage rates.[22]

The second respect in which women are said to represent a reserve army is that of disposability. The massive rise in married women's work and the high level of part-time work leads to these conclusions. These features do indeed show that women workers and in particular married women *have* constituted a labour reserve, but it is far from being disposable. The experience of 15 years of recession bears this out.

If the hypothesis that women are disposable were to be borne out in any way, then recession and public spending cuts would represent a severe setback for women's position in the labour market. In fact the reverse has been the case. Women's position is stronger in virtually every respect. Figures covering the recession years from 1975 to 1986 show that male jobs have been hit far harder overall than female ones. If figures for 1971 are taken as 100, total female employment in 1986 represented 114.8, while male employment had fallen to 86.5. Women made up 44.8 per cent of the workforce in 1986, compared with 38 per cent in 1971. Female full-time employment remained almost constant, while part-time female employment rose from 100 in 1971 to 145.5 in 1986. Part-time work therefore accounted for effectively all the increase in female employment during these years.[23]

The same is true of unemployment rates. The percentage of men out of work has remained consistently higher than the percentage of women. So in 1985, 15.9 per cent of the male labour force was unemployed compared with 9.9 per cent of the female.[24] Even assuming that women's unemployment is harder to gauge because many married women don't register, the figures hardly suggest that unemployment for women is higher than that for men.

How does this situation arise? Some explanation can be found in the experience of women's participation in the labour market during the major recession of the 1930s. Here the experience is highly contradictory. On the one hand, much of the propaganda aimed at married women in particular was virulently against them working. Two ideas

21. See Rubery, p.120.
22. Braverman, pp.382 and 384.
23. Figures quoted in Rubery, p.101.
24. Rubery, p.101.

were pushed equally vigorously: that women should be fully occupied with being wives and mothers; and that if jobs were scarce—as they were virtually throughout the inter-war years—then men and single women should have the first option.

In Britain the introduction of a means test for the unemployed by Labour government minister Margaret Bondfield was accompanied by stringent attacks on benefit during the government of 1929–31. It was estimated that a third of insured women workers were married and therefore likely to have their benefit cut.[25] A marriage bar existed for certain groups of women public servants. Similar conditions existed in the United States, where the AFL craft union confederation did its utmost to maintain jobs for men, if necessary at the expense of women. They argued for discrimination against married women whose husbands had jobs.[26]

Patterns of employment, however, show that exactly the reverse happened. The United States saw a massive increase in the numbers of women working:

> From 1930 to 1940 the percentage of the entire female population in the workforce grew 22 per cent, the greatest single increase of any decade in American history—not quite equalled by the 19 per cent increase during 1965–75.[27]

Similarly in Britain, the number of women working rose steadily during the inter-war years.

How do we explain the contradiction between the ideology of women being in the home and the reality of the increasing numbers going out to work? It lies precisely in the savage effects of the recession on the working-class family. Kolko argues that it is exactly at times of recession that working-class women are most likely to enter the labour market. The reason is simple: "When unemployment or economic adversity strikes families traditionally dependent on the income of male workers, the women in the family are driven into the capitalist labour process".[28]

Women are forced to work for economic reasons. Their willingness to do so for low wages aids their entry into the workforce: "That women workers are absorbed more quickly during periods of recession or depression is aided by the fact that there are always more women ready to work than there are jobs for them".[29]

The experience of the present recession bears this out. Kolko himself demonstrates that in the recession years 1974–75 women's proportion of the workforce grew in 10 out of 15 countries studied in an OECD report.[30]

The question which remains is why men are not substituted for women in these jobs? Such substitution would coincide with the thrust of much bourgeois ideology on the question of married women working. Yet there is little evidence of it having taken place. Indeed the reverse is true. Employers have gone for cheap labour, regardless of gender or marital status.

25. Lewenhak (1977), p.200.
26. Chafe, p.108.
27. Kolko, p.262.
28. Kolko, p.263.
29. Kolko, p.264.
30. Kolko, p.265.

Some people have argued that sexual divisions within the working class are so rigid that it is virtually impossible to substitute one sex of workers for another. Ruth Milkman uses this to explain why women's employment rose so rapidly in the 1930s, arguing that this factor, rather than women's lower pay, was the crucial reason why women continued to be employed.[31]

The problem is that women workers clearly *have* been substituted for men, but not universally, and not at all evenly. For example, women are employed, as we saw in the previous chapter, disproportionately in the newer occupations, especially clerical work and services. Some of these are newly created jobs; others are old ones where new technology or modern production methods have been applied. In some of these, women clearly have been substituted for men—typesetting and bank clerking are two cases in point. In other industries, especially declining ones, there has been virtually no substitution.

The variations cannot be explained by one simple theory. Instead they depend on a number of features: accessibility to "new" (female or immigrant) workers; expansion or contraction of a particular industry; whether union organisation has the strength to resist encroachment on wages or conditions; the nature of the work and the popular perception of it. The relative expansion of the service industries in relation to manufacturing in the postwar years has also helped to cushion women's employment.

The view of women as a *disposable* reserve army of labour is therefore completely erroneous. Women are overall less likely to become unemployed than men. They are also a *permanent* part of the workforce. And future predictions of employment see women as the major part of any increase in the labour market. Of a projected rise in the workforce of 900,000 by 1995, it is predicted that 800,000 will be women.[32]

Women's employment prospects for the 1990s

The prospects for women's future employment are therefore good. Their concentration in industry is in precisely the areas which are continuing to expand rapidly. Neither cuts in public spending nor the introduction of new technology into areas such as shop work and clerical work have had a negative effect on women's work prospects overall.

Yet ideas that women are peripheral to the economy continue to persist. Even those who don't subscribe to the idea that they are a reserve army often take the view that there is a dual labour market, or that there is a "core" labour force, surrounded by a casual, flexible, low-paid periphery. In both of these instances, women are seen as disadvantaged, flexible and disposable.

Part of the reason why these ideas persist is that women workers will of necessity make up a relatively high proportion of those workers who are flexible. Women still provide—and will continue to provide—the bulk of part-time workers, because of the

31. Milkman (1976), p.73.
32. See *Labour Force Survey 1987*, in *Employment Gazette*, March 1988.

needs of child care. For the same reason, young mothers will often want to work in "flexible" jobs. There is evidence to suggest, for example, that women who have been trained to do skilled work (such as nursing) take jobs below their skill level when they become mothers in order to work near home or schools, or to achieve flexible hours.[33]

But this state of affairs is increasingly unsatisfactory for large sections of the ruling class. It makes no sense for them to invest large sums of money in the education and training of women workers, only then to find that the training is wasted after just a few years. Therefore many employers are now introducing time off in school holidays for married women (Dixons and Boots), management job-sharing (Boots) and workplace nurseries (Midland Bank) in order to attract married women back into more permanent work.[34]

Their interests in this coincide with those of many women workers, who now expect to work full-time for most of their lives, and therefore want to ensure that they have access to skills and training on an equal basis with men. There is every sign that women's expectations of employment are rising rapidly. Factors which indicate this include a drop in job turnover among women; massive increases in women gaining qualifications; and increases in union membership among women.[35]

These tendencies point to a better organised and more stable sector of women workers, especially among those who work full-time. This could reinforce the present situation and even lead to "increases in the divisions between different types of female labour, with the employment conditions for the majority deteriorating while an increasing minority acquire more of the characteristics and labour market opportunities traditionally reserved for male labour".[36]

The pattern of women's employment is therefore very different from that put forward by most feminists. Women's employment is not all at the periphery, with male workers exclusively forming a well-paid permanent core. There are contradictory tendencies at work. Some women may be peripheral to the economy, or even easily disposable at certain times, but increasing numbers of women are becoming more skilled and more central to the labour market.

Thus figures for the change in female employment between 1971 and 1981 show that whereas the percentage engaged in unskilled personal service occupations went up by only 1.3 per cent, those engaged in clerical work went up 6 per cent, the professions went up by 6.7 per cent and supervisors by 9.5 per cent.[37]

The implications of these figures for the future organisation of women are clear. Women are permanent workers in centrally important work, in a way they never have been before in the history of capitalism. These facts also lead them to join unions, to take strike action and to defend their conditions in the same way that male workers have traditionally done so. Part-timers are likely to do the same when they work with other

---

33. See Rogers, p.94.
34. For details see "Nursery Times", in *Socialist Worker Review*, 118, March 1989.
35. See Rubery, pp.125–6.
36. Rubery, p.127.
37. Rubery, p.112.

full-time workers. There is a sizeable minority of women with access to various skills which enable them to defend their relatively advantageous position in the labour market.

Yet there are different patterns of women's union organisation and strike action. In order to understand why, we need to turn to the historical problems women have faced in being part of a union, and to the problems of their relationship to the trade union bureaucracy which persist to this day.

CHAPTER SIX

Women and the unions

The history of working-class women under capitalism has always found them organising as part of their class alongside men. When the struggles of the working class rose, women tended to be involved; where those struggles declined, then women's involvement in the organisations of the working class also declined. Yet within the trade union movement there have repeatedly appeared divisions on lines of sex: men and women workers have been all too often pitted against one another when it comes to jobs, wages and union organisation itself.

Such divisions have led to a number of instances where women have attempted to organise separately inside the unions in order to press their own particular demands. Today such separate organisations are often regarded as the means of organising women. Yet separate organisation has never resulted in strong unions for women, and there is a rich tradition of men and women organising together.

Despite the fact that trade unionism, or "combinations", were illegal in the first decades of the nineteenth century, women played a full role. In the years after the end of the Napoleonic wars in 1815, industries where women were heavily employed were also those where combination was widespread.[1] Union activity increased after it was made legal in 1824, and despite restrictions on organising which soon followed, many workers moved towards combination.

In 1834, the same year that the Tolpuddle Martyrs were transported for "swearing illegal oaths", a London conference established the Grand National Consolidated Trade Union (GNCTU). This was the dream of the utopian socialist Robert Owen, and from its outset included women, often organised in women's lodges. The GNCTU paper *The Pioneer* contained a women's page.[2] But the GNCTU, although it organised at one time half a million men and women workers, was short-lived.

Most workers were not organised at all, for most of the time. If they were, their unions tended to be highly specialised and local, organised on the basis of particular skills. This notion of union organisation prevailed throughout most of the nineteenth century, obviously excluding many of the unskilled, including many women.

1. Lewenhak (1977), p.31.
2. Lewenhak (1977), p.37.

In addition, the employers were constantly trying to find ways of undermining the wages and conditions of well-organised groups of workers. This was relatively easy to do while the majority of workers remained outside the unions. So many of the disputes of the early nineteenth century centred around male opposition to women workers who had been brought in to undercut the going rate for the job.

Some of the worst offenders among employers were the publishers of bibles and other religious tracts. So for example the London Union of Journeymen Bookbinders protested in 1825 that the Society for Promoting Christian Knowledge was unfairly reducing wages. Again in 1834, the union supported 200 women folders and sewers against wage reductions by the British and Foreign Bible Society. Fifteen years later, a strike erupted against the bindery works of the Bible Society. It was supported by the union, whose strike committee collected £650. Eventually however the strike failed, but not before the union expelled one of its sections—150 finishers—who objected to the money spent on the women's dispute.[3]

This episode stands in contrast to the situation in the Edinburgh printing trades during the same year, 1849, when a women's print union—the Edinburgh Society of Women in the Printing Trades—was set up. The low rates for which the women worked provoked men's objections to unfair competition. By the 1870s, women were being brought in to break the strikes of male compositors in the city. Women therefore gained a toehold in the industry because they were prepared to act against the men; by the end of the century there were more women employed in typography in Edinburgh than in the whole of England.[4] Meanwhile no women were allowed into the main typographers' union in Scotland until 1916; the situation fed sexism and reactionary attitudes.

The nature of the unions at the time made it hard for any strike or other action to become generalised between different sections of workers. Increasingly male trade unionists saw their best defence of their living standards in attempting to limit competition from women. During the 1840s such attempts—often in the form of resistance to new machinery which could be operated by women—took place in the Sheffield metal file trades, the boot and shoe industry and ribbon making,[5] and in the pottery industry.[6]

A similar struggle took place in the London tailoring industry in 1834 when 9,000 male tailors struck for higher wages, shorter hours and the abolition of piecework and homework. Although not explicitly put, the strike was a protest at women's outwork. Women were soon introduced as scab labour. Owenites inside the union argued against women being excluded from work. The tailors were eventually forced back to work, and a period of sweating, piecework and women's labour in the industry began.[7]

Following the demise of the GNCTU, the tendency was for unions to organise along sex-segregated lines, thereby reinforcing the divisions inside the working class. As

3. Drake, p.8.
4. Lewenhak (1977), p.62.
5. Lewenhak (1977), p.53.
6. Drake, p.6.
7. Taylor, pp.114–6.

Barbara Taylor has put it, these reflected "a growing tension between men and women, as industrial reorganisation and the debasement of craft skills made female labour a growing threat to skilled male workers".[8]

The upsurge in class struggle reflected in the 1830s and 1840s with the growth of Chartism saw many women involved in political activity alongside men. But this did not result in any long-term organisation. The defeat of the Chartist movement following 1848 had serious consequences for the working-class movement. One was the narrow way in which working-class trade union organisation and political institutions developed, which meant that the skilled workers left behind the unskilled, including women and immigrants.[9]

There was only one exception to this picture: the weavers' unions in the Lancashire textile industry, where unions were mixed and a high degree of equality prevailed throughout the nineteenth century. So the Blackburn Powerloom Weavers' Association and the North East Lancashire Amalgamated Association, formed in the mid-nineteenth century, both included women on equal terms. By 1876 the weavers' unions had 15,000 women members—nearly half their membership—and by 1891 women were 62 per cent.[10]

> The question of competition from separate organisations of men's and women's weavers never became a problem. In union there was strength for both men and women. Successful trade unionism for women can then be claimed to begin during the 1850s and 1860s, while a coordinated effort to form separate trade unions by women would not take place until 1874.[11]

The old craftist ideas of the male handloom weavers had been destroyed with the destruction of their livelihoods many years before. Weavers in the factories were much less likely to cling to the old elitist ideas when it came to organising than those who still clung to their craft skills as a defence against the encroachment of manufacturing industry.

Unfortunately the weavers remained an exception until very late in the nineteenth century. Increasingly more typical were the "new model" unions, such as the Amalgamated Society of Engineers (ASE) which was formed of skilled engineers in 1851. Similar structures grew up among ironfounders, carpenters and bricklayers. Many industries were still characterised by local and district union structures. This applied to areas such as mining, tailoring and boot and shoe manufacture.[12] In many ways the new model unions placed their mark on the emerging national trade union movement, and on the Trades Union Congress (formed in 1868). They were marked by political conservatism and extreme narrowness of vision.

The development of women's trade unionism was a mirror image of this conservatism and narrowness. Rather than reflecting struggle, it reflected a history of cross-class alliances and of middle-class philanthropy. Nowhere is this seen more obviously than

---

8. Taylor, p.94.
9. See Thompson, p.137.
10. Soldon, p.6.
11. Soldon, p.6.
12. Soldon, p.9.

in the history of the Women's Protective and Provident League (WPPL), later the Women's Trade Union League.

The Women's Protective and Provident League

The League was established and led for some years by one woman, Emma Paterson. She was the daughter of a London headmaster and had briefly been apprenticed as a bookbinder. She worked again briefly for the Working Men's Club and Institute Union (a middle-class creation to help working people), then for the Women's Suffrage Association, before marrying a cabinet maker, Thomas Paterson, in 1873. Her honeymoon in the United States convinced her of the need for women's trade unionism and the WPPL was founded in July 1874. It was backed by a number of luminaries, including Sir Charles and Lady Dilke, Arnold Toynbee, Harriet Martineau and Charles Kingsley.

From the start, the League was not a union; its aim was merely to foster trade unionism among women. In this, it appealed first and foremost to the middle classes for support. "Emma Paterson did not make the mistake of appealing directly to working-class women. She first sought middle-class support ... for the setting-up of a National Union of Working Women."[13] Nor was the League's aim class confrontation of any sort. Exactly the opposite: "the committee was particularly anxious to avoid antagonising employers".[14]

This approach was reflected in the stated aims of the League: to protect its members' interests, to try to prevent undue depression of wages and to equalise hours of work; to provide sickness and unemployment funds; to act as an employment bureau; and to promote arbitration in the case of disputes between employers and employed.[15] There was therefore no provision for strike or lockout benefit. The League favoured the idea of a general women's trade union; this led to the formation of the National Association of Working Women in Bristol, also in 1874. In addition, the League formed local unions and societies.

However the organisation remained small throughout its life. Between 1874 and 1886 (when Emma Paterson died) the League claimed 30 or 40 women's societies nationally. But as Sheila Lewenhak has pointed out:

> Not many societies had more than a hundred members or lasted for more than a few years; about half disappeared within one year of their being set up. In 1886 the total membership of exclusively women's societies has been estimated as probably less than 2,500; at least half of them in the London area.[16]

The societies also tended to organise among women's skilled or semi-skilled trades (skilled sewing, millinery, bookbinding) and were concentrated in the London area.[17] So by the WPPL conference in 1886 it was reported that of ten London societies originally

13. Lewenhak (1977), p.69.
14. Soldon, p.14. See also Drake, p.11.
15. Soldon, p.14.
16. Lewenhak (1977), p.71.
17. Boston, p.31.

set up, only five were thriving, one was struggling and four had failed. Total membership of the surviving six was only between 600 and 700. Of the 21 provincial societies only nine survived, with a total membership of 1,800. This compares with 30,000 women organised in the mixed textile unions at the time.[18]

Although the League remained small numerically, it retained a level of influence. Emma Paterson became a delegate to the TUC in 1876, and attended in the years after that. The TUC Congress of 1877 reflected a split between the bulk of the TUC leadership and Paterson and her followers in the League when she argued totally against any protective legislation for women. The argument put was on the surface attractive: protection should not come from paternalistic legislation but from trade union organisation strong enough to negotiate with the employers. But "given the low level of organisation of women in the 1870s, parliament continued to offer women workers the only protection most of them had".[19]

In addition, the argument as put by many feminists, including many in the suffrage movement, amounted to the old Liberal *laissez-faire* approach: that there should be nothing intervening between the employer and his workers, and that if women wanted to be equal they would have to compete on the same basis as men. Men in the organised trade union movement tended to be totally hostile to this point of view. They saw protective legislation, with some reason, as improving the working conditions of the whole working class. Marian Ramelson describes their feelings on the subject:

> It is unfortunate that the first women delegates to the TUC should have been the purveyors of a feminist viewpoint which had no relationship to the real problems or their solution. It was nonsense to contend against legislation restricting the hours of work of women and children, when everyone knew that the Ten-Hour Day Act of 1847 had been an inestimable boon and had succeeded in reducing hours for all. To pose organisation against legislation was completely artificial and dangerously wrong. Further, working men considered it outrageous that women, many of whom had never worked in industry in their lives, should pontificate on what was right or wrong for their womenfolk. They rightly rejected the whole approach.[20]

This opposition to protective legislation reflected the weakness and contradictory nature of the League's politics, which were dominated by free-trade Liberalism. On the one hand they wanted to protect women workers, which is why the League was set up in the first place. On the other hand, however, the class interests of some League supporters led to support for untrammelled capitalism. So Millicent Fawcett, the feminist, was a shareholder in the Bryant and May match factory and therefore opposed any restriction on the use of yellow phosphorus.[21]

The relative lack of success of the WPPL lay in a combination of these politics, caution on the part of the middle-class women who were its activists, and a low level of struggle among workers. In addition there were disagreements within the League.

18. Soldon, p.24.
19. Boston, p.33.
20. Ramelson, p.103.
21. Lewenhak (1977), p.74.

A resolution calling for a slightly higher level of activity was carried at the 1886 conference. Emma Paterson was also offered a full-time position, which she refused. She also refused to say whether she would stay on as secretary of the League in the light of the resolution. She died that same year.

The idea of organising separate women's trade unions did not die with Emma Paterson. But for a few brief years it was superseded by a new form of trade unionism which encompassed an upsurge of the unskilled, including thousands of women workers, who took strike action for the first time.

The new unions

The beginning of the new unions can be dated to the matchgirls' strike of 1888. Conditions at the Bryant and May factory in Bow, east London, were first drawn to public attention in Annie Besant's publication *The Link*. She published an article in June 1888 entitled "White Slavery in London", following a discussion at a Fabian Society meeting where the conditions at the factory were discussed. Despite threats of libel action, Besant leafletted the factory and repeatedly drew attention to the terrible conditions of the women there, contrasting these with the massive dividends paid to shareholders. Eventually, on 5 July, 672 of the women struck.[22]

The strike was quickly successful, because of widescale donations and the intervention of the London Trade Council. Wages went up, the hated fines and deductions were abolished and the women formed the Matchmakers' Union. With around 800 members, this was the biggest women's union yet. More important, the strike and its success marked the beginning of a wave of strikes over the next year which were to shake not only the employers but the conservative structures of the old craft unions and the TUC itself.

The crest of this strike wave came the following year, with the strike of the London dockers led by Tom Mann, and many other smaller strikes. The dockers' strike was particularly relevant to women workers, involving as it did thousands of the poorest casual labourers from London's East End. They proved that they could organise and win, and this gave heart to tens of thousands of other unorganised workers. The union drive of the gasworkers had a similar impact. During 1889 and 1890 there were strikes in a range of industries from Silver's cable firm in East London (where Eleanor Marx organised the first women's branch of the Gasworkers Union) to women who skinned onions at Crosse and Blackwell's factory in East Ham.[23] Nor were the strikes confined to London. A strike of Leeds women tailors in 1889 led to the formation of a Society of Workingwomen which grew to 2,000 in a matter of weeks.[24] In Liverpool a number of women's trade unions were established in 1889.[25]

---

22. See Kapp, pp.267–70.
23. See Kapp, pp.337–63 and 392.
24. Drake, p.27.
25. Soldon, p.30.

The net effect was a mushrooming of trade unionism in the last decade of the nineteenth century. In 1886 there were 36,900 women in trade unions, of whom 34,500 were in textile unions. By 1896 there was a total of 117,888 women in all unions. Although textiles were still predominant (106,540) there were increasing numbers in clothing, food and tobacco and clerical unions. By 1906 this trend was clearer. Out of 166,803 women in unions there were growing numbers in these areas and in distribution, general labour and civil service clerical.[26]

The general picture is clear. The impetus of these strikes of the unskilled led to forms of permanent long-term organisation among women as well as men. It had spin-offs even in areas which had not been involved in much industrial action, such as textiles. It led to an opening up of the unions to all. Where women's branches or societies were set up they were increasingly closely connected or amalgamated with the main union. In general the new unions, in the form either of general unions or of "blackcoated" unions (white-collar and "respectable"), tended to admit women from the start.

It is hardly surprising that the strikes led to this change of approach in the unions. The upsurge of industrial struggle from below itself bred ideas of solidarity across narrow trade or sex divisions. Many of the leaders of the new unions had themselves been radicalised by socialist ideas in the previous decade. This was true of Tom Mann, Will Thorne, John Burns and Eleanor Marx. They stressed ideas of general unionism on a mass scale and dismissed the notions of narrow craftism which so dogged the older unions.

This approach, plus the openness of recruitment towards the low-paid and unskilled, brought them quickly into conflict with those stalwarts of the old ways, the TUC leaders. The Liverpool TUC Congress of 1890 revealed some of the problems. This Congress was much more representative than previous ones, with 457 delegates representing 211 organisations and nearly one and a half million workers, compared with less than half the number of delegates representing 885,055 workers the previous year.[27]

Clashes between the new unionists and the old were inevitable. Mann, Thorne and Burns were marginalised by the old trade union leaders. Thorne "had to appeal for a hearing to protest that the representatives of unskilled labour were not receiving any consideration".[28] Eleanor Marx was not even allowed to be a delegate at the Congress, even though she had been delegated by the conference of the Gasworkers Union. She was denied delegation on the grounds that she was not a working woman. Yet Clementina Black and Lady Dilke of the Women's Trade Union League were both admitted to the Congress, as Eleanor Marx pointed out.[29]

The structures of the existing trade union movement were constricting to any real struggle. This did not matter so much when the level of struggles was high. But when they declined and when the employers then moved onto the offensive against the working class, the old unions and their leaders once again were in total control. As

26. Drake, table 1, p.237. Figures for 1886 are rough estimates.
27. Kapp, p.396.
28. Kapp, p.397.
29. Kapp, p.394.

the new unions themselves became established, they too developed a bureaucratised structure and their leaders became more removed from the rank and file. This process gathered pace in the 1890s, and was accompanied by a move to the right among many of the leaders of the struggles of the 1880s. The move was finally consolidated in the first decades of the twentieth century with the establishment of the big general unions, complete with an entrenched bureaucracy. The losers in this process were the rank and file, especially the unskilled—including many women.

Nonetheless, the drive towards the new unions helped to establish trade unionism among women. But the old areas dominated by the craft unions remained much less open to them. There were still disputes in the 1890s in areas such as pottery or printing about women threatening men's jobs with cheap labour. Sometimes the solution was seen as organising women, rather than excluding them from the previously male trades.[30] The London Society of Compositors accepted its first woman member in 1892 on the grounds that she got "the rate for the job".[31] But in other instances there was real reluctance to allow women into areas of work, so "trade unionism was most backward amongst women metal and wood-workers in the 1890s".[32] This fact had serious implications for the working class as the twentieth century dawned and automation and mass production techniques meant unskilled women could often undercut traditional skills. The narrowness of the metal unions and their hostility to women made unionisation on a class basis much more difficult.

There was therefore still the basis for women's trade unionism. Even after the death of Emma Paterson, the Women's Trade Union League continued to campaign for separate organisation. However the League dropped some of its most class-collaborationist aspects. After the passing of the left-inspired resolution which caused Emma Paterson such problems in 1886, the League's annual meetings no longer applauded the *entente cordiale* between capital and labour. The League was careful not simply to attack men for wanting protection from cheap female labour, to appear less as middle-class do-gooders and more sympathetic to the trade union movement.[33]

The official movement in turn adopted certain demands which were consistent with the League's and with a constitutional approach to women's trade unionism. The TUC Congress voted for equal pay for women in 1888, after a resolution was moved by Clementina Black of the League.[34] Emma Paterson had effectively established the forerunner of the Women's TUC by creating gatherings sponsored by the League which discussed women's issues during the main TUC.[35] In 1885 she had also proposed separate women's trades councils.[36]

---

30. Drake, p.37.
31. Lewenhak (1977), p.89.
32. Drake, p.38.
33. Drake, pp.23–4.
34. Lewenhak (1977), p.91.
35. Soldon, p.19.
36. Lewenhak (1977), p.74.

Women's trade unionism still remained weak. This was partly a result of the employers' offensive, which resulted in disputes such as the Manningham strike in Bradford in 1892, which went down to defeat, and the lockout in the cotton industry in 1892–93. It was also a result of viewing women's struggles as separate, which was the whole *raison d'être* of the League, but also affected male trade unionists. So for example a strike of men and women at a pickle and vinegar factory in Gloucester in 1896 resulted in the men going back to work while the women stayed out. Boys were brought in to scab. The local dockers' union supported the women, but called in the WTUL to organise them rather than doing it themselves, though they still agreed to represent them.[37]

Mary Macarthur and the Women's Trade Union League

Mary Macarthur is one of the best-known figures among women in the trade union movement. She became secretary of the WTUL at the age of only 23. Her father owned a draper's shop in Ayr, where she worked. She joined the Shop Assistants Union in 1901, went to its conference in 1902, and won the secretaryship of the League in 1903. She joined the Independent Labour Party about this time.

Mary Macarthur rapidly realised that since the WTUL was not a union, women needed some form of organisation based on the idea of a general union which they could join if excluded from the male unions. In 1906 she formed the National Federation of Women Workers (NFWW), a general women's union which was "rooted in the ideas and militancy of the early general labour unions. In its struggle to improve wages and conditions, it usually found that the strike was the only weapon at its disposal".[38] The NFWW had 4,000 members by 1909.[39]

However the Federation was not seen simply as a means of organising women workers. It also had another aim: to give a voice to a layer of women inside the official labour movement. So Sheila Lewenhak writes: "The setting-up of the National Federation of Women Workers enabled the vocal, educated middle-class women who worked for it to be present at British Trades Union Congresses".[40]

It also enabled these women to pressure for legislation which would abolish the worst of "sweating" among women workers. Mary Macarthur organised a campaign against sweated trades. She had no qualms about involving all sections of society in her support. So the exhibition she organised against sweating in 1906 was opened by Princess Beatrice. The only working-class speakers represented were George Lansbury and Ramsay Macdonald.[41] This agitation led to the formation of the Anti-Sweating League.

Yet although the orientation of the National Federation of Women Workers was to appeal across classes for support, it also had a much more militant approach to struggle.

---

37. Lewenhak (1977), p.93.
38. Boston, pp.61–2.
39. Lewenhak (1977), p.115.
40. Lewenhak (1977), p.116.
41. Lewenhak (1977), pp.118–9.

So Mary Macarthur organised a demonstration in support of the women boxmakers on strike against wage cuts at the Corruganza works in Tooting, south London, in 1908.[42] Although attempts to get a minimum wage centred very much on legislative change brought in by benevolent middle-class reformers, Macarthur was willing to back it up with action.

This was clearly the case with the Trade Boards Act, passed by the Liberal government in 1909, which established boards to fix minimum wages in four industries. Sections of the employing class supported this development, but individual groups of employers, especially in the industries concerned—chain, box and lace-making and clothing manufacture—were hostile. The employers in the West Midlands chainmaking industry refused to implement the new pay rates for their women workers, using a six-month delay clause in the agreement. Some persuaded their workers to sign an agreement to work at the old rates for six months.

Mary Macarthur demanded immediate implementation of the new rates. A mass meeting in August 1910 resolved only to work at the new rates. The Federation put its weight behind the women and organised strike pay, demonstrations and support from other trade unionists. Eventually they beat down the employers of Cradley Heath and won their minimum wage. The result of their success was also strong union organisation, at least for a time.[43]

Campaigns such as these helped the growth of the NFWW. Its paper, *The Woman Worker*, established in 1907, had a circulation of 32,000 by 1909.[44] The membership of the Federation grew from 2,500 members in its first year to 20,000 by 1914.[45] This growth was largely due to the upsurge in struggle which took place from 1910 onwards.

The years 1910 to 1914 were the years of the Great Unrest. Workers responded to something like a decade of falling real wages with an extremely high level of militancy. From the outset strikes broke out which included women. They were very much part of this struggle. There were strikes among an astonishingly wide range of women workers in 1910 and 1911, especially in south and east London.

> Like a chain reaction, in the hot summer of 1911 women in London, jam and pickle workers, rag-pickers, biscuit-makers, bottle-washers, tin-box makers, cocoa-makers, distillery workers—all sweated-factory workers earning between five shillings and ten shillings a week—came out on strike for wage increases. Mostly they were successful in getting rises of between one shilling and four shillings; in many places branches of the Federation were formed and union recognition gained. In all the strikes the League sent an organiser to help the Federation.[46]

The strikes affected some 15,000 women and between 25 and 30 firms in Bermondsey alone. The women came mainly from dockers' families. The Women's Trade Union League reported 21 strikes in 1911–12, of which 18 had satisfactory outcomes. There was

42. Boston, pp.68–9; Soldon, p.57.
43. See Boston, pp.65–8; Lewenhak (1977), p.121.
44. Soldon, p.59.
45. Soldon, p.58.
46. Boston, p.69.

also a massive number of unofficial strikes in 1913–14.[47] Another type of strike took place at Maconochies Jam factory in Millwall in 1911 where women struck to stop young girls doing women's work. Within a week 4,000 women, 80 per cent of them married and with children, were organised in unions.[48]

Not all of the strikes were successful—such as the strike of women at the Idris factory in St Pancras, which was broken by male scabs.[49] But the general mood in these years was of women feeling that they had strength as part of the working class: "one gets the feeling of a sudden welling-up of confidence among women workers".[50]

This confidence was shown in figures for unionisation. There were 166,803 women in unions in 1906. This mushroomed to 357,956 in 1914,[51] largely as a result of the successful years of activity during the Great Unrest. Mary Macarthur and the Federation, as well as the League, played a significant part in this development. The union membership and level of strikes helped to contribute to a growing sense of crisis among the British ruling class. Added to its problems were issues such as women's suffrage and home rule for Ireland. Increasing numbers of those struggling over one issue began to see the links with the other two.

But the crisis of the government was defused in 1914 with the outbreak of the First World War. The Labour and trade union leaders almost all supported the war, at least to some degree. Even their left sections drifted towards some level of support. Mary Macarthur was to play an important role during the war in mediating between capital and labour. In order to do so, she steered the League and the Federation away from their militant policies of the years of the Great Unrest, and back towards much greater class collaboration.

Early on in the war workshops were created by the Queen Mary's Work for Women Fund, intended to provide employment for unemployed women. By January 1915 it provided jobs for 9,000 women, but in conditions which barely improved on the sweating which Mary Macarthur had spent some years campaigning against. Sylvia Pankhurst and the East London Federation of Suffragettes described the scheme as "Queen Mary's sweatshops" and called for a minimum wage of £1 a week to be paid. But the fund's committee, comprised of various women trade unionists including Mary Macarthur, defended the fund's maximum wage of eleven shillings and sixpence a week. It was argued that this was an improvement on women's average wage.[52] It contrasts strikingly with the salary of Mary Macarthur herself in 1914: £350 a year.[53]

Mary Macarthur calmed any worries trade unionists might have had about the involvement of royalty. She told her WTUL colleagues: "The Queen does grasp the whole

47. Lewenhak (1977), p.133.
48. Soldon, pp.70–1.
49. Boston, p.70.
50. Boston, p.70.
51. Drake, table 1, p.237.
52. Boston, p.97; Soldon, p.79.
53. Soldon, p.56.

situation from a trade union point of view. I positively lectured her on the inequality of the classes and the injustice of it".[54]

The workshops had little lasting impact, however, because the needs of wartime production rapidly eliminated most unemployment. Indeed, women's labour was in great demand by early 1915. Large numbers of unskilled and previously unorganised women entered industry. They were hampered straight away by the Munitions of War Act of 1915, which made strikes and lockouts illegal. But they also almost immediately came up against a major struggle which took place in the engineering and munitions industries throughout the war: the struggle against "dilution".

The shop stewards and dilution

The employers saw the war both as a means of increasing their profits, and of curtailing the power of strong union organisation by introducing new practices and undercutting the rate for the job. This process had been going on since well before the war. Automation and mass production techniques, especially the production line, had been used to break down craft skills and to introduce lower rates of pay, often based on time rather than piece rates. Where work was assessed on the basis of the time the employers thought it took to perform a certain task, rather than on the quantities produced, this reduced the control individual workers had over production.

The craftsmen had done their utmost to resist these changes, fighting tough and defensive battles against every encroachment on their power and control. These struggles led to the creation of an extremely powerful shop stewards' movement by the early months of the war which was determined to resist further attacks under the guise of war emergency.

It is sometimes assumed, wrongly, that the engineers opposed women working when the war broke out. What they did was to place all sorts of conditions on women's work in the munitions factories which would prevent the undercutting of their own conditions. They regarded the "dilution" of their skills, which would result if this were not done, as extremely dangerous. So the first major dispute over dilution at Vickers Crayford in 1914 took place when the company, without consultation, took on women for shell-making at about half the male rate. An agreement between the engineering employers and the unions said that women should not be replacements for skilled men, and that women should be restricted to automatic machines.[55]

The limitations of the craft unions were well illustrated by the nature of their approach to women workers. So the Shells and Fuses Agreement between the engineering employers and the ASE, which set out the conditions under which they would accept dilution in this area, stipulated that women would get the rate for the job when they did a job previously done by a man, but only for the duration of the war. In addition

54. Soldon, p.80.
55. Drake, p.69.

pay equality in the munitions industries applied only to piece rates, not to time rates or bonuses. So women's wages (and those of unskilled men) still tended to be well below those of skilled men.

It was against these divisions between the skilled unions and the employers that the Women War Workers Committee, over which Mary Macarthur presided, laid down conditions for women's war work in April 1915. These included trade union membership, the same rate of pay for the same work, no sweating, training for the unemployed, and priority after the war for men whose jobs had been filled by women.[56]

The last point was not a mere aberration on the part of Mary Macarthur, but was part of NFWW policy. So "in return for the Engineers' agreement to act jointly with them in wage negotiations, the National Federation of Women Workers agreed to withdraw its members at the end of the war from any occupation claimed by the ASE".[57] The ASE preferred agreement with the NFWW than with the general unions, although as James Hinton notes, despite ASE discouragement women tended to join the general unions rather than the NFWW.[58]

Nonetheless, women's entry into munitions factories led to an improvement in wages, expectations and unionisation. In particular the Clyde Workers' Agreement of 1916 prevented women from being subject to the worst conditions and wages:

> Of all the agreements negotiated with regard to dilution of war work the Clyde Workers' Agreement won the best terms for the workers, thanks largely to the strength of the newly created Shop Stewards' Movement on the Clyde.[59]

But, Sarah Boston argues, this "stubborn fight to win for dilutees, who were largely women, equal pay or the rate for the job" was waged to protect male position rather than benefit women workers.[60] She is partly right, but fails to take into account the double-edged nature of the struggle against dilution. It was narrow and designed to protect a layer of workers. However its strength was that, through the shop stewards' movement, it was able not only to resist the encroachments of the employers and fight back against them, but in the process also better the conditions of the unskilled.

It is therefore not true that the skilled men fought only for their own selfish interests. Indeed their record in defending women workers was in many ways better than that of the separate women's union, the NFWW. So the 100 per cent NFWW union organisation at Glasgow's Parkhead Forge was achieved through ASE shop stewards. When four girls were victimised following a go-slow at Beardmore's East Hope Street factory in Glasgow, the workforce came out on strike for their reinstatement—but the attitudes of the men's and women's unions were very different. While the NFWW disowned the strike, the ASE members gave it support. The strike spread, with the Clyde Workers'

56. Boston, p.105.
57. Hinton, p.72.
58. Hinton, p.72 note.
59. Boston, p.112.
60. Boston, p.112.

Committee raising money, and at one point a general strike was threatened, although the issue ended with arbitration.[61]

The attitudes of these workers showed the massive strength of their form of trade unionism, but also their limited ability to see beyond their craft interests. Nonetheless, the skilled workers often prevented the employers from getting their own way, and so helped to maintain decent conditions for all workers in the process. In the years of industrial and political upsurge which followed the end of the war, the skilled workers were among the most advanced sectors of the working class which challenged the whole capitalist order.

The impact of the war on women's trade unionism was phenomenal. By 1918 there were over a million women trade unionists. By and large they had joined not the craft unions, but the large general unions. In these general unions there were 216,000 women in 1918 compared with 23,534 in 1914; 54,000 in transport unions compared with only 650 in 1914; 119,000 in the clothing unions compared with just under 26,000; and a substantial leap in the women's membership of the distributive and clerical trade unions.[62] These increases were not just in industries where women took the place of men, but also in traditional women's industries and in the new expanding ones.

Membership of many of the unions survived the end of the war. So in the general unions "it is probable that at the end of 1919 the aggregate female membership was little less than at the time of the armistice".[63]

The membership of the NFWW stood at 80,000 at the end of the war. Despite Mary Macarthur's willingness to work on various government committees she was shunned for being too left-wing once the war was over. She stood as Labour candidate for Stourbridge in the 1918 election and was red-baited by Mrs Pankhurst. She was not included on the honours list because Lloyd George told Queen Mary that she and her husband were too radical![64]

In the immediate years after the war, the separate women's trade unions became fully incorporated into the official machine. The NFWW merged with the National Union of General Workers, and became the Women's District of the NUGW from 1921. The TUC set up a Women's Department, and established two reserved places for women on the General Council.[65] Mary Macarthur died in 1921, the same year that the Women's Trade Union League became part of the TUC.[66] Margaret Bondfield became the first woman president of the TUC in 1923, but gave up the presidency during her term when she won a seat in parliament for Labour.[67]

The emergence of the mass general unions were a feature of the inter-war years, but they did not represent a high level of struggle among workers. In fact, those years

61. Hinton, p.251.
62. Drake, table 1, p.237.
63. Drake, p.181.
64. Soldon, p.100.
65. Lewenhak (1977), pp.172–3.
66. Soldon, p.107.
67. Lewenhak (1977), p.187.

were characterised by high unemployment and employers' offensive. The attempt to reverse this offensive, the widely supported but short-lived General Strike in 1926, was aborted through the timidity of the union leaders. The strike's defeat left its mark on union organisation as a whole, which was severely weakened for over a decade afterwards. Politically, the union leaders moved to the right and preached moderation rather than class struggle.

Once again, policies on women were not immune to these ideas. The TUC adopted a position on organising women which did little to challenge all sorts of prevailing ideas, such as the idea that married women should be barred from certain forms of employment (which occurred in some public sector and local government work) or the idea that women were suited above all to domestic work. Indeed the TUC and the Labour Party promoted the idea that women should go into domestic service as a means of dealing with high unemployment. Despite unemployment, however, they were unsuccessful in persuading women to accept the bad wages and terrible conditions of domestic service, once they had experienced work anywhere else.

The right wing of the movement was dominant for much of the period after the defeat of the General Strike. Although the Communist Party attempted through the Minority Movement (an attempt to organise the left and the militants in the unions) to raise class-wide demands which could benefit women workers, its members were often witch-hunted or at best marginalised. Union membership fell, and this badly affected women workers:

> In 1939 only half a million women belonged to unions affiliated to the TUC, less than half the number in 1918, despite the fact that women workers as a percentage of the workforce had increased from about 27.4 per cent in 1923 to more than 30 per cent in 1939.[68]

There were repeated attempts to recruit women, but on the basis of general appeals, not on activity or struggle. Even when militancy rose in the second half of the 1930s, the TUC still attempted to attract new female recruits on the basis of appeals claiming that trade unionism would enhance health and beauty![69]

But the increased level of strikes and the decline in unemployment in the late 1930s made it easier to organise the unions at work again and this in turn attracted more women workers to them. Labour shortages led to the abolition of the marriage bar (a ban on married women workers) for teachers and medical workers at the London County Council in 1935. But the central issue which came to dominate the once more growing unions from the mid-1930s onwards was the question of equal pay. It was to remain the major "women's issue" for 40 years.

---

68. Boston, p.156.
69. Boston, p.162.

The campaign for equal pay

Equal pay had been voted for in principle by the TUC in 1888. The rate for the job was enshrined in the Treaty of Versailles which mapped out the political settlement after the First World War. It was for most women far from reality. Rates for women manual workers remained far less than those of men, even where they did the same or comparable work—often less than half. It was in white-collar jobs—often "professions" such as teaching or the civil service—that the issue became live in the inter-war years. Here, particularly because the marriage bar often applied, it was considered unjust that single women who had to support themselves should receive less than single men.

By the 1930s, however, manual unions had also taken up the call. The demand was formulated as the "rate for the job": a particular job should be valued for what it was, not for the gender of whoever performed it. The engineering union, now the AEU, passed a resolution calling for equal pay in 1935—eight years before it admitted women members![70] In 1936 the House of Commons went so far as to vote for equal pay for the "common classes" of civil servants. The Tory prime minister, Stanley Baldwin, promptly refused to act on the vote. But a campaign had begun which was increasingly to raise the basic problem of the inequality of women workers.

This campaign received some impetus from the growing number of women in trade unions. By 1939 this had topped the million mark.[71] The number of women in unions reflected a growing unionisation inside workplaces in the late 1930s as well as general recruitment. Wartime conditions after 1939 brought the question of equal pay into sharp relief. Women went into men's jobs in the munitions and war industries, as they had in the First World War, but they were still often paid at half the rate. This caused dissent in two areas: women demanded that they should be paid as the men had been paid, and men, fearful that low-paid women would undercut their rates and therefore eventually their jobs, also demanded the "rate for the job".

Once again, the men's unions were at the forefront of raising equal pay, usually out of concern for preserving a decent rate of pay for all workers. The issue led to a strike at Rolls-Royce, in Hillington, Glasgow, in 1943. The TUC Congress of 1944 passed a resolution calling for the "rate for the job" and in the same year the government established a Royal Commission on Equal Pay. Before this a clause in the Education Act which allowed women teachers equal pay had been narrowly defeated in parliament.

Women workers could expect little better from the Labour government when it came to power in 1945, and chancellor of the exchequer Hugh Dalton deferred a decision on equal pay until after the Royal Commission had reported. When it did report in 1946, it recommended little in the way of equal pay except for the "common classes" of civil servants. In other areas, it was believed that women would be replaced by men

---

70. Lewenhak (1977), p.225.
71. Soldon, p.148.

if equal pay were implemented. The Labour government refused to implement even these findings on economic grounds.[72]

Unfortunately, however, the war years showed the union leaders were still committed to backward ideas about the position of women. The TUC Women's Advisory Conference in 1942 included in its postwar plans that married women should be encouraged to leave work and that the status of domestic work should be raised.[73] Luckily the delegates rejected the plan. But any hope that equal pay would become a reality with the postwar Labour government were soon dashed. Although the TUC had committed itself to equal pay most recently in 1944, its support for a wage freeze under Labour caused it to renege on its promises.

So the question was once again relegated to the fringes of politics. But inside the public sector, the demand was becoming a reality, at least on paper. During the 1950s, teachers and civil servants eventually won equal pay for women. In Europe meanwhile the European Economic Community had adopted International Labour Organisation Convention 100, of "equal pay for work of equal value" as part of the Treaty of Rome in 1956. This meant that women in the original six member countries were given at least a paper commitment to equal pay. In Britain the issue rumbled on until the late 1960s and the tail end of the Labour government led by Harold Wilson. A Bill for equal pay and against sex discrimination was introduced in 1968. Coincidentally, Ford women sewing machinists struck for equal pay the same year. The following year, employment minister Barbara Castle introduced her Equal Pay Bill.

The legislation was pathetic right from the start. Harold Wilson told the TUC Congress that equal pay could only be awarded in exchange for fewer strikes. A TUC delegation visiting Barbara Castle was told that it would take seven years to phase in equal pay, that ILO Convention 100 would not be ratified yet (so avoiding tying the legislation to the concept of equal pay for equal value), and that equal pay could anyway only be introduced at the expense of men's wages.[74]

Barbara Castle was true to her word. The Equal Pay Act was passed in 1970, but did not take effect until 1975. It provided for equal pay only on the extremely narrow definition of the same or "like" work with men ("like" work was to be decided, by a job evaluation scheme). Defining equal pay in this way meant that literally millions of women who did not work alongside men were immediately outside the ambit of the law. The time scale also gave employers years to evade the Act, through discriminatory regrading schemes.

Nonetheless, the passing of the Equal Pay Act made a small but significant difference for many women workers. In 1970, women's gross hourly earnings were 63.1 per cent of men's. By 1975 they were 72.1 per cent, by 1976 75.5 per cent. Since 1978 they have hovered around the 73–74 per cent figure and seem stuck at that level.[75] Even figures for weekly earnings (allowing for the longer hours worked by men) show an increase in the

72. Lewenhak (1977), p.247.
73. Lewenhak (1977), p.241.
74. Lewenhak (1977), p.286.
75. *Employment Gazette*, December 1986.

proportion of women's wages. This can undoubtedly be attributed to the passing of the Act, plus the raised expectations of women workers who demanded and often struck for equal pay. Their improved position on pay may also reflect their more entrenched position in the workforce today.

There were a number of important equal pay strikes in the early 1970s. Here the attitude of the official union machines was important. The fact that the engineering union, AUEW, and the draughtsmen's union, TASS, were keen on pushing equal pay meant that a high number of these strikes took place among their members. Many of the strikes were in protest at regradings which stuck women yet again at the bottom. Several examples show the deviousness of employers in evading equal pay. A two-week occupation at Tetley Tea Bags in Bletchley was in protest at male production workers being given £1 extra on the grounds that they might have to drive a forklift truck—something they never did. Workers at Dunlop Coventry struck for four weeks against new "unisex" grades which put women in the lowest grades.[76]

Strikes which ended successfully often led to further strikes locally, as when the AUEW strike at Nettle Accessories in Stockport in March 1975 led to similar strikes at Friedlands and at Bowbros, both in Stockport.[77] Success or failure in strikes often depended on outside support. So the strike and occupation at SEI in Heywood, Lancashire, was defeated after eight weeks because the women involved in the dispute failed to get outside support, especially from local male trade unionists. But the similar dispute at Wingrove and Rogers in Liverpool won precisely because it attracted solidarity.[78] Here again the role of local union leaderships was key. This accounted for the unevenness of struggle in different areas.

The background to the relatively large number of equal pay strikes in the early 1970s was the high level of class struggle generally. The period from 1969 to 1974 was one of rising class struggle, with significant working-class victories. Women workers took action on an unprecedented scale, especially over pay.

But this situation did not last. Although there were lengthy and impressive strikes in the mid-1970s, such as the dispute at Trico in west London, they were increasingly difficult to win. So the strike by women at Yardley in Basildon, after a decision at an industrial tribunal went against the strikers, was eventually defeated.[79] The fight for equal pay was channelled more and more towards the tribunals by the trade union officials. But without the sanction of strike action the women were often in a weak position. Dependent on the tribunals, they were at an unfair disadvantage. A study of equal pay tribunals in these years showed a massive drop in claims after the first couple of years, as the tribunals proved themselves totally ineffective. The majority of equal pay tribunals found against the claimant.[80]

---

76. Article by Kath Ennis on equal pay, in *Women's Voice* (London) number 19, July 1975.
77. *Women's Voice*, number 19, July 1975.
78. *Women's Voice*, number 14, January 1975.
79. *Women's Voice*, number 4 (new series) April 1977.
80. Campbell and Coote, p.140.

Most women also remained on the lower rates of pay.[81] Faced with a system loaded against them, most women gave up trying.[82] They were often encouraged to do so by the union officials. A few individuals were able to win their cases, helped by the fact that the Act had been amended to bring it into line with the broader EEC definition, but Jeanne Gregory's study shows that of the cases looked at, as many found the union "unhelpful" as found the union instrumental in achieving the outcome of their case.[83]

The "feminist incomes policy"

The explanation for this reluctance to fight and win in equal pay cases lies in the narrow way in which most officials view industrial struggle. Because they see it simply in sectional terms, they are unable, unless they have a wider *political* view, to challenge structural inequality, which is maintained through devices such as job segregation. Nor are they able to challenge the priorities of a crisis-ridden system, which will do its utmost to avoid paying women equally. All too often, union leaders echo the sentiments of a pamphlet produced by the Institute of Personnel Management on the subject back in 1969:

> The trade unions must be persuaded to accept that equal pay for women can only be achieved if women receive larger increases than men until differentials are eliminated, [and] if women are to receive more, men must receive less.[84]

Because the union leaders accept the employers' claim that there is only a certain amount of money to go round, they are unwilling to challenge the existing pay structure in any real sense. In recent years their arguments have been given a feminist tinge, which helps to justify their limited approach, by demands for a "feminist incomes policy". Beatrix Campbell put this argument, although she later backed away from it, as a means of improving women's pay in relation to men's. It suffers from a lack of understanding about incomes policy (which has never benefited the low paid, even when dressed up in such rhetoric). In addition, its whole philosophy is that women can only benefit at the expense of men.[85]

The argument reflects the failure of the struggle around equal pay. It also represents an acceptance of the status quo, and therefore a belief that only marginal changes can be won. The failure of legislative reform has paradoxically strengthened reformist ideas on equal pay, and in particular the reformist feminism which has developed in the past two decades.

The fact that equal pay could become an issue, however, and that legislation was introduced, gives some indication of how the unions have changed since the Second World War. As women entered the workforce during the postwar boom, so they joined

81. Snell, pp.39–43.
82. Gregory, pp.75–89.
83. Gregory, pp.75–89.
84. Meepham (1969).
85. Campbell and Charlton.

unions in large numbers. The number of women trade unionists doubled to over two and a half million between 1951 and 1974.[86] By the late 1960s and early 1970s they also played an important part in the rising tide of class struggle. Some of the strikes involving women, such as the Ford machinists' equal pay strike, or the night cleaners' struggle for organisation in 1971, are well known. Much less well known are the strikes of teachers from 1969 onwards, the many equal pay strikes or the significant struggles of Asian women workers, as at Mansfield Hosiery or Imperial Typewriters (where they also had to fight white trade unionists).

Union membership has continued to grow among women, and at a faster rate than men. But the growth of unionisation among women is uneven. Part-time workers and those who work with women only are less likely to join a union.[87] Women's union membership is higher in the public sector than in private industry. However the size of the public sector workplace makes a crucial difference to unionisation. In workplaces with over 1,000 workers, 58 per cent of full-time women workers are in unions, compared with only 17 per cent in workplaces of less than 25 people.[88] Women are now the majority of members in unions such as the public employees (NUPE), teachers (NUT), local government workers (NALGO), civil servants (CPSA) and shop workers (USDAW).

The growth of women's unionisation has altered the balance of forces inside the trade union movement substantially in the past three or four decades. White-collar unions play an important role in the TUC. Their dependence on women members for future growth means that in recent years token moves towards equality have been apparent. Often the pressure for these changes has come from the rank and file, rather than from the top of the union. In the 1970s, rank-and-file unofficial organisation was important in organising women in a number of white-collar unions.

Now many unions organise women's training programs, appoint women's officers, elect women's committees and give at least verbal support to demands for nurseries and equal pay. The success of the National Abortion Campaign in gaining support across a wide number of unions must be at least partly due to the increased number of women trade unionists.

The large number of women union members at rank-and-file level could not be in greater contrast to the minuscule number of women who occupy top positions in the union machines. The TGWU, with a quarter of a million women members, has only one woman on its executive of 39, and only ten full-time women officials (of a total of 502). In recent years this has begun to change in a number of white-collar unions—partly as a result of reserved places. Some now have a fair proportion of women on their union executives; for example ten out of 26 in NUPE.[89]

This disparity has led to many feminist-initiated calls for positive action or positive discrimination inside the unions. The idea that a woman general secretary or more

86. Soldon, p.164.
87. Martin and Roberts, chapter 5.
88. *General Household Survey 1983*.
89. Beechey and Whitelegg, p.129.

women officials would improve the position of women at every level in the union is a powerful one. In most white-collar and some manual unions there is now commitment to some form of positive action. Yet there is little evidence that much has improved for women members with the establishment of these schemes. They remain a niche for a minority of usually feminist women who "have taken jobs in unions, expanding research departments, and have played a part, as lay activists, in the development of policy".[90]

These women are removed from the rank and file they purport to represent. They form part of a privileged layer of bureaucrats who control the union machines, and who attempt to mediate between capital and labour. Their interests as part of this grouping override any common interest they may have, as women, with women workers. Because of this they end up behaving in exactly the same way as their male counterparts. Far from encouraging the struggles of women workers, which could help to develop their fight for liberation, women officials and executive members will do their best to negotiate and compromise, even at the expense of women workers.

The fact that women have made so little impact at the top of the unions also shows the conservative nature of union structures and their unwillingness to challenge the status quo. But women's unionisation is double-edged: the numbers of women organised, the large struggles of different groups of women workers, from teachers to nurses to cleaners, all point to the immense advances for women that come from being part of the union movement. At the same time, their struggles when they do erupt often go beyond the wishes or the needs of the bureaucracy, which then does its utmost to rein those struggles in.

The limitations of the unions, both politically and economically, go a long way to explaining common attitudes of men towards women inside the unions. The old discriminatory attitude—that women only worked for pin money—has often been broken down, at least among layers of the bureaucracy and local activists. But this has often been replaced by the patronising "we'll do it for you" approach that characterised the politics of the Women's Trade Union League nearly a century ago. Nor is this patronising attitude confined to men. Many feminists take similar positions. In addition, feminist arguments are often used as a cover for a move to the right inside the labour movement. This is true of the arguments against free collective bargaining, and of the idea that women's interests at work differ from those of men.

The argument against free collective bargaining is that it is hierarchical, maintains differentials, implicitly supports a family wage, and that for all these reasons it discriminates against women. The argument was put most forcefully by Beatrix Campbell when she launched her attack on the unions in a series of articles in *Red Rag* in the late 1970s.[91] This she followed up in *Sweet Freedom* in 1982:

> Yet the traditional priorities of union bargaining—focusing on the wage and on the maintenance of differentials—have not helped to lift women out of low-paid ghettos, or

90. Campbell and Coote, p.145.
91. Campbell and Charlton, and Campbell (1980).

to alleviate their domestic responsibilities. On the contrary, the process we know as "free collective bargaining" is primarily a defence of the interests of male workers.[92]

The problem with this argument is simple. Free collective bargaining and standard trade union practices are limited and do not challenge the total priorities of the capitalist system. But what are the alternatives? Either a struggle for the revolutionary overthrow of that system, which involves a political and not just a sectional or syndicalist challenge, or a retreat from even the limited gains of free collective bargaining towards some form of feminist coercion from above.

Unsurprisingly, Campbell chooses the latter option. She argues that the unions need to be politicised and feminised, and that the mechanism for improving women's pay is a "feminist incomes policy". Yet the experience of the 1970s was that wages rose in relation to men's in the middle of the decade largely because of the fight for equal pay—including a large number of strikes. It stagnated as a result of the Social Contract, the incomes policy agreed between the TUC and the Labour government, when those workers covered by wages councils remained stuck below the minimum target of £30 per week for over two years.[93] Incomes policy was a recipe for the decline of real wages, especially those of the lowest paid, under the guise of wage restraint. It is for this reason—and not because of some mythical commitment to free collective bargaining—that many socialists and feminists are opposed to incomes policy, even of a feminist variety.

But while the feminist incomes policy may be too much even for many feminists to stomach, the drift of the argument is taken in unions such as NUPE, which emphasises the minimum wage as the way forward for women as an *alternative* to collective bargaining. Again the emphasis is on a benevolent (Labour) government awarding women the minimum wage, rather than the women workers themselves fighting for a decent wage. But there is no mechanism, other than fighting, to achieve the minimum wage. The employers do not grant it voluntarily and so, predictably, little is achieved. All the evidence still points to the fact that the most significant wage rises for women have been precisely at those times like the early 1970s, when male workers—often better organised—were also fighting and winning.

The other major error of those like Beatrix Campbell who want a feminist strategy for the unions is the idea that:

> Men's and women's priorities diverge not only in the politics of pay but in the economy of time. For women, time is precious in particular ways ... Male trade unionists have been very slow to see time off as a positive benefit.[94]

This argument ignores some of the greatest struggles in working-class history, such as the repeated battles in the nineteenth century for the shorter working day. It is simply fallacious to imply that men fight only for wages while women are concerned with the quality of life. It is true, however, that when workers go on the offensive—as opposed

92. Campbell and Coote, p.166.
93. Phillips, p.100.
94. Campbell (1984), p.135.

to many current disputes defending jobs or conditions—their struggles are often about wages. The real argument is how to involve women more in these types of struggles and so build their confidence and organisation, not about how to hold back wages struggles altogether.

Feminist ideas like those outlined above have a strong purchase on many union leaders today. They fit neatly with the idea that strikes cannot win, that negotiation is the only way forward, that women only join unions on the basis of the services these offer rather than their activity in the workplace. These ideas lead away from collective struggle. In the process they of necessity downplay the role of women workers in fighting to improve their own conditions—a struggle which still continues despite the low level of strikes. Even in periods like much of the 1980s, even limited strikes have resulted in increased unionisation among women workers—for example in the National Health Service and at the BBC.

We should not be surprised at these developments. The history of the working-class movement shows that when offensive struggles do arise, the tendency of women workers is to join men in fighting as part of the working class. This was the experience in the early nineteenth century, during the New Unionism, the Great Unrest, the growth of the CIO organising drive in the 1930s in the United States, and in Britain in the 1960s and 1970s. When it happens again, we will again see the potential of women workers to go beyond the narrow confines of the union leaders and take action on their own behalf.

Part III: The struggle for liberation

CHAPTER SEVEN

Women, Labour and the vote

It is only relatively recently that women committed to feminist ideas have joined the Labour Party. During the 1960s and early 1970s most women who wanted to fight for their liberation would have regarded the party as largely irrelevant. It appeared an old-fashioned and male-dominated organisation. That had all changed by the late 1970s, and today many of those same feminists argue that it is the only place where women can achieve any sort of change.

Labour is, they argue, a mass working-class party which organises more women, both individually and through the trade unions, than any other. And it is, at least in part, open to feminist ideas. In particular the women's sections, the annual women's conference and the various other party structures aimed at women are seen as vehicles for feminist change. Feminists cite in defence of these institutions the early history of the party, when there was also a level of feminist activity.

The early Labour Party and the Independent Labour Party contained substantial numbers of often influential women. But relating to working-class women and their struggles was never central. Despite Labour's desire to improve working-class living standards, the party's record on the question of women was always poor. To understand why, it is necessary to look at some of its history.

The early years: the Women's Cooperative Guild and the Independent Labour Party

The Labour Party itself is as old as the twentieth century. But even before its existence there were attempts to organise working-class women politically. The Women's Cooperative Guild was formed in 1884. The Guild was concerned with promoting the ideals of cooperation and thrifty household management in order to improve the lot of working-class women. Its leadership, however, remained thoroughly middle-class. The Guild's general secretary from 1889 onwards was Margaret Llewelyn Davies, who came from a middle-class family and had been a student at the Cambridge college of Girton.

The Guild's membership tended, however, to be predominantly from the respectable working class. It was "biased towards the upper bracket of the manual wage-earning group. Most of the early Guild members were married and the majority were without paid work".[1]

The campaigns of the Guild reflected this bias, with strong emphasis on issues such as maternity benefit (from 1911 onwards). The Guild was usually moderate politically, although by the 1920s it began to adopt more political stances—linked both with the extension of the vote to women and with the growth of the Labour and Cooperative parties.[2]

Much more significant politically at the end of the nineteenth century was the Independent Labour Party. Formed in 1893, and to become for the next 40 years the predominant left grouping inside the Labour Party, the ILP always had a vociferous feminist current. It contained both women activists on the ground, and prominent women speakers who toured the country forming new branches in the 1890s and early 1900s.[3] These women were under-represented in the party, but encouraged at least a formal commitment to women's equality.[4]

The ILP women were quite impressive. But their ideas reflected a real mixture of influences. In particular, the gradualist approach of the Fabians—who saw themselves as an intellectual ginger group within the labour movement—surfaced in the ILP. Fabian ideas about social change were thoroughly moderate. They combined a sympathy for the working class with an essentially elitist view about how its emancipation could be achieved.

Although the women around the ILP were concerned with many issues, their primary interest was always electoral: how the Labour Representation Committee and later the Labour Party could win seats in parliament and eventually form a government. This meant their main activity was campaigning round elections at local and national level. It involved—at its centre—the argument over votes for women.

The issue of female suffrage had been a live one throughout the second half of the nineteenth century. John Stuart Mill had argued in favour of limited votes for women as far back as the 1860s and a succession of Bills aimed at gaining the vote for a minority of women. Despite a series of laws widening the franchise for men (although always on a property basis), the same right was not granted to women in national elections.

By the 1890s the situation was glaringly anomalous. It affected middle- and upper-class women most deeply, since they were denied rights readily granted to their husbands, fathers, brothers and sons. Since the 1851 census showed that 42 per cent of women between 20 and 40 years of age were unmarried (spinsters),[5] many did not even have access to political power or status through a husband.

However, although the issue was mainly the concern of the middle class, it also attracted a number of working-class women. The National Union of Women's Suffrage

1. Griffin and Thomas, pp.19–20.
2. Griffin and Thomas, p.85.
3. For background to this, see Liddington (1984).
4. See Howell, pp.334–5.
5. Rover, p.14.

Societies (NUWSS)—as its name suggests, a federation of various suffrage groupings—was formed in 1897 and by 1903, a petition for the suffrage was circulating throughout the Lancashire cotton industry. This was only part of widespread agitation throughout the north-west of England.[6]

The most well-known organisation set up to fight for votes for women was of course the Women's Social and Political Union (WSPU), known popularly as the suffragettes. The organisation was formed in Manchester in 1903. It came out of the Labour movement, and at first considered calling itself the Women's Labour Representation Committee.[7] The WSPU's founder, Emmeline Pankhurst, was a longstanding member of the ILP and the widow of one of its leading northern figures, Dr Richard Pankhurst. Her eldest daughter Christabel, then a student in Manchester, was also an ILP member.

The WSPU's tactics and campaigning were extremely imaginative. It first hit the headlines when Christabel and Annie Kenney, a Lancashire millgirl, disrupted the Manchester Free Trade Hall meeting of the Liberal Sir Edward Grey in October 1905. Both were imprisoned. This brought publicity and added support:

> In spite of the press Manchester public feeling largely supported the two prisoners. A great crowd welcomed them at the gaol. Esther Roper and Eva Gore Booth presented them with flowers. Opinion as to their action was divided in suffrage ranks throughout the country. Some sympathised, but showed no sign; many preferred to wait and see. A crowded Free Trade Hall meeting on October 20th gave the prisoners an almost unanimous welcome.[8]

The militant tactics took off from this point. The campaign embarked on a series of stunts and other activities, directed increasingly at ministers in the Liberal administration which formed a government in 1906. In the process the WSPU transformed itself. It went from being a provincial, slightly leftish organisation to a national London-based campaign. As this happened its working-class and Labour roots became much less secure.

> As of January 1906, the WSPU was still a tiny provincial movement, dependent upon the ILP for much of its financial support ... publicity ... and audiences. Only in the wake of the great Liberal victory of 1906 did the WSPU begin to take steps to remove itself from the somewhat parochial world of northern Labour politics.[9]

This particular direction for the suffragettes was increasingly spearheaded by Christabel, who took over as chief organiser of the WSPU soon after she arrived in London. Her attitude to the labour movement was soon made clear with the campaign around the Cockermouth by-election in August 1906.

The suffragette tactics were simple: to attack the Liberal candidate. "Christabel was most pointed in emphasising to the electors that she cared not a straw whether they voted Tory or Labour."[10] Her attitude caused an outcry among Labour supporters.

---

6. See Liddington (1984), chapter 9, and Liddington and Norris.
7. See Rosen, p.30.
8. Pankhurst, p.191.
9. Rosen, p.57.
10. Pankhurst, p.220.

The Manchester and Salford branch of the ILP voted to expel her and Teresa Billington from the organisation,[11] although this had little immediate effect since they belonged to another branch.

But Christabel's approach to the election was not accidental. She felt that the WSPU's connections with organised labour were too close, that it was too dependent on working-class women, and was thus alienating middle-class support.[12] So a break with the ILP was only a matter of time. When the party met the following April in Derby, leading women such as Mrs Despard and Mrs Cobden Sanderson called for backing for Labour in elections and were warmly applauded. Both Emmeline and Christabel Pankhurst resigned from the ILP shortly afterwards.[13]

The WSPU from that point onwards was free to appeal to women across the classes: "The way was now paved for the accession of wealthy donors who would not have supported a Labour organisation".[14]

The ideological basis for the split was more than just the desire of Christabel to free herself and the WSPU from the ties to the labour movement which marked its earliest years. The debate around adult suffrage and women's suffrage became increasingly bitter, with Labour and the women's movement on different sides.

The aim of all the suffrage organisations was to gain the vote for women on the same basis as men. Under existing conditions this meant a property qualification, with the vote being granted overwhelmingly to non-working-class women. The bulk of working-class women, and many male workers, would remain without the vote on the basis of WSPU demands. This approach immediately led to suspicion in the minds of many Labour supporters. Partly they feared that further enfranchisement of the non-labouring classes would not help Labour's electoral fortunes—perhaps hinder them. Partly they saw the issue as one of class, and their task as to help the most disadvantaged in society.

Certainly a debate at the time between Teresa Billington Greig and Margaret Bondfield on women's suffrage or adult suffrage—which would remove property qualifications—put the issues in class terms. Teresa Billington Greig argued that women formed a sex class because of their universal economic oppression, whereas Margaret Bondfield replied that women's suffrage was not real equality because of the economic inequalities which it ignored.[15]

The instinct of many inside the ILP was to support the demands for women's suffrage. Their feelings stemmed from a combination of a residual feminism—close links with the suffrage movement, especially the WSPU—and a feeling that some of those calling for adult suffrage were not really concerned whether women were included in the demand or not. The leading critic of the adult suffragists was the MP Keir Hardie, but he was usually in a minority within the Labour Party as a whole.

---

11. Rosen, p.71.
12. Rosen, p.70.
13. Rosen, pp.84–5.
14. Rosen, p.77.
15. Stanley Holton, p.58.

> The ILP view had dominated the [Labour Representation Committee's] earliest consideration of the issue, but from 1904 LRC support was turned to opposition by leading [members of the Social Democratic Federation] and trade unionists who advocated instead the demand for *adult* suffrage.[16]

On the face of it the issue appeared straightforward. In practice many feminists adopted the view put forward by Sylvia Pankhurst:

> Adult Suffrage was the main refuge of those who did not care for Votes for Women and disliked the militant tactics. The active and advanced minority of the party, which did the main share of the party's work throughout the country, was virtually united behind Keir Hardie for Votes for Women at any price.[17]

Hardie himself echoed this view with the assertion that the Adult Suffrage League, backed by some leading Labour figures, was merely a "dog in the manger".[18]

The argument put by those like Hardie was that a Bill to enfranchise women on the same basis as men would in any case benefit large numbers of working-class women. There was no possibility of winning universal suffrage from one of the major parties, so a partial franchise for women was better than nothing.

The debate in the Labour Party continued in the years up to the First World War, but was at its most heated during 1905 to 1907. These years coincided with the growth of the WSPU into an organisation of some national influence. The action of Christabel Pankhurst and other WSPU activists at the Cockermouth and Huddersfield by-elections in 1906 confirmed the worst fears of the adult suffragists.

The 1907 Labour Party conference in Belfast saw a big swing towards support for adult suffrage and away from simply women's suffrage. Christabel Pankhurst had soured Labour attitudes towards the suffragettes by announcing publicly just a few days before the conference that the WSPU would make no distinction between Tory and Labour when attacking the government. "Her provocative remark played perfectly into the adultist court, alienating undecided delegates from women's suffrage."[19]

Selina Cooper, a working-class suffragist from Nelson in Lancashire and the subject of Jill Liddington's study *The Life and Times of a Respectable Rebel*, spoke for a motion which both supported adult suffrage and called for women immediately to gain the vote on the same basis as men. Her concern was that the demands for women to gain the vote would be lost among general calls for adult suffrage which would not in any case achieve their goal in the near future. Harry Quelch of the Social Democratic Federation attacked as a "retrograde step" this call for women's limited suffrage while some men remained disenfranchised. He won by a large majority.

The impact of the 1907 conference was widespread. Feeling among those who supported women's suffrage ran high. They felt that the conference decision was a defeat for

---

16. Stanley Holton, p.53.
17. Pankhurst, p.242.
18. Pankhurst, p.245.
19. Liddington (1984), pp.174–5.

women's rights. Hardie was bitterly disappointed and even talked of resigning from the Labour Party.[20] To the WSPU the vote confirmed their belief that Labour could not be relied upon to deliver support for votes for women. The hostility shown by them even towards Hardie, who tried to bridge the gap between the adult suffrage and women's suffrage questions, showed that the WSPU leadership was not to be deflected from its course, regardless of what this meant in terms of severing old alliances.

For those women who supported both Labour and women's suffrage the outcome of the conference was confusing and often demoralising. Jill Liddington certainly argues that Selina Cooper felt alienated from both the Labour Party and from the WSPU. She felt that she could no longer work actively for the Labour Party's election campaigns as she had in the past.[21]

The dispute itself is in a sense typical of the reformist and gradualist character of the Labour Party. Its origin, as the voice of the trade unions inside parliament, led it in a very different direction from many of the European socialist parties where the idea of a limited general strike to win the vote for workers took root. The struggles of revolutionaries—for example that led by Rosa Luxemburg against the Prussian electoral system—were directed at workers *themselves* fighting to win reforms. Labour's approach, on the other hand, started not from principle but from opportunism: what would benefit it most electorally?

It was in this sense that Labour looked at the question of the vote from a class point of view. The party did not want middle- and upper-class women enfranchised while working-class men remained without the vote. Labour's leaders understood that the party could not but gain from universal adult suffrage—and at the expense of the Liberals in particular. Simply in order to ensure that it could eventually form a government, Labour had to back universal suffrage. The party made a number of compromises on the way, including calling for women's suffrage as well as adult suffrage. But it is hard to see—while recognising Labour's opportunism—how socialists at the time could have supported limited suffrage for women as opposed to adult suffrage.

Many feminists justify the argument in support of women's suffrage by claiming that the adult suffragists really weren't interested in women getting the vote. But the evidence is that those arguing for adult suffrage were for the most part sincere. As Constance Rover points out: "From its inception ... [Labour] affirmed its support for adult suffrage, frequently making it clear that by this term it meant the enfranchisement of men and women".[22]

No doubt a number of people backed this position out of opportunism, and because they preferred not to have to support the women's suffrage organisations for essentially misogynist reasons.[23] But it is equally clear that many of those who were committed to

---

20. Pankhurst, p.246.
21. Liddington (1984), p.178.
22. Rover, p.147.
23. A number of writers make this point, see Rover, p.146, and Liddington (1984), pp.178–80.

adult suffrage were also in favour of women's equality—including many working-class women.[24]

What was really at stake were political differences over the question of class. Christabel Pankhurst was the key and often most vociferous proponent of the view that women had no particular allegiance to any political party. In practice this led increasingly to support for right-wing ideas.

In time, some left-wing critics came to look upon the WSPU as supporting the Conservative Party. Some substance was given to this by the increasingly Conservative tendencies of Mrs Pankhurst and Christabel.[25]

The scepticism towards the WSPU from left-wingers was more than justified by its behaviour. From 1906 it appealed explicitly to women of all classes. Its first big militant demonstration outside parliament in October of that year

> marked the end of the WSPU's almost exclusive dependence on working-class women for deputations ... the groundswell of support that the WSPU received in the autumn of 1906 came from the educated and well-to-do, rather than from the rank and file of the Labour movement.[26]

From this point on the paths of the WSPU and the Labour Party increasingly diverged. However, the Labour Party was under some pressure to deliver on the question of women's rights. Margaret Macdonald, wife of Ramsay Macdonald, set up the Women's Labour League in 1906. Some at least saw it as an attempt to undercut the growing support of the suffragettes—this was the view of Sylvia Pankhurst and Keir Hardie.[27]

Certainly Labour felt under pressure from some of its activists. Selina Cooper, for example, refused to work for the Women's Labour League after the 1907 Labour conference because of the party's line on the vote. This led to the collapse of her own branch of the League, of which she was president.[28] Even though in the years following that conference things began to change to make the issue of the vote more important for Labour, the League itself remained small—5,000 by 1910—and mainly middle-class in composition.[29]

However as the WSPU moved away from Labour, the "constitutional" suffragists—organising through the National Union of Women's Suffrage Societies (NUWSS)—moved closer towards it. Increasingly the NUWSS endorsed Labour candidates and by 1912 had established an election fund to help Labour win by-elections. This represented an abandonment of the Liberal Party by even many middle-class feminists, since it had shown itself intransigent on the question of votes for women. The Labour leadership, on the other hand, was becoming more sympathetic to the cause. Although Labour was more strongly pro-adult suffrage than ever, the resolution at the 1912 conference stressed

---

24. See for example Drake, p.104, and Nield Chew.
25. Rover, p.94.
26. Rosen, p.74.
27. Pankhurst, p.244.
28. Liddington (1984), p.178.
29. Richard Evans, p.176.

that women's suffrage was clearly seen as part of adult suffrage. The years from 1912 to the outbreak of war in 1914 therefore saw a more friendly and fruitful cooperation between the suffragists and Labour (although this still did not win seats for Labour in by-elections).[30]

Meanwhile these years saw the increased isolation and splintering of the WSPU. The first major split took place in 1907 when leading women such as Charlotte Despard and Teresa Billington Greig formed what eventually became the Women's Freedom League. The origins of the dispute are not entirely clear, but lie at least in part in the lack of democracy inside the WSPU and the Pankhursts' autocratic behaviour.[31]

During the next four years the WSPU—run by Emmeline and Christabel Pankhurst and a married couple, Emmeline and Frederick Pethick Lawrence—staged a number of spectacular demonstrations. They took a variety of forms. There were the "rushings" of parliament when thousands of women thronged Parliament Square and tried to enter the building. There were window-smashing protests where government buildings and West End shops and offices would be simultaneously assailed by suffragettes clutching hammers. The aim of these operations were to gain publicity, often through mass arrest. The Liberal government willingly assented to brutal police and prison tactics in their efforts to curb the suffragettes.

The suffragette tactics became increasingly removed from those of the constitutional suffragists, and the WSPU found itself in a cycle of activity which constantly raised the level of commitment needed to be a WSPU member. Activity meant illegal actions, frequent imprisonment and often damage to health. It therefore depended more and more on women who had the time and energy to give it that commitment—certainly not working-class women.

By 1912 the WSPU was effectively at crisis point. An unannounced mass campaign of window-smashing led to Christabel's forced and secret exile in Paris.[32] Between that time and the outbreak of war, suffragette activity was almost totally directed towards acts such as arson and serious damage to buildings. Those arrested went on hunger strike and were force-fed. In response, the Liberal government passed the vicious and repressive "Cat and Mouse Act", which allowed the authorities to release those seriously ill through hunger-striking, and then to re-arrest them once their condition became less serious. The hunger strikers were left in a semi-permanent state of sickness, which was often irreparably damaging to their health.

The strain of this activity took its toll on the organisation. Andrew Rosen shows that there was a massive decline in the fees paid by members between 1909–10 and 1913.[33] Anyone challenging the direction of the organisation or the autocratic behaviour of Christabel Pankhurst in particular was squeezed out. The Pethick Lawrences returned from a North American trip in 1912 to find the WSPU offices moved and themselves

30. See Liddington (1984), chapter 13.
31. Rosen, pp.89–90.
32. See Dangerfield, pp.158–62.
33. Rosen, p.211.

without a role.[34] And Sylvia Pankhurst, who from 1912 had attempted agitation in the East End of London, was told to break with the labour movement or with the WSPU.

The East London Federation of Suffragettes

The East London Federation was in many ways the most impressive feature of suffragette organisation. Certainly most socialist feminists use it as an example of how working-class women can be organised on the basis of feminist politics. It stands in marked contrast to the main organisation of the WSPU, in that it made a serious effort to organise around issues concerning working-class people.

Sylvia Pankhurst's aim in establishing branches of the WSPU in the East End of London was to interest working-class women in the question of the vote. The opening of WSPU shops in Bethnal Green, Poplar, Limehouse and Bow towards the end of 1912 also coincided with a by-election which once again outlined the official WSPU's hostility to Labour.

George Lansbury, the well-known supporter of women's suffrage and Labour MP for the East End constituency of Bromley and Bow, had put forward the idea that Labour MPs should vote against the government until women were granted the vote. When he didn't gain official support from the Labour Party he resigned his seat to stand in a by-election as Independent Labour, largely on the issue of women's suffrage. Despite the WSPU's support for his candidacy, in practice its intervention was not particularly pro-Labour. On election day itself, the well-off WSPU would not at first even allow Lansbury's supporters the use of their cars to take voters to polling stations.[35] Lansbury was defeated.

This incident highlighted the fundamental differences which now existed between the approach of Sylvia Pankhurst and pro-women's suffrage Labour MPs such as Hardie and Lansbury on the one hand, and the majority of the WSPU on the other, for whom "social reforms for working-class women, let alone 'socialism', had long since ceased to be the primary goal".[36] By 1913, Sylvia had formed the East London Federation of the WSPU. It advocated universal adult suffrage, was not anti-men, was working-class and did not base its tactics on arson.[37] All these features marked it out in distinct opposition to its parent organisation.

The WSPU in fact continued with its campaign of clandestine arson and other attacks up to the outbreak of the First World War. The politics of Emmeline and Christabel Pankhurst became increasingly right-wing. In 1913 they embarked on a campaign against the "great scourge"—sexual disease—and launched a moral crusade which was anti-marriage. Their hostility to the Labour movement and working-class politics now took a number of forms. They wanted property qualifications and opposed universal adult

34. Rosen, pp.173–4.
35. Rosen, p.182.
36. Rosen, p.183.
37. Rosen, p.217.

male suffrage.[38] They disliked any connection with the working class. The demand for the extension of class privileges led almost inevitably to a defence of those privileges on an extremely narrow basis.

The wave of strikes in the years immediately preceding the war—the Great Unrest— they treated with hostility:

> "Why," they asked coldly, "does not the government bring in legislation to make strikes illegal?" "Why does Tom Mann get away with only six weeks imprisonment [for his famous 'Don't Shoot' appeal to soldiers not to fire on strikers]—whilst Suffragettes are being so cruelly imprisoned?"[39]

Sylvia's interest in working-class women was particularly incomprehensible to her sister, who saw workers as weak and impotent. Matters came to a head in 1913 when Sylvia spoke at an Albert Hall meeting organised by the *Daily Herald* in support of the thousands of workers locked out in Dublin. This infuriated Christabel, who felt that it connected the WSPU too closely with left-wing issues. Shortly afterwards, Sylvia agreed that the East London Federation should separate from the parent organisation; it became the East London Federation of Suffragettes.[40]

By this time the WSPU's decline was terminal. At the outbreak of war in 1914 it was the "harried rump of the large and superbly organised movement it had once been".[41] Emmeline and Christabel Pankhurst were jingoistic to the extreme, supporting the war effort, renaming their paper *Britannia* and leading anti-German sentiment. Christabel stated that women were better off in Britain and the US than anywhere else, and that stewards who had evicted suffragettes from meetings before the war were "Huns" with "guttural accents".[42]

Sylvia on the other hand, through the East London Federation of Suffragettes, opposed the war as a pacifist and continued her general social agitation. For much of the war this tended to centre on various welfare projects, such as a creche in an old pub, workshops and food provision. These were aimed particularly at alleviating the hardships of working-class mothers.

Like many others at the time, her politics moved to the left as the war progressed. Her ideas, already class-oriented, tended further in this direction, and she left agitation for the vote behind. She produced a paper called the *Worker's Dreadnought* directed at agitation around a number of working-class issues.

The impact of the Russian Revolution in 1917 was to push Sylvia even further to the left. After the war, she briefly joined the newly formed Communist Party. But she retained a number of disagreements with Leninist politics. The most important of these was her attitude to participation in parliaments by revolutionary socialists. She regarded such participation as both irrelevant and wrong politically. Lenin's pamphlet

38. Richard Evans, p.197.
39. Ramelson, p.157.
40. Rosen, p.223.
41. Rosen, p.242.
42. Richard Evans, p.197.

Left-wing Communism: an infantile disorder—which argues that standing in elections for parliament was a tactical question rather than one of principle—was a polemic aimed partly at Sylvia Pankhurst. This was a sign not only of the influence of these ideas, but of Sylvia Pankhurst's own significance in left-wing politics in Britain.[43]

Once the revolutionary wave following the end of the First World War had subsided, Sylvia, like many others of her generation, also withdrew from revolutionary politics. She remained committed to left-wing causes—although of an increasingly bizarre nature. Her ILP-influenced politics, strongly stamped by Keir Hardie, led to a number of political confusions. The ILP started from an essentially moralistic standpoint. It was influenced heavily by feminist ideas, but in addition was capable of moving to the left or right under the influence of workers' struggle. Sylvia Pankhurst's political development was very much a product of these vacillations.

The balance sheet of the suffrage movement

Women won the vote on a limited basis (essentially it was given to older, middle-class women) in 1918, and this was extended to all women over 21 in 1928. The popular right-wing myth is that women were given the vote as a reward for their patriotism and hard work dining the war. Many socialists, on the other hand, explain it purely in terms of the heroic struggles of the suffragettes up to 1914. The answer probably lies elsewhere. Fear of revolutionary struggle—which was breaking out in many European countries in the immediate aftermath of the war—forced the ruling class to concede reforms. One which resulted in relatively little social upheaval and yet fulfilled working-class aspirations was the extension of the vote. So universal manhood suffrage was granted in 1918—and it would have been politically inconceivable for any extension of the vote to men not to be given at least in part to women.

But it did not by this stage represent any radical challenge to the status quo. Evidence of this is that the first woman to take her seat as an MP was the Tory Lady Astor. Despite the misgivings of the Liberals before 1914, women's suffrage could easily be incorporated into the system.

The suffragette movement had all but disappeared by 1918. Emmeline and Christabel Pankhurst remained right-wingers, and soon faded into political obscurity. Sylvia espoused a series of causes. But the movement itself and its direction contain lessons for today. Primarily, the experience of the WSPU shows that women cannot be organised successfully across classes for any length of time. Attempts to do so end in the domination of any movement by middle- and upper-class women. Even Sylvia's attempts to break from the class-collaborationist approach of the WSPU was a failure, because it tried to link class politics with those based on gender.

The social crisis which erupted after the war led to an increased class polarisation. In the short term this benefited revolutionary ideas. But as the ruling class was once

43. For a detailed critique see Lenin, pp.556–65.

more able to stabilise the situation and place itself firmly in control, so the attraction of reformist ideas grew. Many of those influenced by the ideas of the suffragettes and other feminist ideas from the pre-war years now gravitated towards the growing Labour Party, which was set to replace the Liberals as Britain's second major party. Women were taken much more seriously by Labour now that they could help vote the party into office.

The Women's Labour League, founded in 1906, was integrated into the party's mainstream as the Women's Sections in 1918. It was campaigned for, full-time organisers were appointed to run it, and an annual conference was instituted. These measures were highly successful:

> By the end of 1922 there were over 1,000 Women's Sections, not including Ward Sections or Groups, and the sections had a membership of over 120,000. By the middle of 1924 there were 1,332 sections and the membership had risen to 150,000. Two areas, Woolwich and Barrow-in-Furness, had each more than 1,000 members enrolled.[44]

This enthusiasm reflected both the new women voters and, as GDH Cole points out, women's greater Labour and trade union activity as a result of the war. It also reflected the much greater roots which Labour was developing, and the increasingly bureaucratised structure of the party.

Yet although Labour was to benefit particularly from individual membership of women in the party, and from the active role which many women took in organising locally, its attitude towards fighting for women's issues was in general poor. So both the Labour Party and the trade unions supported cutting married women's benefit in 1922 and were again in favour of directing unemployed women towards the hated domestic service.[45] Once in office Labour took similar attitudes—especially with the acceptance of Means Test and benefits cuts by the majority of the Labour cabinet in 1931. These hit women as married or part-time workers particularly hard. Margaret Bondfield was to report in 1933 that in the intervening two years a quarter of a million married women had applied for unemployment benefit—only about a fifth had been allowed it.[46]

It is hardly surprising therefore that many women activists inside the Labour Party turned to issues where they felt they could have some influence. The question of birth control was pressing. Birthrates were falling, but most working-class women were forced to obtain contraceptive advice in secrecy and were often totally ignorant on the subject. Illegal and highly dangerous abortion was widespread. Many feminists—often those earlier active campaigning for the vote—took to campaigning on this question.[47]

Despite the work of a number of women "pioneers", major issues concerning women were to remain submerged. Only in the 1960s did things begin to change fundamentally.

---

44. Cole, p.141.
45. Lewenhak (1977), pp.184–5.
46. Lewenhak (1977), p.201.
47. See for example Rowbotham (1977), and Liddington (1984), chapter 18.

CHAPTER EIGHT

The women's movement of the late 1960s

The modern women's movement has existed for around 20 years. Its birth in the United States in the late 1960s was the result of specific historical circumstances. In that sense, although there was obviously a continuity of ideas between the new women's movement and the campaign for women's suffrage around the turn of the century, the modern movement was in major respects unique.

Three factors lay behind the founding of the movement. The first was the changed position of women at work. Women as workers—and especially as sometimes well-paid workers—demonstrated some of the contradictions of women's role in capitalist society. They were increasingly expected to play a role in the world outside the home, but they were also treated as second-class citizens. Women's inequality was there for everyone to see—demonstrated through low wages, "women's jobs" or part-time work.

Even where women had access to their own income, they were all too often treated as children, rather than responsible adults. So throughout the 1950s and early 1960s, for example, it was extremely hard for women to make any major credit purchase, such as a house or even a washing machine, without the permission and financial backing of a man.

This situation created a sense of grievance among many women. This was particularly true among women of the professional and middle classes. These grievances encompassed a lack of financial and legal equality with men, but went much further. There was also a sense of lack of fulfilment, of boredom with what even middle-class marriage—and its material comforts—had to offer. Betty Friedan spoke for a generation of such American women when she called this feeling "the problem which has no name".[48]

The problem for these women was no doubt compounded by a factor which was of real benefit to a layer of women, but which nonetheless tended to increase their frustration: the expansion of higher education after 1945. A substantial layer of women, including a number from working-class backgrounds, gained access to higher education

---

48. Friedan, pp.15ff.

and consequently to usually better paid and higher status jobs. By the late 1960s, there were 150,000 full-time women students in Britain[49] and this was steadily rising.[50]

Greater educational opportunity was both a stairway to much better prospects than even most middle-class women would have thought possible a generation earlier, and at the same time a demonstration of how inferior the position of women really was. So women found they were disproportionately at the bottom of the pile inside higher education itself. They found also that when they obtained jobs such as teaching, they were again disproportionately in the lower grades. The grievances underlying Betty Friedan's problem with no name continued to grow.

Education itself fuelled this process. Despite the real limitations of the education system, young men and women found their horizons widened. They discussed ideas and concepts which in some small ways began to challenge the ideas they had grown up with. Some of these new ideas tended to bring them into conflict with some of the basic tenets of capitalist society.

The third factor in the birth of the women's movement was in some ways a product of the changing structure of capitalism itself: the political explosion of the mid- and late 1960s and the growth of what became known as "the movements". It is impossible to understand the growth of the demand for women's liberation, and the flourishing of women's groups, without understanding this explosion—and particularly its effect in the United States, birthplace of the women's movement.

The founding of the American women's movement

The US movement was a product of factors similar to those in Britain. There were, however, a couple of major differences, which had a bearing on the different development of the women's liberation movement in each country.

The expansion of higher education was much greater in the much richer United States; the academic milieu was, and remains, an important feature of American political life. Also the impact of the organised working class on the women's liberation movement, or on the student or anti-war movements—which was very great in Britain—was virtually non-existent in the US.

This was particularly true of the US student left. It had no real connection with the working class or with working-class organisation in any real sense. That organisation was in any case extremely weak. It had been dealt major blows in the late 1940s and 1950s through a combination of the anti-Communist witch-hunts of McCarthyism and the Taft-Hartley anti-union laws. Any working-class *political* tradition—such as that represented by the Communist Party or the Trotskyists—had been severely weakened and effectively wiped out in many parts of the country.

---

49. *Social Trends 1970.*
50. *Social Trends 1986.*

The student new left was also a product of its time, and its class composition. Its members were the children of Betty Friedan's generation. They had grown up in the middle-class prosperity of the boom. Sara Evans in *Personal Politics*, her invaluable book about women and the left of the 1960s, describes what this meant. Although the left had a radical and liberal approach to the question of civil rights, its position on women was much worse than the previous generation of Marxist-influenced left-wingers: "the new left embodied the heritage of the feminine mystique far more strongly than the older left had".[51]

This heritage was incorporated into the growing civil rights movement. Politics in the United States was dominated and shaped by one movement throughout the whole of the 1960s: the movement against black oppression. This had a fundamental effect first in the form of the civil rights movement, which was then superseded by black power. The student movement was intertwined with it, the anti-war movement heavily influenced by it, and the women's movement was directly affected by its political repercussions.

Pressure for civil rights for blacks of the southern United States had been growing since the Second World War. Even as late as the 1960s, southern blacks could not vote and were segregated from whites. The few reforms accorded to them by the federal government were reforms which the white bigots in the south were unable or unwilling to implement.

Young radical students—blacks and whites (including some southern whites)—got involved in the movement for civil rights. By the early 1960s, many of them were not just giving moral support from northern university campuses but living in the south, registering voters, organising campaigns. They organised mainly through the Student Non-Violent Coordinating Committee (SNCC), and often faced real physical danger from hostile whites.

The politics of these students was egalitarian. They often lived lifestyles based on those of poor southern blacks. "Let the people decide" was a favourite slogan. But their egalitarianism didn't extend to women. Women took a secondary role, although many able women organisers went south.

In personal relations too there were problems. White women found sexual relationships with black men sometimes difficult, because of the prevailing ideas in their society. Writing of the period 1963 to 1965, Sara Evans says, "the patterns of sexual exploitation set in the south were transferred to the northern new left". She went on to explain future developments inside the left and in the women's movement when she stated: "When the same treatment came from white men in a white movement it would eventually prove easier to apply the categories of 'sexual exploitation' and 'objectification'".[52]

Meanwhile discontent with the male leaders of SNCC was growing among some of the women members. The inferior position of women in the organisation, the usually failed attempts at liberating sexual relationships between white women and black men,

---

51. Sara Evans, p.116.
52. Sara Evans, p.82.

and the growing alienation from the male leaders, prompted some black and white women in the SNCC to write a conference paper in late 1964 cataloguing instances of sexual inequality in the movement. The response from a leading black SNCC member, Stokely Carmichael, was the now notorious "the only position for women in SNCC is prone".[53]

Things were changing in the SNCC in different ways however. The civil rights movement was becoming eclipsed. Against a background of riots in Harlem and Watts, and the growth of black nationalism around Malcolm X, whites became much more marginal in the SNCC. Two white women, Casey Hayden and Mary King, wrote a paper in 1965 considering what black and white women had in common.[54] But increasingly the movement was splitting on grounds of race, partly as a result of the frustration of failure inside the campaign.

But despite their increasing ineffectiveness in this area, students continued to want to campaign over rights for blacks—though their attention turned now to the northern black ghettos and the appalling conditions there. It also turned increasingly to the movement against the Vietnam War.

The main vehicle for this protest was the Students for a Democratic Society (SDS). This involved itself in campaigns on a number of issues, but was marred by its practice in all sorts of ways. Students in SDS tended to direct their liberal guilt towards the oppressed of the ghettos, where they set out to organise the economically marginal. In doing so they ignored the working class as a force for change and concentrated instead on those with no economic or political power to change society.

They also based their politics increasingly on personal experience. An SDS leader, Tom Hayden, argued as far back as 1962 that "the time has come for a reassertion of the personal".[55] But the personal politics came to mean living the same ghetto lifestyles as the most oppressed urban blacks. This meant among other things accepting the most backward cultural and political ideas of some of those blacks—including a thoroughly sexist attitude to women. The identification of these radical white students with the struggles of the oppressed did not extend to any understanding of the oppression of women, who continued to be treated as second-class within the movement.

Despite this, the oppression of women gradually became an issue inside the movement. It appeared at the "We won't go" Conference against the Vietnam War, at SDS meetings and at the 1967 SDS conference where a "Women's Liberation Workshop" developed. Perhaps unsurprisingly, the first theorising of women's subordinate position from this conference equated women's oppression with the colonial oppression of the blacks in Africa or the Vietnamese. "Women are in a colonial relationship to men and we recognise ourselves as part of the Third World."[56]

This clearly absurd political position was derided by the bulk of the conference—but usually for the wrong reasons. Women were ridiculed at the conference. They were

53. Quoted in Sara Evans, p.87.
54. Sara Evans, pp.98–100.
55. Quoted in Sara Evans, p.104.
56. Quoted in Sara Evans, p.190.

pelted with tomatoes and driven off the stage. An offensive and sexist cartoon deriding women's rights appeared in the next issue of *New Left Notes*, and, in Sara Evans' words, "SDS had blown its last chance".[57]

The general fragmentation of the various movements by 1967–68 led the women further along the path to the founding of the women's liberation movement. Jo (Joreen) Freeman called a meeting in Chicago in 1967 to organise a women's intervention in the forthcoming National Conference for the New Politics (NCNP). The conference, held in August that year, "provided the final precipitant to an independent women's movement when white men, engaged in a wave of guilty liberal capitulation to black demands, patronised and ridiculed women making similar demands".[58]

Jo Freeman and Shulamith Firestone, who tried to raise women's liberation demands at the conference, were told that there were more important things to discuss than women's liberation. But for these and other women activists, the women's issue *was* the most important. The following week a number of women in Chicago produced a paper, "To the women of the left", which raised the idea of women's liberation with a layer of women disaffected by the new left. Within a year, there were women's liberation groups in most major US cities.

The nature of the movement

The American women's movement was therefore not born in a vacuum. It was a definite product of the American left, which itself was weak. There was no organisation comparable to the British Labour Party, and the US Communist Party was small. The left had been decimated by McCarthyism, while trade unions too were weak compared to Europe. This background formed the movement's politics and its practice. The women's movement started as a left-wing, radical movement. The women who founded it had been formed by the student politics in which they were active, and they retained many of its ideas. So the National Organisation of Women (NOW), founded in 1966 by Betty Friedan, was regarded (quite rightly) as thoroughly middle-class and limited in its fight for reforms. Celestine Ware, an early participant in women's liberation, described NOW as "regarded much as black militants regard the civil rights organisations. The typical NOW member is middle-class, employed full-time, and married".[59]

Women's Liberation Movement members tended to be very different from this. They often challenged the notion of marriage, stressed the importance of alternative lifestyles, and—even if only in a small way—tried to challenge the whole basis of capitalist society itself. They also often identified with other radical political issues. They protested at state persecution of the black power organisation, the Black Panthers. One group organised a protest demonstration over Nixon's inauguration in 1969. The movement

---

57. Sara Evans, p.192.
58. Sara Evans, p.197.
59. Ware, p.21.

was anti-war. And, as befitted a movement for women's liberation, it organised a famous protest against the "Miss America" contest in Atlantic City.

The women's movement was much weaker than the other movements however. It never succeeded in organising mass actions, and the numbers involved in it were surprisingly small. Far from there being a large and united sisterhood of women, the movement was diffused and fragmented from the start.

The politics adopted, even when overt, were also limited. Soft Maoism—characterised by a cheering of spontaneity, a lack of orientation on the working class, a contempt for theory—or else forms of libertarianism dominated. The old slogan "Let the people decide" summed up the attitude of much of the new left and hence of the women's movement.

In addition, massive stress was put on the expression of personal feelings and on the process of consciousness-raising. Today, these are practices which are considered unique to the women's movement. But in reality they did not originate there, but were already established in the student movement from which it came. Sara Evans has pointed to a number of similarities between the two movements: the anti-leadership bias; the emphasis on personal experience (SDS meetings in the mid-1960s began with the campus organiser describing his or her background and how he or she became radicalised); the emphasis on the internal procedure of the meetings.[60] Women's consciousness-raising—the central tenet of the women's movement—was the logical conclusion of this practice. There may also have been a Maoist influence: consciousness-raising has been likened to the process of "speaking bitterness" during the Chinese Revolution.

The weakness of even the most radical politics showed quickly. As women's oppression became the deciding factor of everything, so all other political problems were subordinated. The 1969 statement of principles of the New York Radical Women put it like this:

> We ask not if something is "reformist", "radical, "revolutionary" or "moral". We ask: is it good for women or bad for women? We ask not if something is "political". We ask: is it effective? Does it get us closest to what we really want to do in the fastest way?[61]

New York Radical Women soon split. A group which emerged from its three-way division was Redstockings. It continued and developed this view in its own statement of principles:

> We are critical of all past ideology, literature and philosophy, products as they are of male supremacist culture ... we take as our source the hitherto unrecognised culture of women, a culture which from long experience of oppression developed an intense appreciation of life, a sensitivity to unspoken thoughts and the complexity of simple things, a powerful knowledge of human needs and feelings.[62]

---

60. Sara Evans, p.214.
61. "Principles of New York Radical Women", in Morgan, p.520.
62. Ware, p.40.

This anti-intellectual approach, raising individual feelings to the level of theory, was to become the "common sense" of the women's movement. Overt political positions tended to go out of the window. Women who had never felt they really "belonged" in the black, student or anti-war movements now had a movement of their own. The women's movement became a natural home for those women who wanted to work round the question of women but also, and just as important, felt left out of the existing political scene. An atmosphere and the beginnings of a theory had to be created which would justify this movement of all women.

An example of the confused thinking which prevailed can be seen from the statement of Judy Laws, quoted in 1970 in *Mademoiselle* magazine. Laws was sacked from the University of Chicago for wanting to do research into the sociology of women's oppression.

> I see the woman problem as the greatest neglected ill. I'm pessimistic about our impact on the war, and I'm convinced that white people can't participate in the black movement, but I'm not a socialist, and I'm not a revolutionary, I mean—I wear a bra.[63]

But if politics was not a word which guided the early Women's Liberation Movement, nonetheless political differences soon emerged which caused all manner of divisions inside it. Redstockings, already the most important splinter from New York Radical Women, confirmed the consciousness-raising approach to fighting women's oppression: "Redstockings believes that liberating women has priority above every other idea; it dispenses with formal political language and finds the key to a woman's liberation in her own experience".[64]

In 1969, the New York Radical Feminists (NYRF) was founded from a combination of the feminists and the Redstockings. Its membership included Shulamith Firestone, Anne Koedt and Celestine Ware. These people moved increasingly and explicitly away from any notion of socialist politics. So the NYRF manifesto declared: "the political oppression of women has its own-class dynamic".[65] Firestone developed this view in her book *The Dialectic of Sex*.[66]

Some took the logic of a separate female class dynamic even further. Valerie Solanis stated in the SCUM (Society for Cutting Up Men) Manifesto: "the male is an incomplete female, a walking abortion, aborted at the gene state".[67]

Any idea that there might have been of a strong, collective and centralised movement against women's oppression was beginning to disappear. A Congress to Unite Women in 1969 came to nothing. Even the ultra-respectable NOW ran into problems, when its New York branch nearly split in two in 1970 over the question of lesbianism. Some of NOW's respectable members did not want themselves associated with political lesbians or with any challenge to dominant ideas about sexuality. The writer Rita Mae Brown,

63. Quoted in Ware, p.21.
64. Ware, p.39.
65. Ware, p.59.
66. Firestone, chapter 1.
67. Solanis, "The SCUM Manifesto", in Morgan, p.514.

who was a NOW member at the time, argued that: "Lesbianism is the one word which gives the New York NOW executive committee a collective heart attack".[68]

The movement was therefore diffused and splintered: because of its legacy from the movements; because of its avoidance of political argument; and because of its orientation on personal lifestyles. Increasingly real political differences manifested themselves in supposedly personal disagreements, which just led to the setting up of more groups.

The story of the city-wide Women's Liberation Coalition which met weekly in New York is an illustration of the fragility of the groups at this time. It had a left-wing, pro-working class orientation and tried to attract working-class women. It supported a Panther demonstration in November 1969 against the terrible jail conditions of pregnant Panther women in New Haven. But some coalition women felt that the demonstration was too pro-Panther, and there was a split over the extent of left involvement. By December 1969 the coalition had ceased to meet.[69]

The movement faced one further contradiction.

On the one hand, its influence grew to a massive scale. By 1971 , there were over a hundred women's liberation publications. By 1973 the mainstream feminist magazine *Ms* had a circulation of 350,000. By 1974 there were women's studies programs at 78 educational institutions—with another 500 campuses offering 2,000 courses.[70]

But the number of activists involved in the movement remained relatively small in comparison with the general influence of feminist ideas. NOW claimed 30,000 members by 1973—hardly a mass movement and, given the limited nature of NOW's demands, a very small number. The more radical wing of the movement fared no better. The Women's Liberation Coalition attracted just 150 women each week from the whole of New York City. The 1969 Congress to Unite Women attracted just 200.[71]

The discrepancy in these figures created a problem which still exists for the women's movement today: there is vast but passive support for some of the ideas of women's liberation, but there is no connection between these ideas and any consistent activity. This in turn leads to tokenism, to passivity and to a sectarian refusal on the part of the women's movement to acknowledge anyone other than itself as having the right to speak on behalf of women, or to act in the interests of women.

The American women's movement was from the beginning by far the largest and most influential. It exported its ideas, especially to Europe, and thereby ensured that many of its preoccupations and problems—although sometimes not its vitality—would also emerge elsewhere.

68. Quoted in Deckard, p.375.
69. Ware, pp.50ff.
70. Deckard, p.385.
71. Ware, p.50.

The early women's movement in Britain

The existence of women's liberation in Britain is usually dated from 1968. It was in that year that the first modern equal pay strike—by women machinists at Ford—took place. The same year a body with the unwieldy title of the National Joint Action Committee for Women's Equal Rights (NJACWER) was set up. This committee was based on the unions and in 1969 organised a demonstration in support of the demand for equal pay.

Throughout 1969, a number of women's liberation groups sprang up. They were often comprised of women who lived with or were married to active male left-wingers. But as Sheila Rowbotham has written: "It was really from the Oxford Conference in February 1970 that a movement could be said to exist".[72]

More than 500 women attended that first conference. Most found it an exhilarating experience. For the first time women in Britain were organising along the lines that American women had been following for two years. There were, however, from the outset major political differences between the early British movement and its American counterpart.

The movements in Britain were of a totally different nature to those in the US which had exerted a strong and often negative influence on the women's movement there. The civil rights and black power movements did not exist in Britain in any real sense. The student movement was important but limited in its impact. The mass anti-war movement had an important politicising effect, but did not have the same cutting edge as that in the United States, where it was at the heart of the aggressor nation.

The mainstream political situation in Britain was also much more favourable. The second half of the 1960s saw the passage of liberalising laws on divorce, abortion, gay rights and equal pay. In addition, the high rate of unionisation in Britain (about half of all workers were in unions as opposed to around 28 per cent in the US in the late 1960s) led many of those on the left and in the women's movement to see working-class struggle—through the trade unions—as a major feature of the fight for women's liberation.

These attitudes were reinforced and strengthened by the high level of class struggle in the years around the birth of the women's movement. One feature of this was the large number of strikes involving women, many of which were taken up by the early women's movement. The Leeds clothing workers in 1970, the Post Office telephonists in 1971, May Hobbs' struggle to organise the London office night cleaners, all were seized as opportunities to build the movement.

Sometimes socialists and women's liberationists were instrumental in helping these disputes. This happened in the case of the night cleaners, as one contemporary report describes:

> A combined picket was set up of cleaners, IS [International Socialists] and Camden Women's
> Action Group, Socialist Women and the Workshop, which was joined by cleaners of another

---

72. Rowbotham (1972), p.97.

building which came out in sympathy. As a result of these actions a representative of the TGWU negotiated with the cleaning company and it was agreed that the two shop stewards were to be reinstated; the company was forced to recognise the union, and to agree that there would be no intimidation against union members.[73]

It is hardly surprising that these sorts of results encouraged women to look towards the working class and to the unions as vehicles of struggle. The same year as the night cleaners' strike, 1971, International Women's Day (originally organised by the socialist movement near the beginning of the century) was celebrated again. The focus was a demonstration around the four demands of the women's movement: free abortion and contraception on demand; equal educational and job opportunities; free 24-hour nurseries; and equal pay.[74]

So the movement in its early years had a lively and outward-looking orientation. One of its first major successes was the picket of the "Miss World" contest at the Albert Hall in 1971 which caught the imagination of many women. But, as in America, the freshness and vitality of a few early activities were quickly replaced by problems and difficulties. The reasons for these were often very similar.

The rationale of the movement was that it was capable of uniting all women to fight against their oppression. At first it seemed possible to win women to this through working-class struggle. But as the political differences inside the movement became clearer, this possibility became more remote.

The Oxford Conference did not bring these political differences out. But the Women's Liberation Conference at Skegness just over a year later pointed to some of the major problems. The conference has become somewhat notorious in recent years. Dissent started over the structure of the conference itself. Some women walked out of the Saturday plenary to discuss on their own. It was agreed that evening that there would be more small group discussion the next day. In the plenary the following afternoon, however, a row broke out involving some Maoists. A Maoist woman was removed from the chair, and a male Maoist ejected from the meeting for disruption. The conference then proceeded to vote to disband the Women's National Coordinating Committee (WNCC) which had been set up at the Oxford conference, at least partly on the grounds that it was wracked by sectarian division.

This conference marked a turning point. From then on, men were not welcome at such gatherings, and the already existing hostility to socialists was becoming more marked. "It is clear from the outcome of this conference that the apparent agreement in the Women's Liberation Movement which was sometimes seen at WNCCs does not exist in reality", commented the magazine *Socialist Woman*.[75]

Another report of the conference, in the women's liberation workshop magazine *Shrew*, pointed to some of the problems: "We were worried by the widespread opposition

---

73. Report in *Shrew* (London) volume 3, number 1, February 1971.
74. Rowbotham (1972), p.97.
75. *Socialist Woman* (London), number 1, 1972.

that there seemed to be to any form of organisation ... Organisation and intellectual analysis are too simply seen as authoritarian and therefore masculine; hence bad."[76]

Even here, however, the authors agreed that men should in future be excluded from such conferences.

This argument continued at the Manchester conference in March 1972, where it centred on whether men should be allowed to attend the conference social on the Saturday night. The next day the conference split for or against men. One delegate encapsulated the anti-men position:

> If there is one woman present who would like to be with her sisters for two days of the year and not be oppressed by the presence of any men, surely we could respect that sister's wish and have a conference for women without men.[77]

This was an important step in two respects. Firstly it meant that the movement was becoming far more internalised, and concerned with the structure and form of meetings themselves, rather than with what the meetings decided. Secondly the step was in practice away from the idea that the working class—and in particular men as part of the working class—was part of the solution to the fight against oppression. Instead men were increasingly seen as part of the problem. By the late 1970s, viewing men as the problem had become an immensely influential theory.

Of course, the argument about men was a reflection of much greater divisions—between those who wanted change in a socialist direction and those who subscribed in some way to a "women's revolution". An interesting report in *Shrew* tells of a public meeting on women's liberation held in Ealing, west London, in 1971, where the argument got round to whether changes in personal lifestyles were enough or whether social change was needed. A speaker from the Women's Liberation Workshop stated: "there is nothing in socialism in which women are freed. If women are viewed as conservative they would be suppressed in a socialist system".[78]

Similar arguments were being repeated in groups around the country. As the movement progressed, it was clearly the socialist ideas which were losing out. In some ways this was partly the fault of the socialists themselves. *Socialist Woman*, a magazine produced by the orthodox Trotskyist International Marxist Group, stressed class issues but did so in a remarkably formalistic way. Increasingly its theoretical debates hinged round the question of women's domestic labour—a sometimes sterile and often obscure debate conducted at "an abstract level".[79] The group's concrete intervention was around the Working Women's Charter, a list of demands for women at work. This campaign was, however, aimed at influencing the lower levels of the union bureaucracy rather than at mobilising working women.

---

76. Mitchell and de Winter.
77. *Shrew*, volume 4, number 3, June 1972.
78. *Shrew*, volume 3, number 9, December 1971.
79. See for example *Socialist Woman*, Autumn 1974.

Women's Voice, the women's paper of the International Socialists (forerunner of the Socialist Workers Party), had a consistently working-class and activist orientation. It was based from its inception in 1972 on workers' struggles (especially those for equal pay and later around the National Abortion Campaign). But it tended to ignore any arguments taking place within the women's movement, so in practice it did not challenge the anti-socialist ideas which were coming forward.

But the main reason for the growing weakness of socialist ideas inside the movement lay in the distorted view of socialism which predominated. Most feminists' view of socialism was a completely eclectic variety of ideas, as one veteran feminist—late of the *Spare Rib* collective—articulates:

> By the late 1960s the politics coming out of [such] struggles included observations, analysis and practice which women in turn seized hold of to help them define themselves ... Mao, black power, Fanon, Vietnam, Reich, libertarianism, sexual liberation.[80]

This political confusion coloured the new Women's Liberation Movement, which adopted the voluntarism of Mao, the cheerleading of the oppressed from the national liberation movements, sexual radicalism and individualism from the libertarians. Because the politics were so unclear and eclectic, there were many things which these women could not begin to explain. If, following Stalin and Mao, one third of the world was already socialist, why were women in these countries still oppressed? Why did women's liberation not come about as a result of colonial revolution?

The questioning of "socialist" theory grew, especially in the mid-1970s. The "crisis of militancy" produced by the failure of the struggles of the late 1960s and early 1970s to change the world had its effect on many women. For them, the women's movement provided a convenient stepping stone out of organised socialist politics. Involvement in left-wing groups was increasingly regarded as unacceptable by many feminists.

The American experience was transferred wholesale to Britain, and left-wing organisation was accused of sexism, as if its members had been in any way comparable with the Tom Haydens and Stokely Carmichaels of the US left. In reality, many of the women articulating these ideas had always been hostile to left groups—and had at best been on their margins. There were even some who had shown little interest in ideas of women's liberation while in left groups, yet who now turned against the left.

It was widely accepted that all left-wing men were the problem. Some left-wing feminists went along with this and some—at first tentatively—asserted that they were feminists first.

Red Rag, produced by a collective of various left-wing women but increasingly under the influence of the Communist Party, stated in its first issue: "The organised labour movement—that is, the trade unions, the co-ops and the left political parties—is the decisive force in this country for social progress and for socialism".[81] The language

---

80. O'Sullivan, p.72.
81. *Red Rag*, number 1, 1973.

may have been Stalinist, but at least the commitment was to working within mixed working-class organisations. By the fourth issue of the magazine a change was under way: "our first commitment is to the Women's Liberation Movement".[82]

As the socialists moved closer to a cross-class feminism, so the non-socialist feminists became more confident. A Women and Socialism conference was held in Birmingham in the autumn of 1974. Even here radical feminists went on the offensive against socialist feminists:

> Socialist women were challenged to demonstrate their commitment to women, all women, even "fascist" women, and to put women above their "politics". Violent statements about men have appeared in the Women's Liberation Newsletter unsigned; women with boy children have been turned away from the Kingsway Women's centre; women in the office have refused to speak to men over the phone.[83]

Although such antics were greeted with a sense of outrage, they became more and more common as radical feminists tried to impose much greater separatism on the movement. The politics of the socialist feminists were so muddled that they were incapable of taking the radical feminists on. Eventually, as we shall see, they were to capitulate on a theoretical and a practical level.

But the weakness of the movement, and its division over class and gender, did not lie simply in the politics of the women involved; rather, the politics were a product of the social composition of the movement itself, and of its underlying basis. Like the American movement, the British movement was not based on working-class women. It attracted women from that thin layer who were educated, aware, higher earners if they were in work.[84] Sheila Rowbotham describes one group:

> They were predominantly American and in their mid-twenties. Some of them had been active in the Camden Vietnam Solidarity Campaign, most of them had husbands who were very deeply involved in revolutionary politics. Many of them too had small children and felt very isolated both as housewives and as foreigners. They started to meet in Tufnell Park and were later to have an extremely important influence.[85]

A survey in *Shrew* in 1972 gives a similar picture. A student interviewed seven out of twelve women in a London group. Four were over 30, and only one under 25. They were all from middle-class backgrounds. Three had been born in North America and four in Britain.[86] Their political views were as usual diverse: "there was no one coherent radical ideology that was expressed. We had not sorted out the relationship between the class struggle and women's struggle".[87] But this lack of coherence was beginning to show a negative side. "Only one of us was optimistic about the future. The most pessimistic of

82. *Red Rag*, number 4, 1974.
83. Alexander and O'Sullivan.
84. Sheila Rowbotham interviewed by Elana Dallas and Alastair Hatchett, *Socialist Review* (London), number 3, June 1978.
85. Rowbotham (1972), p.93.
86. *Shrew*, volume 4, number 1, 1972.
87. *Shrew*, volume 4, number 1, 1972.

us felt that the movement, because of its lack of concrete purpose, might fizzle out and felt it necessary for us to work for concrete goals."[88]

This study, together with Sheila Rowbotham's recollections of the Tufnell Park group, is impressionistic but fascinating. Two points are worth making: the women were not particularly young or new to the political milieu. They had been around the left and clearly looked to the women's movement to provide them with a political purpose greater than that of passive spectators. In this they were quite different from the people who, new to politics, tended to gravitate to the revolutionary left at the time. In addition, there was also a high proportional involvement of Americans in the early British movement. This is evidence of the huge influence of the American movement on the British, and explains how many of the political ideas first developed in the US were carried into the movement in Britain in a very direct way.

The nature of the movement—the fact that it was not linked to struggle, the fact that it could at best only relate to a very small number of working-class women on an individual basis—led to the sense of powerlessness and pessimism experienced by the women cited above. It also meant that the central belief of the movement—consciousness-raising—fitted perfectly. Middle-class women could spend endless hours talking about what was oppressing *them* as individuals; the practice of consciousness-raising automatically led away from class struggle.

An article in *Shrew* in 1971 entitled "Organising Ourselves" described what a women's liberation group was like. Each group would be small—between 10 and 15 members—and locally based. The point of the group was to act as "a model for political work and a microcosm of a future good society".[89] So the group was not there primarily to organise in the outside world but to raise the level of ideas of its own members—and therefore to create a pleasant, feminist consciousness regardless of the objective circumstances in the wider world.

This attitude had an effect on the practice of the women's movement in more ways than one. The groups became more and more inward-looking. Some became closed to new members, which meant that the movement really was developing into an internalised, charmed circle.[90] Because "the personal is political" became the accepted slogan, discussion of personal problems became as valid as fighting for social change. The orientation on the personal also meant the movement stayed small. It seems that there were never more than 60 women's liberation groups in London[91] and given the optimum size of between 10 and 15, these could only have organised a few hundred women.

Conferences and demonstrations also tended to be small. For example the International Women's Day demonstration in 1971 attracted 2,000 people, of whom a quarter were

88. *Shrew*, volume 4, number 1, 1972.
89. *Shrew*, volume 3, number 2, March 1971.
90. Of 41 groups listed in *Shrew* in 1972, 28 were open to new members, 13 were closed (*Shrew*, volume 4, number 5, October 1972.)
91. "Organising Ourselves", in Rowbotham (1972), p.103. Figures for groups listed in *Shrew* tend to be much lower, so this is a generous estimate.

men.[92] The publications fared a little better. *Spare Rib* was launched in 1972 and quickly built up a wide circulation, although not on a mass scale. But even by December 1971, *Shrew* contained an article about its production problems which bemoaned the fact that "we don't even sell the 3,000 copies that are printed each month".[93] *Red Rag, Women's Voice, Socialist Woman, WIRES* and the others only had similar circulations at best.

Given all these factors, it is hardly surprising that even by 1974 signs of crisis were everywhere. The initial enthusiasm of the movement had gone, many of the activists had run out of steam, the radical feminists were going on the offensive. *Shrew* didn't produce an issue for two years from late 1974 to 1976.[94] *Socialist Woman* wrote in 1974: "most working-class militants do not turn to the WLM (Women's Liberation Movement) to centralise and coordinate their struggles".[95]

Yet the period was one of significant struggles among women. Equal pay was the impetus for many: SEI and Wingrove and Rogers in 1974, Electrolux in 1975, and there were many other struggles by women: Asian women at Kenilworth Components; teachers in Hackney; Rolls-Royce and Dunlop workers in Coventry. The list went on and on in the early and mid-1970s.[96] Members of the women's movement related to the strikes as individuals—there was no sign of a mass movement of women committed to helping these women win. Instead, where struggles were successful, this tended to be where fellow trade unionists had played a key role—often men.[97]

The abortion campaign

In 1975, surprisingly, a new struggle developed. If anything was a key "women's issue" this was. It provided the opportunity for mass mobilisation for the first time since the formation of the movement. But, when it was tested, the movement was found wanting.

The issue was abortion. In 1967, an Abortion Act had been passed which allowed legal abortion for women if continuing with the pregnancy would affect the mental or physical health of the woman. Although this criterion obviously imposed restrictions, it also allowed far more women to obtain safe and legal abortions.

The rate of legal abortions shot up. In 1969 there were 53,000 legal abortions. By the mid-1970s the annual figure had reached well over 100,000.[98] The anti-abortion lobby, unhappy with the original Act, attempted to restrict the law further. A right-wing Labour MP, James White, introduced a private members' Bill which aimed to restrict the grounds for abortion and the abortion clinics which provided essential back-up to the NHS.

---

92. *Shrew*, volume 3, number 3, April 1971.
93. *Shrew*, volume 3, number 9, December 1971.
94. *Shrew*, Autumn 1976.
95. *Socialist Woman*, Autumn 1974.
96. See the strike compilation in *Red Rag*, number 5, 1974.
97. For example at Wingrove and Rogers in Liverpool, and equal pay strikes in Glasgow and Coventry (usually TASS/AUEW).
98. *Abortion Statistics 1985*.

A meeting at the House of Commons in April 1975 heralded the beginning of the National Abortion Campaign (NAC), set up to fight White's Bill and to defend the 1967 Act. From the start the campaign was heavily influenced by socialists, who carried a lot of the work. Members of the International Marxist Group in particular (then numbering several hundred) were involved in the national structure of NAC. The International Socialists were very active in the campaign, especially at a local level. The largest left organisation at the time, the Communist Party, supported the campaign, but was much more passive in its approach.

The campaign had great success in its early months. The NAC petition was used to organise street meetings, factory gate meetings and local activities. Labour MPs were pressurised to oppose the Bill. Most important, the issue was taken up in workplaces and in union branches. This line was particularly pushed by IS, which argued that the attack on abortion rights was essentially a class issue, since rich women always had the money for safe and legal abortion—it was the poor who were penalised by restrictive abortion laws.

The right to abortion proved surprisingly popular. Petitioners received a lot of support from many sources—that of middle-aged and older women was particularly noticeable (many of them would have experienced illegal abortion, which before 1967 ran at an estimated 100,000 a year). Even all-male workplaces or union branches could be committed to support for the campaign. In June 1975, NAC's first national demonstration in London mobilised 40,000. A further 700 marched in Glasgow and 100 in Dundee. On the London demonstration, banners included the Hull Docks shop stewards' committee, a couple of AUEW branches, and branch banners from the UPW (Post Office workers), NUJ (journalists), COHSE (health workers), NUT (teachers), ASTMS and NALGO (white-collar workers) and 18 trades councils.[99]

Where the issue was raised among workers, it was clearly getting a good response. Beth Stone, a member of the NUT executive and of IS, struck a chord when she told the demonstration that White's Bill was "part of a concentrated attack on working people".[100] The demonstration was a great success. But divisions within the campaign came quickly to the fore, divisions which reflected those growing in the women's movement itself.

Women members of IS who attended the NAC steering committee argued that the June success should be built on and repeated as the most effective way of defeating White. Others in NAC put increasing faith in sympathetic Labour MPs to win their case. Yet although a Labour government was in office, the abortion issue continued to be regarded as a matter of individual conscience by Labour, and a substantial minority of Labour MPs continued to support White.

A NAC planning meeting in September 1975 split. Representatives of the IMG, the Communist Party and the Labour Party opposed the call for another national demonstration. The IS won its position for such a demonstration in the local NAC groups

---

99. *Women's Voice*, number 19, July 1975.
100. *Women's Voice*, number 19, July 1975.

where activists were represented, but was unable to do so at the national meeting. As an article in *Women's Voice* put it, the majority of those leading NAC were "effectively arguing for the burial of the campaign".[101]

Similar divisions occurred at NAC's conference in October that year. Women grouped around IS and *Women's Voice* argued for and successfully won the adoption of the slogan "Free abortion on demand—a woman's right to choose" as that of the campaign. But a mass mobilisation by the anti-abortion organisation SPUC was consciously ignored by the conference organisers. It was left to a *Women's Voice* initiative to call a picket of SPUC. Two hundred women left the conference and joined the picket.[102]

Revolutionary politics could clearly appeal to a minority of the activists. But the main direction of the campaign was going elsewhere. It tended to reflect a growing inclination among much of the left to look to the Labour Party for change. So the IMG put more and more faith in MPs such as Jo Richardson (even though Labour minister Barbara Castle was already trying to restrict private abortion "abuses"—thereby throwing a sop to the anti-abortionists).[103] The fact that James White's Bill was ultimately defeated by parliamentary means—although largely because of extra-parliamentary pressure, which demonstrated the anger of many people on the issue—increased this orientation.

In addition, the socialists in the campaign tended to be on the defensive. Individuals on the steering committee were granted as much weight as whole political or union organisations, and the atmosphere was always against the socialists. Any attempts by socialists to raise the political level of the campaign were denounced as attempts to split the movement. The bulk of women in organisations such as the IMG or Communist Party tended to tail-end and sometimes encourage these sentiments.

So instead of NAC becoming a campaign which could genuinely involve large numbers of workers and so transform the nature and priorities of the women's movement, it became just one small, and increasingly marginal, part of it.

The movement itself meanwhile had come a very long way. In some ways the growth of NAC hid certain developments. But by the mid-1970s the excitement of the new movement had died. Sisterhood was revealed to contain all sorts of contradictions and as many political differences. By then too, radical feminist attitudes were hardening. Their "common sense" views were to crystallise around the theory of patriarchy—a theory which was increasingly adopted by the socialist feminists to explain women's oppression. So the women's movement faced the second half of the 1970s, major recession and economic crisis, with confusion, diffuse politics and practice, and its own crisis. The later story of the women's movement was therefore a very different one.

---

101. *Women's Voice*, number 21, September 1975.
102. *Women's Voice*, number 23, November 1975.
103. *Women's Voice*, number 23, November 1975.

CHAPTER NINE

The decline of the women's movement

The hopes of the early years of the women's liberation movement quickly turned sour. By the mid-1970s and into the 1980s, the movement and the feminist ideas which underpinned it were charted on a different course. Two separate trends—which reinforced each other as time went on—began to dominate the movement. The first was the legitimising and sheer respectability of much of the movement, which meant its incorporation into society and the state at all sorts of levels. The second was the development of radical feminism as the dominant trend within the movement as a whole.

Respectability became a hallmark of the US women's movement, as a thin layer of women moved up into top jobs or into newly created "equality" posts in government. An interview with Robin Morgan, a leading US feminist, in 1978 showed the extent to which this had happened. She herself worked on *Ms*, a mainstream women's magazine, and saw no contradiction between this and her feminist politics. She spoke approvingly of the acceptance into mainstream politics of a friend of hers:

> Eleanor Holmes Norton I first met almost fifteen years ago when she was counsel to the black women's liberation committee of SNCC. We have been teargassed together. She now heads the Equal Opportunities Commission, and I would stake my life that she is not selling out.[1]

American capitalism was well able to incorporate a layer of former radicals from the women's, black and student movements into the system. This it consciously set out to do. Today 44 per cent of accountants in the US are women, compared to only 16 per cent in 1960. In 1986, 30 per cent of Business Administration masters' degrees were awarded to women, as against 8.4 per cent in 1975.[2]

This trend was accompanied by a high level of ideological conservatism. Some women returned to the traditional roles that many had eschewed only ten years before. The feminist historian Linda Gordon described herself in 1978 as "very alarmed" about the baby boom then taking place among many feminists. They seemed to be valuing all the

---

1. Interview with Robin Morgan in *Spare Rib*, number 77, December 1978.
2. *The Economist*, 14 March 1987.

things—marriage, the family and motherhood—which they had always believed were at least part of the causes of women's oppression.

> I know a million women here with babies, and I'm the only one who is working full-time. Everyone else is living in families with a restoration of straight sex-roles ... practically every one of them has got married. I've experienced the conservatising effect on myself; having a baby throws me in more and more on the little quasi-family that I live in.[3]

A sure sign of the incorporation of much of the movement lay in the designation by the United Nations of 1975 as International Women's Year. As with all the unfortunate causes singled out by the UN for special attention, International Women's Year did nothing to alter the unequal position of working women within society. It did, however, produce a massive jamboree—a conference in Mexico.

The conference served only to highlight the massive class differences which existed between its different participants. These class differences were particularly accentuated by the presence of women from the third world, such as Domitila Barrios de Chúngara, the wife of a Bolivian tin miner. Tin miners in Bolivia worked in the most appalling conditions and died at an average age of 34. The main struggle of these workers and of their wives was against the mine-owners and the government, not against each other. Domitila was shocked at the priorities of the bourgeois feminists at the conference. Betty Friedan, leader of NOW, criticised her and other women like her for talking about politics too much. Discussion of politics clearly demonstrated the divisions between them too sharply for Betty Friedan's liking. Domitila answered the bourgeois women:

> Every morning you show up in a different outfit and on the other hand, I don't. Every day you show up all made up and combed like someone who has time to spend in an elegant beauty parlor and who can spend money on that, and yet I don't. I see that each afternoon you have a chauffeur in a car waiting at the door of this place to take you home, and yet I don't ... Now, señora, tell me: is your situation at all similar to mine? Is my situation at all similar to yours? So what equality are we going to speak of between the two of us? If you and I aren't alike, if you and I are so different? We can't, at this moment, be equal, even as women, don't you think?[4]

Two years later another massive women's conference took place, this time at Houston in Texas in 1977. The Equal Rights Conference was, like Mexico, hailed as a huge success by many feminists. Yet it marked the degree of rightward drift of the American movement. It was graced by the presence of three First Ladies (wives of American presidents): Rosalynn Carter, Betty Ford and Lady Bird Johnson. All three were extremely rich members of the ruling class, who could know nothing of the problems of ordinary women.

The conference attracted 15,000 people. But an estimated 20 per cent of delegates were "pro-family" conservatives who were opposed to abortion, lesbian rights and the US Equal Rights Amendment. An all-white delegation from the racially segregated

---

3. Interview with Linda Gordon in *Spare Rib*, number 75, October 1978.
4. Barrios de Chúngara, p.198.

state of Mississippi, which included four male members of the American Nazi party, was admitted to the conference.[5]

The idea that politics could be forgotten as feminists celebrated the sisterhood of all women proved totally false. The conference, far from being a force for change, was able to become a reaffirmation of the most conservative and traditional values. This was something which most feminists didn't understand at all. Robin Morgan heralded it as a breakthrough because it attracted so many women:

> Women came who had never been involved in the women's movement, in politics or anything of the sort. They came because they were angry about a traffic island on the corner for their kids, or a job, or because they'd been raped. They discovered that feminists were against pornography, and that was a big shock.[6]

But the breakthrough was in the opposite direction from women's liberation. The mass of women Robin Morgan talked about were not adopting the ideas of women's liberation; instead one-time women's liberationists were making concessions to the right. The net effect was a shift to the right which has continued ever since.

Those who did not join in this shift tended, in the US at least, to move into lifestyle politics as an attempt to build a feminist culture and society in the here and now. This lifestyle feminism was often built around lesbianism as a political theory and practice. Women could build a lifestyle—at least in a few big cities—which cut men out of politics, out of social life, out of sexuality—sometimes even out of work.

In Britain it was much harder for feminists to go as far as their American counterparts along the paths of respectability or lifestyle politics. Nonetheless these two developments were repeated in Britain, although in less extreme form. The theory behind much of the lifestyle approach increasingly challenged and eventually displaced socialist feminism as the dominant set of ideas inside the women's movement. The most notable feature of the British movement in the mid- and late 1970s was, therefore, the rise of radical feminism.

At first this was not always discernible as the major trend. It was hidden by a number of factors, particularly the still substantial level of class struggle, which enabled those still arguing for socialist ideas within the women's movement to find an echo. There were, for example, major strikes involving women of which Trico, in 1976 for equal pay, and Grunwicks, over union recognition a year later, are the two best-known. Both were in London. There were fights against cuts in public spending and against hospital closures, such as that over the Elizabeth Garrett Anderson Hospital in London. There was another attempt to restrict abortion (the Benyon Bill) which had to be fought off in 1977.[7]

But the direction in which the movement was going became increasingly clear. The four demands of the movement—for equal pay, equal education and job opportunities, contraception and abortion, and nurseries—were added to in this period. In 1975, the demand for legal and financial independence was added, and in 1978 demands for an end

5. *Spare Rib*, number 68, March 1978.
6. Interview with Robin Morgan in *Spare Rib*, number 77.
7. See *Women's Voice*, number 2 (new series), February 1977.

to discrimination against lesbians and an end to male violence. The increased emphasis on issues which women faced as individuals represented a shift away from a collective solution to women's oppression. This was logical: the movement was travelling away from class struggle and towards separatism and lifestyle politics.

Violence against women first became an issue inside the movement in 1974, when Women's Aid came into being. By 1975 there were 90 women's refuges around the country.[8] These were mainly funded and run by volunteers. Women's Aid served to highlight a major scandal: that many women lived in fear of physical beating from the men they lived with, and that the capitalist state itself colluded in this situation. The police would not normally interfere in domestic disputes, and local councils would not rehouse women made homeless through violence. The idea of the refuges was that women would at least have somewhere safe to go where they could be safe from battering. They became quickly accepted, even by some Tory councils.

Similar arguments arose over issues such as rape and pornography. There were a number of controversial rape cases at the time, and in 1975 the first Rape Crisis Centre was set up. The following year saw the establishment of Women Against Rape. WAR was influenced by the same people who had set up the Wages for Housework campaign two years previously. It therefore combined a strong radical feminism, a theory which located women's oppression in the home, with a level of activism which ensured that it gained some support.[9]

Pornography was provoking similarly strong responses. The movement to "Reclaim the Night" took off in 1977. Its aim was to reclaim the streets for women, especially in areas such as Soho, in London's West End, where sex shops and porn cinemas abounded. Tactics were often extremely militant, and the women clearly annoyed the porn racketeers. A demonstration through Soho in October 1978 was brutally attacked by the police, and 16 women were arrested. Many women continued to march in different cities around the country, however, and by the late 1970s Reclaim the Night was one of the most dynamic features of the women's movement.

But this change in orientation—towards individual problems of rape or violence, and away from class struggle—was not an accident. It resulted from the increasing adoption of a theory which saw not capitalism or class society as the enemy, but all men. So the women arrested for "reclaiming the night" were described as "the victims of men's defence of pornography".[10] An extremely influential and cogently argued book, *Against Our Will* by Susan Brownmiller, stated as its main thesis that rape is "a conscious process of intimidation by which *all men* keep *all women* in a state of fear".[11] The italics are in the original.

Theories of violence were ideal from a radical feminist point of view. They did not fit neatly into a class analysis; the ruling class was not obviously culpable; indeed a more

8. Kappel and Leuteritz, p.196.
9. Women Against Rape.
10. "The Soho Sixteen and Reclaim the Night", 1978 leaflet reproduced in Feminist Anthology Collective, p.223.
11. Brownmiller, p.15.

direct guilt appeared to lie with individual men. Hence the need, so the argument went, for a separate "women's revolution" against male power and dominance.

A whole spate of radical feminist theory backed up these ideas. Women such as Mary Daly and Dale Spender represented a new and forceful trend in radical feminist ideas, as they denounced all things male and recreated their own parallel of bourgeois history by emphasising the history of bourgeois women.[12] The socialist feminists, who had been in the ascendancy in the early days of the women's movement—at least in Britain—now found themselves pushed onto the defensive and challenged in every area of basic theory.

The development of the theory of patriarchy as a major force in the movement dates from this time. It marked the defeat of socialist feminism. The term "patriarchy" had always been in use, and "patriarchal" has also been used to describe various sorts of feudal and peasant families, where the "patriarch" (often the grandfather) dominated socially and economically within the family and oppressed all its other members. (This sort of patriarchal family was, of course, a productive unit—unlike the capitalist family.) But the term took on a much wider usage. By 1979 Sheila Rowbotham expressed problems and reservations with the whole concept:

> The term has been used in a great variety of ways. "Patriarchy" has been discussed as an ideology which arose out of men's power to exchange women between kinship groups; as a symbolic male principle; and as the power of the father (its literal meaning). It has been used to express men's control over women's sexuality and fertility; and to describe the institutional structure of male domination. Recently the phrase "capitalist patriarchy" has suggested a form peculiar to capitalism.[13]

By the late 1970s it had come to mean virtually anything to do with male domination. It tended to replace theories of the family as the root of women's oppression. Its conclusions were fairly uniform: that male domination is not simply a product of class society or—specifically—capitalism, but is something quite separate which will endure after the overthrow of capitalism. This was used as the theoretical justification for women's separate organisation. Typically two socialist feminist historians, Sally Alexander and Barbara Taylor, embraced this view in 1980:

> It was precisely because a Marxist theory of class conflict, however elaborated, could not answer all our questions about sexual conflict that we tried to develop an alternative. If we need to keep the two areas of analysis apart for a time, then so be it.[14]

The strength of patriarchy theory among socialist feminists meant that many were already making major concessions towards idealist and non-materialist theories. These concessions led to a major retreat among socialist feminists. For it meant rejecting the idea that male workers could play a role in the struggle for women's liberation. If men

---

12. See for example Spender.
13. Rowbotham (1979).
14. Alexander and Taylor.

were at least in part the oppressors of women, then at least part of the struggle had to be against them. This led to an acceptance of more radical feminist ideas.

The early radical feminists in America had identified men as a major enemy, on the basis of biological differences. Here was a theory which once again stressed the biological difference between men and women as a major source of oppression, rather than the social system within which they existed. From the late 1970s onwards, theories of the family as the root of women's oppression, which explained oppression in class terms, were increasingly replaced by patriarchal theories based not on class but on gender.

By 1982, two socialist feminists could, while defending socialist feminism, demonstrate how far it had strayed from basic Marxist ideas. Beatrix Campbell and Anna Coote's book *Sweet Freedom* pointed to aspects of women's oppression which "cannot be accounted for in Marxist theory of class exploitation".[15] They claimed that:

> Socialist feminists have begun to develop an exacting critique of theories of class exploitation. They insist on the centrality of ideological struggle, which has been all too glibly nudged to the periphery of politics by much of the left. Reproduction and family relations are placed at the heart of social and economic theory and strategy.

> It is at this point that the gap between radical feminism (in its non-biological determinist form) and socialist feminism is at its narrowest. What distinguishes the two is that socialist feminists' politics entail neither a rejection of men nor a withdrawal from them, but an urgent necessity to fight both in and against male-dominated power relations.[16]

Campbell and Coote were right to say that the gap between radical and socialist feminist theory was growing narrower. But what they didn't understand was that the balance of forces was swinging towards radical feminism, with serious implications for the future. The wholesale adoption of patriarchy theory only served to strengthen the radical feminist wing of the movement.

Things were in any case moving fast. The national women's liberation conference in Birmingham in 1978 was an indication of that. The conference is remembered, somewhat notoriously, as the last to be held in Britain. Its debates were so acrimonious that no one individual or grouping took it upon themselves to organise a repeat. More than 3,000 women attended the conference. All the different wings of the movement were represented, but some were more dominant than others.

Many radical feminists were becoming increasingly impatient with any strategy for change which involved men or socialist politics (which they saw by implication as male-defined). Among them were the Revolutionary Feminists—so-called not because of any adoption of socialist ideas, but because of their uncompromising hostility to any collaboration with men.

Revolutionary Feminism had emerged at the previous year's women's liberation conference, when Sheila Jeffreys organised a workshop entitled "The Need for Revolutionary

---

15. Campbell and Coote, p.32.
16. Campbell and Coote, p.33.

Feminism—against the liberal takeover of the Women's Liberation Movement". Two hundred women had turned up to discuss "a *political* feminism". There was sex-rolism, lifestylism, and socialist feminism. "I [Jeffreys] was in a desperate search for radical feminist theory which talked of the power of men and how to take it from them. Politics was taken to mean socialism, and theory the extension of Marxism."[17]

Jeffreys hit a nerve. By the time of the 1978 conference anti-socialist ideas were much more widespread. The conference was split on every major issue, The report in *Spare Rib* indicated this. The conference was divided into workshops which discussed three issues: "how do we oppress each other; what is the nature of campaigns, how effective they are and what is the alternative; and how do we come together in terms of our own internal organisation?" The atmosphere was acrimonious. As the report's writers, Anny Bracx, Gail Chester and Sara Rance, put it: "one concept which we have developed hardly surfaced in this set-up: sisterhood ... there was little sympathetic listening; it was mainly a question of attack and defence".[18]

Debate centred around the phrasing of the new seventh demand of the movement—against male violence. Should it be preceded by the phrase "male violence against women is an expression of male supremacy and political control of women"? "After a protracted shouting match, it was voted to delete the incriminating sentence from the new seventh demand."[19]

But the damage had been done. Women who had gone to the conference hoping to experience the movement as a real sisterhood of women were bitterly disappointed. This was reflected in *Spare Rib*'s letters pages in the following months. A Birmingham woman wrote: "The threatening stances, arrogant posturings and self-indulgent introspection I and my friends witnessed at the conference have ensured that none of us will ever try to establish contact with the movement again".[20]

A number of feminist groups, including Lesbian Left, Rights of Women, and Women against Racism and Fascism wrote, on the other hand, that the movement had to be "broad enough to accommodate our differences".[21] Members of Brighton Women's Liberation wrote defending those who had argued: "While the plenary was disastrous and upsetting it revealed genuine political differences within the movement which we have been afraid of facing up to".

This statement was undoubtedly true. There *were* real political differences. The letter described them thus:

> Our politics are feminist. We analyse our oppression as due to male supremacy, to the patriarchy. Men are our oppressors, the enemy, and not some-abstract "system". The system is created and perpetuated by men for the benefit of all men. Capitalism, class, racism,

---

17. "Women's liberation 1977", in *Spare Rib*, number 58, May 1977.
18. *Spare Rib*, number 70, May 1978.
19. *Spare Rib*, number 70, May 1978.
20. Letter in *Spare Rib*, number 71, June 1978.
21. Letter in *Spare Rib*, number 71, June 1978.

fascism, colonialism and imperialism are all male institutions, current manifestations of male rule—the patriarchy.[22]

These feminists were absolutely clear about their politics, and they were developing more confidence in expressing them: oppression came from the patriarchy; it could be fought not by focusing on issues such as class or imperialism but by fixing on male rule as the primary source of women's oppression. Such an analysis clearly left no room for any political activity which involved men.

This analysis was miles away from the established socialist feminism—Sheila Rowbotham's writing on history, the domestic labour debate, issues like the night cleaners, the National Abortion Campaign or the fight for equal pay at Trico. But the socialist feminists had a problem. They had conceded the theory of patriarchy and therefore at least some of its conclusions. Now many feminists were taking these conclusions much further than the socialist feminists had wanted. It was at this time that socialist feminism really went into crisis.

A reflection of how far socialist feminism moved politically during the 1970s can be seen in a comment from a leading American socialist feminist, Kathie Sarachild, a former founder of Redstockings. Interviewed in *Spare Rib* in 1978, she said:

> New York Radical Women had always contained a contradiction between what then were called the politicos and the feminists; later you would call it the socialist feminists and the radical feminists. But then, the politicos didn't call themselves feminists. They were against feminism.[23]

By the late 1970s the "politicos" certainly weren't against feminism. Their defensiveness at being socialists was indeed reflected in nearly all the socialist feminist publications. *Red Rag*, by now totally dominated by Communist Party feminists, went through a crisis in 1980. Its editorial stated:

> Our crisis ... came from our assumption as socialist feminists that because the WLM existed, men would change. But the pain of our personal and political lives over the past couple of years has been the discovery that the second doesn't follow from the first.

The editorial continued: "socialism has not only failed to confront patriarchy, but socialism in Britain has just about killed off socialism".[24]

Socialist Woman went through a similar crisis in 1978, over whether to organise a socialist feminist current;[25] and the Socialist Workers Party's *Women's Voice* saw in the bitterly divided 1978 women's liberation conference a sad betrayal of the earlier unity of the movement. In an open letter issued after the conference it looked back to the 1970 founding conference in Oxford and said:

---

22. Letter in *Spare Rib*, number 73, August 1978.
23. *Spare Rib*, number 79, February 1979.
24. *Red Rag*, August 1980.
25. *Socialist Woman*, Spring 1978.

There we were, not knowing how our movement would develop, not knowing each other, not yet having proved that we could build any campaigns among the masses of women who hadn't even heard of us. But there was far more sisterhood and solidarity and sense of purpose in that meeting than there was in Birmingham. Is this what we've achieved in our eight years?[26]

All these statements provided evidence of the deep crisis in which socialist feminism found itself. But the solutions to this crisis weren't forthcoming. Or if they were, they tended in every direction other than towards an attack on radical or separatist feminism. Feminists around *Red Rag*, particularly Beatrix Campbell, increasingly adapted radical feminist theory to attack the male working class and the trade unions—with predictably reactionary results. The SWP and *Women's Voice* went through its own internal crisis, partly at least centred on the need to resolve the relationship between Marxism and feminism.

Other feminists turned to a form of organisation which did not exclude men and indeed welcomed them. But they did so by launching a major attack on "Leninist organisation", which they alleged had nothing useful to say or offer to women. Sheila Rowbotham, Lynne Segal and Hilary Wainwright published their influential book, *Beyond the Fragments*, in 1979. It drew strongly on libertarian politics and polemicised against "Leninist forms of organisation". Its main thesis, however, was that left politics had to be transformed by women and by the experience of the women's movement.

Beyond the Fragments was praised by nearly everybody on the left. It was even the subject of an adulatory article written by Jill Tweedie on the *Guardian* women's page. She wrote in support of the book that:

> Political and industrial jargon is too often used to make people feel inferior, ignorant, powerless. Godheads like Lenin and Marx are invoked to put you in your place and the ordinary person fights back in the only way possible—by dropping out.[27]

This really was standing things on their head. Women's liberation had started as a movement against oppression which it believed was caused by the system, and perpetuated through the dominant ideas in that system—those of the ruling class. Now, the argument was exactly the opposite. Women's oppression was maintained not just by men, but by socialist men—the very ones committed to ending this oppressive system! Just to rub the argument in, the article was accompanied by a picture of two women pensioners captioned "waiting for the revolution: are they failed by the organised left?"

This was the message which many would-be socialists took from *Beyond the Fragments*. As Lynne Segal later admitted, some saw it as justifying abandonment of class politics, others as the green light for joining the Labour Party.[28] This may not have been the intention of its authors, but it was nonetheless the outcome. The *Beyond the Fragments* conference in Leeds in 1980 was hugely popular. Yet little came of it organisationally.

---

26. *Women's Voice*, number 17, May 1978.
27. Jill Tweedie, "What every fragment knows", in *The Guardian*, 29 January 1980.
28. Segal, pp.209–10.

Attempts to set up local "fragment" organisation foundered on two things: the decline of local "fragment type" groups around the end of the 1970s and the massive influx into the Labour Party of those influenced by such arguments. This was the key political direction for socialist feminists in the 1980s.

Women and Labour—a force for change?

The left had become increasingly disillusioned by the period of the late 1970s. The viciously anti-working class policies of the Wilson-Callaghan Labour governments of 1974–79 seemed to provoke bitterness rather than a clear move to any left-wing alternative to Labour. The upward advance of far-left political groups, internationally a hallmark of the late 1960s and early 1970s, had been halted and in many cases put into reverse. Disillusionment with Labour led to increasingly bitterly fought strikes—especially in the "Winter of Discontent" of 1979—and disillusionment was so strong that many workers turned to a Tory government under Margaret Thatcher as preferable to Callaghan.

The effect of election defeat was to strengthen the left inside the Labour Party. Labour's right-wing, anti-working-class policies were seen as responsible for the defeat of 1979. The movement around the former cabinet minister Tony Benn, which aimed to transform the party through a process of democratisation which would commit the leaders to party policy agreed by conference, took off from this point. Its climax was in the campaign for the deputy leadership of the party in 1981, where Benn came within an inch of beating the right-winger Denis Healey.

The activists of the Benn campaign and some of his keenest supporters were often former members of left groups. They, like thousands of others, were frustrated and disillusioned that years of operating in left groups, in movements or campaigns had not resulted in any real social change. They saw transforming Labour as the alternative. From the beginning the movement around Benn always had a feminist component. Many of those politicised from 1968 onwards—either in far left organisations or in the women's movement—now found in the Labour Party a much more comfortable home.

Benn always made clear his support for feminist issues. In a major interview carried in *Spare Rib*'s hundredth issue in 1980 Benn argued, in the face of some hostile questioning, for a form of socialist feminism, operating through the Labour Party.[29]

There was another feature of the Labour Party which made it a challenge for feminists: the under-representation of women at all levels. This was a reflection of wider society—a 1967 Labour Party survey of 2,000 local authority committees showed that only 10 per cent were headed by women[30]—but it reflected badly on the party. There were five reserved seats for women on the party's national executive, but apart from these virtually no women were elected to party positions. The few there were came from the constituency section, not the parliamentary party or trade unions. Women

29. "Talking with Tony Benn", interview in *Spare Rib*, number 10, November 1980.
30. Quoted in Lovenduski and Hills, p.21.

made up only 11 per cent of party conference delegates and only 5 per cent of trade union conference delegates.[31]

Women's membership was higher than these figures suggest, standing at around 40 per cent in 1970. Yet the party women's organisation reflected the more passive women members, not the more active. As recently as the mid-1970s, the authors of a study on women and the Labour Party could write: "The women's organisation is strongest in the rural areas and the north of England, where traditional attitudes to women's roles still tend to flourish".[32]

There were increased demands among Labour women for feminist change inside the party to rectify some of these problems: calls for the revival of women's sections, for women's committees attached to local councils to ensure that women's demands were met, and for positive discrimination in order to create more women MPs, council leaders and so on. Labour made a party political broadcast on the question of women in 1981, and in 1982 organised a women's festival in London. The Greater London Council (GLC) in particular became identified with women's issues, and its women's committee attracted a great deal of publicity.

The attraction of Labour for so many feminists had nothing to do with its record or its policies on issues of women's rights. It had, indeed, a particularly poor record. The Callaghan government had gone out of its way to stress the virtues of traditional family values, and at one time had even proposed a Minister for Marriage.[33] So why were feminists attracted to Labour? The answer lay, at least in part, in the nature of the party itself. An editorial in *Feminist Review* put it like this:

> A number of features peculiar to the Labour Party and its left wing may have made it attractive to feminist "entryism" in the past year or so ... the Labour Party seems more like a forum than a political party and it is not, of course, a democratic centralist party. It is not a party that's claimed to have a worked-out line on the emancipation of women or a worked-out policy for them. Women may therefore have expected less of the Labour Party than they did from Marxist groups, and perhaps also felt that their feminism was less under attack—or remained more intact, simply because the Labour Party is less "ideological".[34]

The Labour Party had always been a "broad church", in that it contained wide divergences of opinion—and sometimes directly contradictory views—within its midst. In the late 1970s and early 1980s in particular, when the left in the Labour Party was on the ascendant, this made it a much more attractive option than a more rigorous, Marxist organisation. It was also true that Labour was attractive to a layer of educated women in high-paid full-time work who, along with their male counterparts, have tended to become the backbone of the party in recent years.

---

31. Lovenduski and Hills, pp.18–19.
32. Lovenduski and Hills, p.18.
33. *Spare Rib*, number 75, October 1978.
34. "Feminism and the political crisis of the Eighties", in *Feminist Review*, number 12, 1982, p.6.

The central organising base for young activists inside the Labour Party was local government. Activists were often welcomed as candidates in moribund Labour parties and found themselves elected as councillors and occasionally even MPs. A number of left-wing councils took office in the early 1980s, especially in London but also in Sheffield, Lothian and Liverpool. The jewel in the crown of the local government left was Ken Livingstone's GLC. It had a strong commitment to equal opportunities for women, blacks and gays.

The GLC's Women's Committee eventually had a budget of £8 million and a substantial staff. Its establishment caused an outcry, with the press accusing the council of funding lesbians and gays on the rates. Although some money was justifiably allocated to promoting lesbian and gay rights, the vast bulk of funding actually went elsewhere. Half of the £8 million budget in fact went on child care.

Yet much of the mud stuck, as the Tories orchestrated an unpleasant backlash against positive discrimination and equal opportunities policies. The situation was made worse by the political collapse of the Labour-controlled councils in the face of Tory ratecapping by 1985. The successive rounds of cuts that followed hit women hard as workers, and as consumers of council services and equal opportunities policies. Islington council in London, for example, which boasted a woman leader and deputy leader in the early 1980s, abandoned its equal opportunities policy—still under its woman leader Margaret Hodge.

The political pressure of capitulation to ratecapping—and the cuts in education, health and welfare services that had to be implemented as a result—took its toll. An internal inquiry into the GLC's women's unit in 1984 found mismanagement and institutionalised racism. Although the highly paid head of the unit was initially backed by the chair of the women's committee, Valerie Wise, she soon left with a golden handshake. The two black women leaders of councils in London—Merle Amory in Brent and Linda Bellos in Lambeth—both resigned. Linda Bellos capitulated to cuts in Lambeth. She later took a job as women's officer for another London Labour-controlled council, Hackney.

The hopes of the local government left were therefore short-lived. It hardly needs spelling out that the victims of ratecapping and the cuts were overwhelmingly the poor, single parents and various groups of the oppressed. By the end of the 1980s it was also clear that the main long-term beneficiaries of the left's equal opportunities policies had been a small handful of women who staffed the women's units, often at high salaries.

The early 1980s were characterised, however, by the blind faith of many feminists in local government and what it could achieve. This led to passivity around issues which could mobilise numbers of women. An example was an incident on the biggest demonstration yet in defence of abortion rights—against the Corrie Bill in 1979. The demonstration had been called by the TUC. In itself this was unprecedented. It was built for in trade union branches all over the country, and 80,000 women and men turned up on the day. Union and workplace banners were well represented. The TUC had, however, called the demonstration for its own ends, and was determined to control it. The National

Abortion Campaign—led by Labour Party women, often former revolutionaries—was all too happy to comply. A number of women activists, many of them radical feminists, objected to men leading the march, and several hundred spontaneously took over the front of the march, to the fury of the TUC bureaucrats.

The socialist-radical split again came to the fore. Women bureaucrats and Communist Party members Judith Hunt and Terry Marsland defended the march order in *Spare Rib*; Susan Hemmings justified the breakaway in the same issue.[35] Yet again, the actions of men on the demonstration led to an increased alienation from what was seen as the left. A letter in *Spare Rib* from Lesbian Left said that they had met after the march to discuss their future. At the meeting they talked of

> the contradiction between feminist politics on the one hand and male-defined left politics on the other. Most of us decided at the meeting that we can no longer accept the term "Left" because its politics does nothing to challenge Patriarchy.[36]

Yet both sides in the argument were wrong. The march should have been led by women, yes, but by women rank-and-file trade unionists—the people most oppressed and exploited—not by male (or a few female) union bureaucrats. Nor should it have been led by the radical feminists, who couldn't involve working-class women in their struggle and had no conception of the need to win working-class men to support for abortion rights.

This one incident encapsulated much of what was wrong with the movement by the early 1980s. Socialist feminists looked passively to Labour and to the trade union bureaucracy to deliver reforms for women. In practice this often took the form of advancement for themselves and women like them, in the employ of the GLC or other left councils, or as women councillors or MPs. Radical feminists were often activists in the movement, but were totally removed from any notion of class struggle.

Yet the two reached a synthesis in the extreme separatist action of the Greenham Common peace women, and the uncritical support they received from feminists inside the Labour Party. The peace camp and the movement which arose round it was one of the major influences on politics in the early 1980s. The women were part of a gigantic, if largely passive, movement for peace which swept Europe in response to US plans to site Cruise missiles at various European bases, including Greenham Common. It was sparked by the notion that Europe could be used by the superpowers as a "contained" or "limited" theatre of war.

The Greenham women originated in a march organised by one woman to the proposed missile base in Berkshire in 1981. Once there, the marchers set up a women's peace camp. The camp won strong support from CND members and others concerned with the threat of war. The privations suffered by the women, and their brutal treatment at the hands of military personnel and the local council, only added to this support. Demonstrations around the base attracted many thousands. Tony Benn added his support and stressed

---

35. *Spare Rib*, number 89, December 1979.
36. *Spare Rib*, number 89, December 1979.

that the actions of the Greenham women should be followed. Here once again was an issue where a women's campaign could attract mass support.

But the campaign had two major weaknesses. The first was that it relied on a small number of women to act on behalf of others. This added to the passivity of the movement, which could cheer on the actions at Greenham while doing virtually nothing. The second weakness lay in the politics of the campaign. Non-violence, both as a political ideal and as a tactic, was central. But this non-violence was celebrated as a particularly female thing. It was argued that nuclear weapons were a product not of the capitalist drive to war, but of male aggressive values. "Take the toys from the boys" was a popular slogan. As one view put it:

> Our present hierarchies are based on the need to control and feel superior. The model for this is men's domination of women ... women have a different consciousness. Although we have believed in our own passivity and helplessness, few of us are really taken in by male heroic values.[37]

But what values were to replace these "male heroic values"? The argument was that women's traditional roles as wives and mothers were, almost by definition, peace-loving occupations. These therefore equipped them for campaigning for peace. Such a view was embellished by a whole series of mystical and semi-religious ideas about female goddesses, dragons, and weaving mystic webs around the base. This last action was inspired by women who wove a web round the Pentagon in Washington as a protest against war:

> There were cheers, chants, and whistles, and women sang as we wove. Generals minced their way through woman-made webs, amidst laughs and admonitions about their daily work. At the end there was a braid around the Pentagon, and beautiful weavings at all the entrances. Women who were not arrested held a closing ritual circle.[38]

Women looked back to pre-capitalist times in order to celebrate their femaleness, and—following Mary Daly in *Gyn/Ecology*[39]—adopted the term "spinster" with pride. A peace group in Vermont, US, called itself the Spinsters and used spinning and weaving as a means of combatting male violence. A leaflet they issued started like this: "We will meet, all of us women of every land, we will meet in the center, make a circle; we will weave a world web to entangle the powers that bury our children".[40]

These politics were ultimately reactionary. They harked back to a mythical golden age and, because they did not confront the power of the capitalist state, in the end they could point no way forward to getting rid of nuclear weapons. The movement around Greenham Common underlined the dominance of radical feminist ideas inside the women's movement—and showed the lack of any form of class analysis of how to fight women's oppression.

---

37. "Working as a group: Nottingham Women oppose the Nuclear Threat", in Jones, p.28.
38. Ynestra King, "All is connectedness: Scenes from the Women's Pentagon Action, USA", in Jones, p.56.
39. Daly, *Gyn/Ecology* (London 1979), pp.392–4.
40. Catherine Reid, "Reweaving the web of life", in McAllister, pp.298–90.

Fragmentation

The difficulties in counterbalancing this sort of analysis were immense. Those so-cialists who pointed to class struggle as the means to achieve women's liberation found little to back up what appeared to be utopian claims about the working class. The level of class struggle in the early years of the Thatcher government was low, unlike in the early 1970s. There were, it is true, a number of significant strikes involving women. In 1981 women textile workers at Lee Jeans in the west of Scotland occupied to prevent closure. Typists employed by Liverpool City Council embarked on a long strike over regrading in the same year. Asian women at Chix in Slough struck for union recognition in 1980, again beginning a dispute which was to bring them widespread support. In 1982 hospital workers took action over pay. But all the disputes eventually ended in at least partial defeat, and none generalised to such an extent that other workers took up their example.

Fragmentation was the order of the day. The movement went in dozens of different directions. One indication of this was the crisis of the collective which produced *Spare Rib*. The magazine had always been hailed as one of the great successes of the movement, and had been produced monthly since 1972. It was by and large accessible and lively. But as its hundredth issue approached in 1980, the collective was forced to bring in a group counsellor to sort out its problems. These were caused by bitter political divisions. Initially these took the form of whether or not to publish an article criticising lesbians. As *Spare Rib* put it: "Publication was blocked. Personal rifts and political disagreements opened up that had until then lain relatively dormant. Since then it has been difficult to produce work and get along in a sisterly spirit".[41]

The group counsellor did not solve what was basically a political crisis, as was admit-ted in a later issue. Further splits continued, especially on grounds of race. Allegations were made that white feminists were oppressing their black sisters. A row broke out over whether by supporting Palestinians and attacking the state of Israel, some feminists were not also oppressing Jewish women. The net result was an almost total turnover in the composition of the collective, and the dominance of a much stronger Third Worldist approach—pushed especially by many of the black women who now comprised much of the collective.

The black-white split was characteristic of the movement's fragmentation. The logic of seeing oppression as the central determining factor in society, and therefore concentrating on organising only against that oppression, meant that different oppressed groups became more concerned with how others oppressed them than with looking outwards to fight that oppression. The result was moralism rather than political analysis.

The establishment of the Organisation of Women of African and Asian Descent (OWAAD) in 1979 as a separate black women's organisation was a sign of this. OWAAD was dogged from the beginning by sectarianism. It always looked to what separated it

41. *Spare Rib*, number 98, September 1980.

from the rest of the left and the rest of the movement. This can be seen, for example, in the statement issued at its second Black Women's National Conference in 1980:

> Those of us who tried to involve ourselves in the anti-racist and anti-fascist movement (primarily the Anti-Nazi League) found that the mainly white membership was ignoring *institutionalised racism* (e.g. racist immigration laws...), preferring instead to channel its energies into combatting the *symptoms* rather than the cause.[42]

This simply wasn't true, as the record of the Anti-Nazi League and its participating groups shows. All too often, indeed, campaigns on issues such as immigration laws were set up and found little or no resonance in the black communities. But it was a convenient peg on which to hang separatism. The result was still more fragmentation and internalisation inside the movement.

There was only one beacon of light during these years for women who had a socialist approach to organising, and who believed that working women had to organise as part of their class in order to achieve liberation. The movement of miners' wives in support of the strike of 1984–85 took everyone by surprise. Women Against Pit Closures (WAPC) showed the strength and solidarity of the wives and families of the miners.

Women started by duplicating their traditional roles in the home—cooking, buying food—but quickly went on to do much more. They spoke at meetings, collected money and picketed. They travelled the country in the process. A national demonstration in London in August 1984 attracted thousands, as did a rally in Chesterfield at the end of the strike.

The women were an inspiration for socialists and feminists. Many feminists were involved in building support for the strike, and socialist feminists such as Jean McCrindle were instrumental in building WAPC. But the campaign was inevitably bound up with the fate of the strike, so could not be sustained after its defeat. Attempts by the women to win affiliation to the National Union of Mineworkers at its 1985 conference failed following the opposition of those, like the Communist Party, who opposed the union's president, Arthur Scargill. Although the campaign represented a real advance for many of the women concerned, it remained firmly in the control of the union leaders and their wives, Betty Heathfield and Ann Scargill.

Nonetheless, Women Against Pit Closures offered a glimpse of the strengths of women workers. It helped at least temporarily to win the argument that the key division in society was one of class, not of gender. Unfortunately the defeat of the strike not only led to the dominance of much more right-wing feminist ideas, it also dealt a blow to the idea of class struggle as a means of changing the world. This in turn affected the development of the women's movement—for the worse.

---

42. *Spare Rib*, number 95, June 1980.

The women's movement today

We are told that today the movement is going from strength to strength. Feminist ideas, according to the gurus of the movement, have never been stronger. Just look, we are told, at the success of feminist publishing, or the plethora of women's studies courses. Women are in more positions of power than ever before—from private industry to the prime minister herself. Even some socialist feminists who should know better are influenced by these arguments. But encouragement from these changes can only be sustained by totally abandoning the original principles of the women's movement. For although there have undoubtedly been major advances for women in the past decades, these have been nearly all advances for bourgeois feminism. A minority of middle- and upper-class women have gained access to the once closed worlds of men—in business, finance, journalism and higher education. This sort of advance has in fact made the dominant ideas inside the women's movement more right-wing than ever. This, in turn, has brought fewer real gains for working women, and indeed some major attacks on hard-won rights.

As usual, it is in the US women's movement that these features are most apparent. Sylvia Ann Hewlett's book on the movement, *A Lesser Life*, showed how most women's rights groups were supporting a court case—the Garland case—which sought to deny women the right to reinstatement in their jobs following maternity leave, and so effectively denied maternity leave. She quotes Dianne Feinstein, mayor of San Francisco and a feminist, as supporting this on the grounds that if women wanted equality, they had to be treated equally with men and not expect any special privileges!

> What we were asking was to create a special group of workers that, in essence, is pregnant women and new mothers. I just don't happen to agree with that. I don't think the work market has to accommodate itself to women having children.[43]

This is also apparently the position of the National Organisation of Women. As Hewlett points out, it results in women having less right to leave for childbirth than if they are incapacitated in a skiing accident—because only women can have children, whereas anyone can have an accident.

It is an astonishing position for anyone who calls herself a feminist to take. Yet it shows precisely what is wrong with American feminism. Its ideas may be extremely widespread and influential but it is moulded by the society in which it exists. So it is not based on ideas of working-class activity or even on basic egalitarian ideas. In present-day America, with less than a fifth of workers in unions, it adapts to all sorts of backward and anti-working-class ideas.

The Equal Rights Amendment to the US constitution also fell during the 1980s presidency of Ronald Reagan. It had been passed in the US Senate in 1972 by 84 votes to 8. Ten years later the deadline for ratification passed with only 35 of the necessary 38

---

43. Hewlett, p.146.

states having ratified.[44] The Equal Rights Amendment had been the hope of the mainstream feminists. It had been a central plank of the strategy at the Houston conference. Yet the support for women's liberation had been frittered away.

To give another example, while abortion remains legal in the US, only 13 out of the 50 states provide any abortion funding for women who cannot afford to pay—a fact which NOW chooses to ignore in all its activity for a woman's right to choose.

Twenty years of the US women's movement have won some chance of self-advancement for a sizeable minority of women—while poverty, unemployment and discrimination remain the lot of most women workers.

In Britain, once again, the situation is not quite as polarised. But the patterns are nonetheless clearly repeated. Activity inside the women's movement has declined dramatically, and sometimes ground to a virtual halt. The campaign against Victoria Gillick, the reactionary who won a court case in 1985 preventing doctors and clinics from giving contraceptive advice to under-16s, is an example. Demonstrations organised against this ruling attracted a mere 3,000 women—half the strength of one demonstration was brought by the SWP. Luckily the ruling was reversed; but had it not been, there was little evidence that the women's movement could have mobilised to defeat it.[45]

Neither are International Women's Day demonstrations serving as any sort of focus for feminists. In some years they have been virtually non-existent. In 1986 there was a demonstration at Rupert Murdoch's printing plant at Wapping in support of the wives and families of sacked printers. It was composed mainly of striking women and wives, and left-wing groups. The women's movement organised little. In 1987, the International Women's Day demonstration was unpublicised and tiny. Publicity went instead to International Women's Week—a series of events usually organised and funded by Labour-controlled councils. Once again, municipal feminism became a substitute for any serious mobilisation.

Why is the women's movement today in such a sorry state? The answer lies in a combination of organisation and politics.

The decline in class struggle over the past ten years has led to major crises among socialists and feminists. They have had to come to terms with defeat and with a massive ideological shift to the right. They have seen their ranks depleted. But the socialist organisations have survived this process incomparably better than the women's movement. Although some groups have disappeared completely and the Communist Party has lost its once dominant industrial role, there are still many thousands of socialist activists. The very structurelessness of the women's movement—so beloved by the authors of *Beyond the Fragments*—has resulted in disintegration and decay.

This is a logical conclusion of the movement's politics. If you believe that the purpose of liberation is consciousness-raising, then why not carry on with that in the privacy

44. Mansbridge, p.1.
45. See *Socialist Worker Review*, number 76, May 1985.

of your own home? If academic feminism is equally as valid as struggling to change the world, then why engage in activity?

But the women's movement nonetheless survives, although it becomes harder and harder to talk of it as a single movement. Its ideas are widely accepted inside whole sections of society today—in academia, in local government, in bourgeois politics and even in some private industry. But it now has an ideal life support system—the Labour Party.

Labour is today a major prop for feminism. Funding for local council women's committees ensures that a feminist profile is maintained in many inner-city areas—because professional feminists are paid to ensure this happens. There are therefore a number of high-salaried jobs earmarked for feminists, at least in London. Publications such as *Spare Rib* and *Outwrite* are partly subsidised by advertisements for these jobs and for other women's committee activities. Until the abolition of the GLC, they also received direct grants from its women's committee.

Feminism on the rates is not just a right-wing slur, but an actuality. However, given the crisis of British capitalism—and given the reformist and gradualist nature of the Labour Party—this brand of feminism becomes less and less able to deliver.

What remains for feminists inside the Labour Party is an increasingly constitutional fight to get even the most minimal commitment to equality. An important component of that fight is the Women's Action Committee (WAC), formed in 1980 as part of the Campaign for Labour Party Democracy. Its aims centre on the party constitution, demanding more power and control for the party's annual women's conference—its right directly to elect the women's section of the national executive, and to be able to refer resolutions automatically to the annual conference—and demanding women on parliamentary shortlists.

This last demand was won at the 1988 national conference. The response of most of the left and feminists was euphoric. A Campaign Briefing conference leaflet stated that the vote was "a huge step to ensure that future parliaments will have a much larger number of Labour women".[46] But there is nothing to compel constituency parties to select women candidates, and the number of women becoming Labour MPs in the foreseeable future is unlikely to rise dramatically.

There are few signs of WAC's other demands being accepted—if anything the reverse. The trade union leaders are demanding a form of electoral college in the women's conference, so that their voice is represented more strongly. The only beneficiaries of this move will be the union machines, dominated by the block vote, which will be able to impose their policies more easily.

The dominance of feminist ideas inside the Labour left has led to a blurring of politics. WAC has constantly stressed what all women inside the party have in common, arguing that the crucial question is not left or right but white men against blacks, women and other oppressed groups. Ann Pettifor was quoted in 1985: "There is a set of interests

---

46. "Campaign Briefing", leaflet for Labour Party Conference, 4 October 1988.

which unite women which the white middle-class men who run the party can't divide up into right and left".[47]

WAC also argued that political differences and divisions were due to male-dominated, macho behaviour, rather than to real and material divisions. As one WAC conference bulletin put it:

> *Macho* politics is destructive politics. It is about division, polarisation, competitiveness and political conflict. Women in general recognise there is little to be gained from this competitiveness ... Men in the Labour Party, however, take great pride in gaining competitive supremacy for their particular "line" or strategy.[48]

Events clearly showed the potential for disaster in such arguments. During the right-wing backlash following the miners' defeat in 1985, WAC tended to the attitude that feminists should be above political feuding. It described the party leadership's attack on the NUM and its witch-hunt against the left-wing Liverpool council as being about "different camps led by strong male heroes [which] compete fiercely for our support".[49] This could only play into the hands of the right wing, which adopted a veneer of feminism while attacking anyone who wanted to fight back against the Tories and the employers. The view of trade union struggle, or any other struggle, as inherently macho and old-fashioned has been seized on by all sorts of people who want to argue against any sort of fight.

More recently, leading members of WAC have taken a more class-oriented view. Ann Pettifor has come down in support of the party's hard left, and spends a lot of time attacking the ideas of *Marxism Today*. However, some of the formulations in the WAC bulletin are very similar to the sorts of views put forward in *Marxism Today*.

The key problem feminists face in trying to institute change through the Labour Party is the nature of the party itself. The party is undemocratic. Its MPs' lack of accountability on issues such as abortion is a disgrace. The reserved section for women on the national executive is a sick joke, since male trade union bureaucrats decide its composition in their caucuses. Issues concerning women are rarely considered when choosing the lucky five.[50] This lack of democracy is endemic to the party, which grew originally from the need of the trade union bureaucracy to gain representation in parliament. Its structures stem from the control the bureaucracy wields even today. Constitutional changes therefore represent a political challenge to right-wing domination—which explains both the fear that movements for constitutional change cause, and their eventual lack of impact.

The reselection of MPs has become little more than a token; leadership elections a test of loyalty to the existing leadership; the consideration of women on shortlists will probably prove similarly ineffective. The system is still stacked against those who do not have official backing—especially those without union backing:

---

47. Quoted in Seyd.
48. Labour Women's Action Committee bulletin for Labour Party Conference 1985.
49. Labour Women's Action Committee bulletin for Labour Party Conference 1985.
50. See Ann Pettifor's description of the Solidarity meeting at the 1984 TUC Congress, in *New Socialist*, number 20, October 1984.

Labour women candidates are less likely than men to have the trade union backing necessary for placement on the B list (the party keeps an A list of ordinary approved candidates and a B list of candidates sponsored and nominated by the unions).[51]

The importance of being on the B list cannot be overestimated: "In 1983, 114 of the 153 union-backed Labour candidates were elected, a success rate of 74.5 per cent. Only seven of the 153 were women, five of whom were elected".[52]

The obstacles appear nearly as great as ever. Even when changes are won, these are highly unlikely to bear fruit. For example the women's conference will only be able to elect the women's section of the executive *if* the women's conference comes firmly under the sway of the union leaders—which means, if the block vote is implemented there. The ideas put forward by WAC, that women should be given access to the forums of political power inside the party, are therefore only realisable on terms unfavourable to the left and to most feminists.

Feminists inside the Labour Party who want change are at an impasse. They have no real power to challenge anything, so settle increasingly for low-level reforms which represent a retreat from their original aims. Feminists in local government, for example, have always argued they could at least achieve something—such as more nurseries— which would help working-class women. Today, as great chunks of public spending are cut, even that claim seems hollow. The promise of the Labour Party in the early 1980s for some degree of women's liberation has not been fulfilled.

The crisis of socialist feminism

The dominance inside the movement of either bourgeois or radical feminism—or a combination of both—is a problem for socialist feminists. How do they resolve the dilemma of the relationship between class and gender? Can they comfortably remain in left-wing organisations? These are major questions which have not yet been settled. Because they have been thrown on the defensive by the dominance of anti-working-class ideas, many socialist feminists too accept that a large part of the problem of women's' oppression lies with men—and especially working-class men. Indeed such is the strength of this argument that it has become the accepted "common sense" of the movement.

Its chief and most polemical propagator is the Eurocommunist journalist Beatrix Campbell. She has now been on the offensive over this question for more than ten years. In an influential *Red Rag* article titled "Work to Rule", written with Valerie Charlton in 1978, she attacked the "craft-defensive male trade union movement in excluding women from the labour process. A singular feature of this process seems to have been men's assertion of their wage as the family wage".[53]

---

51. Lovenduski (1986), p.141.
52. Lovenduski (1986), p.141.
53. Campbell and Charlton, in *Red Rag*, number 14.

The article argued that men's and women's interests as workers were basically antagonistic, attacked the notion of free collective bargaining and called for a redistribution of wages in favour of women. She took this further in another *Red Rag* article in 1980, typically entitled "United We Fall".[54] Again in *Sweet Freedom*, with Anna Coote, she returned to the theme.[55]

Over the years, Beatrix Campbell's attitude to male workers and to the trade union movement has become more hostile. The substance of these arguments has already been dealt with. What is important here is to stress their impact on an already retreating and fragmented movement. They aided the right by serving to strengthen the arguments of those who were moving away from socialist politics and towards a cross-class feminism. After all, if men had traditionally been as great a problem as the capitalist system itself, then there was surely little point in engaging in struggle alongside them. This indeed was the conclusion of many feminists, who regarded the trade unions as the "men's movement".

Other socialist feminists sometimes found all this too much to stomach. Some, like Angela Weir and Elizabeth Wilson, tried seriously to bring the question of women's liberation back to that of class and in the process aimed some effective blows at Beatrix Campbell's theory on feminist incomes policy and the family wage.[56] Others, like Anne Phillips, vacillated about class, gender and much more.[57] Nonetheless, the idea that male workers have used the unions as a means of oppressing women has become widely accepted. It is propagated with ceaseless and monotonous regularity by Beatrix Campbell through *Marxism Today*. Yet studies which seriously challenge such ideas remain locked into an academic debate and are not nearly as well known.[58]

One feminist who has tried to come to terms with this crisis of socialist feminism is Lynne Segal, a co-author of *Beyond the Fragments*. In her book *Is the Future Female?* she begins by stating her worries over the direction of the women's movement:

> I wanted to write this book because I was disturbed by what has been emerging as the public face of feminism in the 1980s ... What is most troubling to some older feminists such as myself is the turnaround in feminist writing from an initial denial of fundamental difference between women and men in the early 1970s to a celebration of difference by the close of that decade.[59]

She goes on to lambast currently widespread theories, such as those concerning rape, pornography and violence. She is scathing of those who present men as the enemy. It isn't as simple as that, she argues. Men aren't an undifferentiated biological mass. Are those who are socialists or pro-feminist to be treated in the same way as those who want

---

54. Campbell (1980).
55. Campbell and Coote, chapters 2 and 5.
56. Weir and Wilson.
57. Phillips (1987).
58. See Humphries (1977), note 40.
59. Segal, pp.ix–x.

to keep women in the home? She pleads for a real socialist feminism which can direct its energies to fighting the real enemy.

Sheila Rowbotham has also recently written a book which reiterates the same theme.[60] Their approach is—compared to most of their contemporaries—a breath of fresh air. But the analysis, too, is flawed by two major features which also, in their different ways, affect Angela Weir and Elizabeth Wilson too.

The first is that all accept variations of the patriarchy theory as the key to understanding women's oppression. This is both wrong theoretically and gives ground to anti-working-class and anti-socialist theory. For writers like these, who want to remain true to the name of socialist feminist, this leads at best to contradiction and to fudging in an attempt to explain against whom and against what women must fight to end their oppression.

The second problem is their understanding of socialism itself. Angela Weir and Elizabeth Wilson support the Stalinist wing of the Communist Party. Their view of socialism and women's liberation is therefore distorted by their support for countries which claim to be socialist but aren't. Lynne Segal and Sheila Rowbotham are libertarian socialists, which means they reject most forms of party organisation (except of course the Labour Party which puts no demands on anyone). Instead they favour autonomous movements. Yet today one thing at least is absolutely clear: these movements have not grown, often they have not even held together, and they are farther away from their aims than ever before.

Women's oppression is a result of class society, which today means capitalism. Only a political organisation which attempts to challenge class society itself can offer a strategy for the successful overthrow of capitalism, and so a strategy for the complete liberation of women. The failure to understand this means that even the best of the socialist feminists cannot see a way out of the problems of women's oppression today. That is why those seeking genuine liberation will find anything other than socialist organisation a blind alley.

---

60. Rowbotham (London 1989).

CHAPTER TEN

The left and the women's movement

[T]he Trotskyist movement as a whole ... "forgot" the question of women's liberation throughout the period from the Second World War to the end of the 1960s, that is until it was imposed on us by the rise in the women's movement, first in America and then in Britain.[1]

This statement by John Molyneux probably sums up the attitude of most of the left towards the women's movement today. The movement may have its faults, so the argument goes, but without it the left would never have recognised the specific oppression of women and the problems that women face.

But is it true? The answer must be no. Firstly the left did not "forget" the question of women. In the United States, the left was publicly forced away from the question of women's oppression, along with most others to do with social change, by the impact of McCarthyism and the rise of the right wing. So for example in the late 1940s the Progressive Party organised a campaign for black and women's rights; it was defeated by the right-wing backlash.[2]

There is evidence to suggest that, despite the impact of Stalinism on the Communist Parties, attitudes of individual Communists and socialists on questions of women's equality remained rigorous and self-searching. Sara Evans, herself a separatist feminist, points out that the socialists of the 1940s and 1950s were far superior to those of the 1960s with regard to issues such as the equal sharing of housework.[3]

In Britain there was nothing comparable to the right-wing backlash experienced in the USA. But here the weight of right-wing social democracy, in the form of the Labour Party, and a trade union bureaucracy with similar politics, ensured that issues concerning women's equality tended to be taken up only at a token or bureaucratic level. The largest organisation to the left of Labour, the Communist Party, maintained a strict division between industrial activity and "politics". So its often impressive industrial

---

1. Molyneux, p.121.
2. See Deckard, p.323.
3. Sara Evans, pp.116–18.

militants all too often did not take up wider political issues, including those relating to women's equality.

In addition, the revolutionary socialist tradition in both Britain and the US was marginal to the working-class movement. It had been all but destroyed by the rise of Stalin in the USSR and the defeat, exile and eventual murder of Trotsky. The dominance of Stalinism inside the workers' movement on a world scale meant that all sorts of questions were hidden or ignored for over 30 years. It was precisely the rebirth of a revolutionary alternative to Stalinism in the late 1960s internationally which put these questions back on the political agenda.

Yet despite the major difficulties facing revolutionaries in the years after 1945, issues concerning women *were* taken up within the working-class movement. Equal pay became an issue in many unions during the 1940s and 1950s, and it is arguable that pressure from union machines forced the passing of Equal Pay legislation in 1969 by the Labour government led by Harold Wilson. Indeed, most of the major postwar reforms concerning individual sexual freedom were passed before the advent of the women's movement either in the United States or in Britain. The British law reforms concerning abortion (1967), homosexuality (1967), divorce (1971) and equal pay (1970) were all enacted or well under way by the time the women's movement began.

Organisations which campaigned for women's rights also existed. The National Organisation of Women was founded in the US in 1966. In Britain long-standing organisations such as the Abortion Law Reform Association (ALRA) had continued to campaign, while new ones as such as NJACWER were set up largely through trade union initiatives in the late 1960s.

Women workers were also active in a number of disputes in the same period. For example in late 1968 women engineering. workers at CAV Lucas, in north London, staged a one-day strike in support of their union's claim for equal pay.[4] At around the same time, a headline in *Socialist Worker* read: "Round-the-Clock Shift Work Threat to Women". The story below it told of attempts by the then Labour government to repeal sections of the Factory Acts; the effect would have been to increase the exploitation of women workers.[5]

If anything, the women's movement was a response to these events, not the creator or instigator of them. So why the feeling, common even among socialists, that without the women's movement nothing would have happened? Partly the reason lies in the deep-seated antagonisms, outlined above, between the emerging US women's movement and the American New Left. Many individual women were deeply scarred by the process.

Yet in Britain, again, the process was quite different. By the late 1960s and early 1970s, there were no large numbers of women—or even a small number—who felt themselves embittered or estranged from organised left politics. Many of those influenced by ideas of women's liberation joined left-wing groups at precisely this period.

---

4. *Socialist Worker*, 16 November 1968.
5. *Socialist Worker*, 21 December 1968.

If any of those women did believe that the revolutionary left had "forgotten" ideas of women's liberation, then certainly they considered this forgetfulness pardonable. Sheila Rowbotham, briefly a member of the International Socialists in the late 1960s, wrote an article on equal pay in *Socialist Worker* in February 1970 to help build for the first women's liberation conference in Oxford that month.[6] The report of that conference in *Socialist Worker* hardly gives the impression of a left hostile to or ignorant of issues of women's liberation:

> A mixture of old and young, housewives, workers and students, they came as individuals fighting for emancipation. There were members of Women's Liberation Workshops, trade unions, radical single-issue pressure groups and from many left tendencies including more than 50 from IS.[7]

But it *is* true that from the early 1970s onwards there was always a tension between IS (and other revolutionaries such as the International Marxist Group) and the women's movement. This was not an argument about whether or not to relate to strikes, or to other issues concerning women. The record of IS, from the night cleaners to equal pay and later on to abortion, was extremely good. The argument lay rather in the nature of the women's movement itself. And here there was a contradiction. The movement had, especially in America, attracted many women to its ideas. For many, it provided a vitality and energy which seemed lacking elsewhere. It had a level of dynamism. But it remained at the same time a thoroughly individualistic movement. While the movement itself was capable of tapping a well of bitterness against women's oppression, it was and is totally incapable of giving a lead to a real fight against that oppression.

The reason for this lay in the class nature of the movement. It was not based on collective working-class struggle but on changing individual ideas. Its ideas appealed strongly to a section of the middle class, stressing as they did changes in individual lifestyles, fulfilment and so on. It therefore drew heavily from the middle classes, and especially the technical-managerial "new middle class", in its support.

While the movement could therefore act as some sort of inspiration for many women, including those of the working class, it could offer them little in terms of real change. This was apparent relatively early in the history of the movement. There was not a great deal for the movement to contribute to working-class struggle in practice, precisely because of its class nature.[8]

During the early 1970s the contradictions within the women's movement were reflected in arguments within the revolutionary left. Should socialists work in or with the movement? Were its members just middle-class? But weren't a lot of socialists from a similar class background? Did the women's movement have anything to offer the growing number of struggles involving working women? None of these conflicts

---

6. *Socialist Worker*, 12 February 1970.
7. *Socialist Worker*, 5 March 1970.
8. See Ennis.

was resolved. In the meantime, some women members of IS, with the backing of the organisation, set up first a newsletter, then a magazine.

The magazine, *Women's Voice*, first came out in 1972. Like *Spare Rib* (launched at around the same time) it attempted to relate to women through a "women's magazine" format. Unlike *Spare Rib*, it had an uncompromising orientation on women workers. But the contradictions of the movement were not resolved by *Women's Voice*. Indeed it reflected them. It tended to combine feminism with a sort of syndicalism: cheerleading the working class, with rhetoric about women fighting.

In the early 1970s, this lack of clarity was a problem, but it tended to be swept aside by the rising tide of class struggle. There was little disagreement that workers had the power to change the world, nor was there any doubt that women workers could play a full part in the class struggle. The problems arose as things changed.

The crisis of the revolutionary left was an international phenomenon. This had become apparent by the mid-1970s. The reasons were twofold: it became clear firstly that the mass upsurges of the 1960s did not simply herald increasing revolutionary struggle everywhere; and secondly that the established leaderships of the working class were more than willing to do deals with a crisis-hit capitalism in order to preserve it. As the Communist Party made the "historic compromise" in Italy, the TUC made the Social Contract in Britain and similar deals were made elsewhere, revolutionaries watched in dismay as the mass of the working class acquiesced.

The result for many was disillusionment with the working class, and so a search elsewhere for possible sources of revolutionary change, especially in the movements—students, blacks, women, the Third World. In addition, the revolutionary left was hit by a massive crisis of confidence: a feeling that all its efforts had been in vain because the world had not changed.[9]

The process was most advanced in Italy, which had boasted the strongest revolutionary left in Europe in the early 1970s. There revolutionaries were numbered in tens of thousands, and were able to sustain three daily papers to the left of the Communist Party. But theoretical cloudiness, coupled with a total inability to understand the downturn and what it meant for socialists, left the movement disarmed.

The theory and practice of the Italian revolutionary left drew heavily on both Maoist politics and spontaneist ideas. These fitted with a period of rising struggle, but could not come to terms with the later period of defeat. So the revolutionary left lost confidence and direction precisely at the time when the Italian women's movement was growing and gaining a confidence of its own.

The Italian women's movement had emerged later than those of Britain and the US. Its background was an extremely male chauvinist society, with a lower proportion of women working outside the home than most of the rest of Europe. The fight for women's liberation seemed an immense task, a battle against the Catholic church, a large peasantry, and the legacy of 20 years of fascism. On top of that the behaviour of

9. For details see Harman (1988), pp.345–55.

many members of the revolutionary left over the question of women left much to be desired. The divorce referendum of 1974, however, gave the movement an impetus and by the end of 1975 it was calling for a large national women-only demonstration. The event proved to be a turning point. It was to mark

> not only the height of the confidence of the women's movement, but also the beginning of a long and bitter battle between the women's movement and the organisations of the revolutionary left. For, at this women-only demonstration, Lotta Continua [with 40,000 militants, one of the biggest organisations on the left] refused to accept to be excluded and physically attacked the women in an attempt to join the march.[10]

Many women members left Lotta Continua as a result. A year later the group's Rimini conference collapsed in confusion, as the organisation took its increasing "movementism"—the tail-ending of the various "autonomous" movements—at face value and collapsed into those movements.

The bitterness, recriminations and sheer confusion over these happenings reverberated widely. Nearly everyone on the left accepted that its collapse and the crisis of the revolutionary movement was the fault of the left itself, rather than the result of the ideas of separatism and feminism.

The Italian experience cast its stamp on the international feminist experience, just as the US women's movement had done in the late 1960s. The dominant feminist view of left groups became much more negative. It seemed as though many of the women now regarding themselves as feminists were former members of revolutionary organisations, and that they had left those organisations because of their experiences with revolutionary men, male leaderships and so on. This came out clearly in reports of two socialist feminist conferences in Paris and Amsterdam (two were held because of various splits). One report from Celia Deacon, a former member of IS, is particularly revealing:

> I was struck by how many women there are internationally who used to be in left groups but have left them. Many similarities emerged in our experiences of the sectarianism, economism, narrow conception of Marxism, the resistance to women's ideas and the characterisation of feminist ideas as "bourgeois", the rigid adherence to a formally correct line and the male authority structures that characterise most of the revolutionary left.[11]

The effect of this on the revolutionary left was dramatic. In Italy it resulted in disintegration and the creation of a political desert in a place which had once been the most fertile in Europe. In Britain the effect was much less severe, but nonetheless profound. The relative weight of the movements *vis-à-vis* the left increased. Left-wing organisations became more in favour of autonomous organisation for women, blacks and other oppressed groups. Even within their own organisations, they accepted a degree of

---

10. Holborow (1979).
11. Report by Celia Deacon in *Spare Rib*, number 61, August 1977.

autonomy from black and women members. The once monolithic Communist Party, for example, tended to collapse in this direction.[12]

Although the IS/SWP did not go anywhere as far as most other left organisations, it was nonetheless increasingly influenced by these developments. At first it tended to call for more militancy and more orientation on working-class women, but in time it too came more under the influence of feminist arguments and ideas. This pressure was reflected in changes in *Women's Voice*.

As early as 1976, an article on the first *Women's Voice* group, in North London, stated that "like men workers, perhaps even more so, women are suspicious of left-wing groups".[13] Autumn of 1977 saw an attempt to build a full-scale women's revolutionary organisation, with local groups and supporters' cards. By now the magazine claimed a circulation of 10,000 copies per month.[14]

Right from the beginning there were major problems with this orientation. There were always internal divisions among women members of the SWP about the nature of the organisation and what they were trying to build. Some shied away entirely from the notion of building the groups, others were highly enthusiastic about the prospect, yet others had doubts about the political basis of the groups themselves. These divisions tended not to surface publicly, although they were the underlying reason for many tensions and arguments. The SWP leadership didn't really face up to these political problems. There was no reply to Joan Smith's articles on the family—these were the theoretical basis of the *Women's Voice* Organisation—for some years.

Meanwhile the line projected through the magazine was highly enthusiastic, even triumphalist. By early 1978, the magazine had gone "glossy", with a shiny cover and more human interest stories. It prominently advertised the groups and the need to build them.[15] Its general approach to the women's movement was to stress what socialists had in common with feminists rather than the other way round. The burden of its criticism of the disastrous 1978 women's liberation conference in Birmingham was that the formerly amicable atmosphere of such events had disappeared.[16]

Internal arguments began to develop inside the SWP. Some argued that the groups and the magazine were politically too "soft" on the women's movement, and needed to be aligned more closely to the party itself.[17] Others felt the process of building the groups had not gone far enough, and that the *Women's Voice* Organisation had to become an independent revolutionary women's organisation, a "sister" organisation of the SWP.[18]

---

12. See for example the defence of women's autonomy in Campbell (1978).

13. Report on North London *Women's Voice* group by Mandy Hurford and Diane Watts, in *Women's Voice*, number 30, June 1976.

14. See *Women's Voice*, number 10, October 1977.

15. See *Women's Voice*, number 15, March 1978.

16. See the open letter from *Women's Voice* to the conference, in *Women's Voice*, number 17, May 1978.

17. This was the position taken by the present author, and others such as Gill Brown. It was also probably the position of much of the leadership, for example Chris Harman and Alex Callinicos. This wasn't always clear, since there was a delay in arguing openly (although not privately) for internal reasons. There was also a further complication, since the organisation was split over a number of other questions—such as the role of *Socialist Worker* and whether there was an industrial downturn.

18. The position taken by, for example, Joan Smith, Sheila McGregor and Linda Quinn.

What was behind this confusion and disagreement? At root there were two things: a complete misunderstanding of the political period in which we were operating—the downturn in working-class struggle—and a major theoretical misconception about the nature of feminism. The two fed each other. So most of the participants in the discussion had a false overestimation of what could be achieved. Few doubted, at least initially, that a substantial movement of working-class women could be built; the differences were over how close its links should be with the SWP. This overestimation also led to a form of voluntarism.

In turn, this fitted neatly with the idea that when it came to the question of women's liberation, left groups were the problem. Such a conclusion was a disaster politically. It led to a deep mistrust of the "male left" and a strengthening of the notion that women needed to organise autonomously in order to achieve their liberation.

Indeed, the rationale that underlay the creation of the *Women's Voice* Organisation was an accommodation to autonomous organisation. The idea was implicit that socialist mixed organisation would always be dominated by men and that women therefore had to organise separately. This was in turn underpinned by the notion that all women had something in common against all men; and that all men had an interest in the oppression of women.

The argument had little factual or theoretical basis, predicated as it was on the idea that gender was a more central division inside capitalist society than class. By the late 1970s, however, it had become widely accepted among socialists. In organisations such as the Communist Party and the IMG, adoption of autonomy theory meant a total separation of struggles. Women had to decide for themselves what their best course of political action should be, and individual men on the left—let alone "male" groups—should not be able to influence or even argue with them.

The increasing number of feminists who were joining the Labour Party found this separation of struggles particularly convenient. They could justify membership of a male-dominated, pro-family and highly sexist organisation on the basis that it gave them "space" as women to organise autonomously. The fact that Labour Party conferences were able to pass meaningless paper resolutions supporting women's rights further encouraged such feminists to stay in the Labour Party along with its more sexist members.

If the theory of autonomy effectively let sexist men off the hook inside the Labour Party, it had a disastrous effect on revolutionary organisation. It led away from collective struggle, away from any attempt at theoretical rigour and towards a celebration of some of the most vague spontaneist feelings.

This was true of the argument in the SWP over *Women's Voice*. The women's organisation had caused worry and disagreements from the start because it was based on a misconception. There was no understanding that organising working-class women separately from men led to separatism and lifestyle politics. It was therefore not surprising that the problems reflected inside the women's movement were reproduced around the SWP. In particular, there was a subtle but marked move in *Women's Voice* away from issues such as strikes and towards specific "women's issues" such as violence, Reclaim the Night—and even toxic tampons![19] In other words, collective struggle tended to be given a lower priority when it appeared to lack a "women's dimension"; instead individual issues were stressed.

Alongside this went an inability to recognise the real nature of the women's movement and what it was becoming. So for example an open letter written by Anna Paczuska in 1981 took *Spare Rib* feminists to task for abandoning the term "women's liberation" in favour of "feminism". There was little understanding that this wasn't an accidental occurrence, or a question of semantics, but stemmed from the movement's shift to the right.[20]

In 1979, the argument came to a head in a fight inside the SWP over how closely the *Women's Voice* groups should be tied to the party. Those favouring tighter control won their argument at the SWP conference that year. The following eighteen months saw constant unresolved tensions surfacing in arguments about the individual or the collective, feminism or socialism, and many other issues. At the same time the groups failed to make headway, often declining and sometimes even disappearing, as SWP women members "voted with their feet" and became less and less involved in running them.

This was not because of a lack of commitment to ideas of women's liberation or to organising working-class women. But it was evidence of increasing divergence between the *Women's Voice* groups and the party branches, with "women's work" being left to the groups while the branches dealt with everything else—including industrial work concerning women workers. This meant that many individual women party members found themselves in a ghetto.

The logic of the situation became increasingly clear; *Women's Voice*, far from winning a layer of women "put off" by male-dominated organisation towards a revolutionary party, was itself becoming a bridge out of the party. In 1981 there was a bitter argument along these lines within the SWP, and at party conference a clear majority voted to close the *Women's Voice* groups down. The following year the magazine was also closed.

Although the prolonged nature of the fight and the bitterness of some of the arguments left their mark, the eventual outcome was a greater theoretical clarity. Part of the problem with the debate had been a general lack of such clarity, a theoretical confusion and a lack of knowledge about the Marxist tradition on the question of organising women.

It was generally recognised that the notion of an independent revolutionary organisation of women separate from that of men had no foundation in Marxist theory, and was an attempt to accommodate to feminist theory. This was true even for many of the women (and men) in the SWP who had supported *Women's Voice*. The number who left the party was small, especially when it became apparent that the retreat from separate organisation did not mean an abandonment of commitment to women's liberation, as some had argued it would.

---

19. See for example *Women's Voice*, number 47, December 1980.
20. See *Women's Voice*, number 52, May 1981.

Perhaps more decisive in shifting many people was the terrible state of the women's movement by this time. This was recognised even by some of the movement's most partisan supporters, as a gloomy *Feminist Review* editorial from 1982 testifies:

> Socialist feminists as a group have initiated relatively little political activity and have been at the forefront of few campaigns although individual socialist feminists have been politically active. The November 1980 socialist feminist conference on imperialism, although important, also had the effect of minimalising women's struggles in this country and of discouraging organisation.[21]

The choice was stark: stay with revolutionary organisation, drop into inactivity or join the Labour Party. A minority took the first option, and were often encouraged to do so by what they saw of those who had chosen the other two. In particular the dominance of reformist feminism became an object lesson to the left, as those who had once fought for the fundamental change of class society now opted for less and less "in the here and now". Many of the feminists of the 1970s were those who presided over the welfare, education and health cuts implemented by Labour councils in the middle and late 1980s. Their fate shows the result of the women's movement's failure to confront the structures of class society which oppress women.

---

21. "Feminism and the political crisis of the Eighties", in *Feminist Review*, number 12, 1982, p.5.

CHAPTER ELEVEN

The class struggle for women's liberation

Twenty years ago, the fight for women's liberation might have seemed to many people a relatively easy affair. A combination of education, legislation and positive discrimination would lead to a greater awareness and a greater impetus towards women's equality. After all, the demands were eminently reasonable. As one strike picket placard from the early 1970s put it: "We only want women's rights". Experience showed, however, that they were much harder to win.

The past two decades have been an example of being so near, yet so far. There have been instances of real progress for women's rights—women are now much more accepted as workers; childbirth and marriage are both in decline; divorce has gone up steeply; far more women go through higher education. All these also indicate that women's massive involvement in wage labour is not some transitory phenomenon, but a permanent feature of late capitalism.

But these changes are a *partial* challenge to the old roles—not a complete change. This freedom from the straitjacket of the traditional role as mother and housewife only exists within the confines of a society dominated by the needs of capital accumulation. So the freedom is illusory: it has little to do with real liberation. On the contrary: such freedom means much greater likelihood of exploitation, *coupled with* the continued existence of privatised reproduction.

This is the contradiction which lies at the heart of women's oppression under capitalism. The competitive nature of the system means, as we have seen earlier, that the family continues to be the major instrument for the reproduction of labour power. So the fight for liberation—to end the oppression of women through the family—is of necessity interconnected with the fight to end the system which gives rise to both exploitation and oppression.

Yet the dominant ideas within the women's liberation movement and among feminists do not start from this analytical framework. On the contrary, the theory of patriarchy offers them no clear strategy for how liberation can be achieved. This in part explains the failure of the Labour Party, the unions and the women's movement itself on the question of women. Settling for reforms within the system has always meant accepting less than what is required to win women's liberation.

So the demands of most feminists have become more and more tailored to the limited advances which they believe are all that can be achieved. At the same time it is more obvious that reformist feminism cannot even deliver these limited changes. Women's liberation will not be achieved without the revolutionary overthrow of capitalist society.

To understand why this is so, we have to develop a clear analysis of why oppression exists. At the centre is the existence of class society. Engels' work explicitly ties the development of class society to the "world historic defeat of the female sex".[1] The full title of his book, *The Origin of the Family, Private Property and the State*, makes this clear. Once society produces a surplus of wealth, those who have access to that surplus have a need to maintain their control over it. Hence the connection between the production of a surplus and the rise of class society. Inside class society monogamous sexual relations within the family become necessary in order to pass wealth from one generation to another. With the emerging ruling class comes the development of the state, in order to protect the wealth and power of those who rule.

The analysis put forward by Engels is much maligned by some feminists, who criticise it for being based on inaccurate anthropological evidence. It is true that some of the evidence has been proved incorrect. It is also true, however, that a number of more recent anthropological studies have substantiated the bulk of Engels' assertions.[2] His basic thesis still stands.

What Engels achieved over a hundred years ago was the demolition of the myth that male domination had always been the norm—or that it was even typical of many societies. He argued that male domination and female submission were social constructions, not an eternal truth. He did so by pointing to very early societies—what he described as "primitive communism"—where there was no *necessary* stigma or inferiority in being a woman. There was, it is true, the earliest division of labour between the sexes. But that division was not based on one sort of labour being valued more highly in society than another. Therefore there was no material basis for women's oppression. Indeed there is evidence that in various and differing societies, women's status was extremely high.

To Engels, and to Marx, the argument was relatively simple: societies had existed where there was no oppression of women; the development of that oppression was connected to the rise and the continued existence of class society; it was only with the end of class society that the oppression of women could become a thing of the past.

This argument knocked a hole in the prevailing set of ideas of bourgeois society: that women's natural place was in the home, caring for children and looking up to a man. More recently, however, it has been challenged by feminist theorists precisely because it locates women's oppression not in the behaviour of individual men, but in class society.

---

1. Engels (1978), p.65.
2. See for example Leacock (1981); and Reiter (1975).

At the centre of patriarchy theory—however much it is dressed up as being an analysis of class society—is the idea that there are given biological and gender differences which determine the oppression of women. Those who support it therefore deny that class society lies behind women's oppression; and this denial leads to the conclusion that *individual* change rather than collective class action is the answer to oppression.

Patriarchy theorists carry the argument further: not only do they say that class society is at best secondary in causing the oppression of women, but also that class is not the key division within society. All women, they say, have something in common (just as all men have patriarchal privileges in common), and from this they argue that every woman, regardless of class, can empathise with the problems of women.

But in reality there are massive differences between women of different classes. Ruling-class women benefit directly from the surplus value extracted from working men and women. Many middle-class women constitute part of the technical and managerial new middle class; others are professionals such as doctors and lawyers, who in status and income are far removed from most working-class people. There are all manner of ways in which oppression can be alleviated by the material advantages which middle- and upper-class women enjoy. This does not mean that their oppression disappears. But access to nannies, to various services which can be bought on the market rather than performed in the home, to their own car and the like—all these make a difference.

More important, economic and social power is not denied to *all* women. Many middle- and upper-class women have access to such power. Although they may be oppressed *within* their own class, they can also act as the oppressors (and sometimes the exploiters) of others.

The corollary of this argument is that working-class men are not the oppressors of women. The exploitation of the working class leads to their individual powerlessness and alienation. And it is this exploitation which ensures that class divisions are by far the most important and fundamental divisions inside society.

So the oppression of women is embedded in class society—alongside an exploited class, the working class, men and women, which has every interest in overthrowing class society, *and the ability to do so*. The key to women's liberation lies in the process of social revolution, which alone can end class society.

Women's liberation and revolution are not just pipedreams. Every revolutionary movement of modern times has brought with it an upsurge in women's activity and the blossoming of new ideas about women's liberation. Women have rejected their traditional roles and have played a leading part in changing their own destinies.[3]

The reason is simple. Struggle for social change causes our ideas to change, not on an individual basis but on a wide scale. Workers and oppressed groups struggling side by side brings the acceptance of ideas of freedom, liberation and socialism by people who had previously never thought of such things.

---

3. See Cliff, chapters 1, 2 and 3.

The Russian Revolution of 1917 marks the highest point of such changes, when workers' revolution meant that one of the most backward countries of Europe ushered in changes undreamt-of anywhere else. Despite mass poverty, illiteracy and superstition the Zhenotdel (the women's department), set up by the Bolshevik Party, was able to achieve pathbreaking success. It had to start from a very low level, since women under the rule of the tsar were still treated as chattels and the property of their fathers or husbands.[4] Yet socialised child care, laundries, restaurants—all were provided as a means of helping to shift the burden from the individual family (and therefore the individual mother) towards society as a whole. Legal restrictions on women's rights were removed: abortion, contraception and divorce were made available, and marriage was separated from religion. All sorts of special provisions were made for pregnant and nursing mothers. As Sheila Rowbotham has pointed out: "These seem like unspectacular and extremely fundamental reforms now, but in the Russian context they were an extraordinary achievement".[5]

Trotsky made a similar point when interviewed by an American journalist in the 1930s. The position of women in post-revolutionary Russia was far in advance of any of the more advanced capitalist countries. When asked "Is it true that a divorce may be had for the asking?" he replied: "Of course it is true. It would have been more in place to ask another question: 'Is it true that there are still countries where divorce cannot be obtained for the asking by either party to a marriage?'"[6]

Just as in all other areas of life, the revolution changed the position of women—and men's attitudes to women—dramatically. Of course, it could not overcome in the space of a few short years the legacy of generations. Some reforms proceeded with painful slowness. The poverty of the revolution—beset with civil war, blockade and famine— meant that those reforms fell short of the ideal.

They were, in any case, relatively short-lived. By the late 1920s the revolutionary gains had been overthrown in the effort to catch up with and overtake the West, as Stalin put it. The needs of women's liberation were subjugated once again to the drive for accumulation. By the 1930s women, still part of the workforce, were again also expected to shoulder the burden of privatised child care. Motherhood was glorified in the name of nationalism, and women were awarded medals for producing a certain number of babies. Only the increasingly privileged bureaucrats lived anything approaching a liberated lifestyle.[7]

Nonetheless, the experience of the early years of the Russian Revolution stands as a testimony to revolutionary change as the only means of achieving women's liberation. No other event in history has come anywhere close to it.

This conclusion leads some feminists to accuse revolutionary socialists of wanting to postpone all struggle for women's liberation until "after the revolution". But

---

4. For a graphic description of the scale of women's oppression in tsarist Russia, see Rowbotham (1974), pp.138–9.
5. Rowbotham (1974), p.141.
6. Trotsky (1974), p.54.
7. Trotsky (1972), pp.144–159.

revolutionaries do not counterpose the two. As Rosa Luxemburg put it, revolutionaries are the best fighters for reforms precisely because they have the goal of revolution. It is those who profess to limit themselves to reform of the system who repeatedly sell short on those reforms—including reforms in women's lives.

The experience of recent years has borne this out. The fight around issues like abortion and equal pay has been led by socialists. Revolutionaries are at the forefront of these campaigns because they understand that a successful fight both helps individual women *and* strengthens the overall fighting capability of the working class. It therefore helps build the confidence of all of the working class and the oppressed and so helps build towards the revolutionary overthrow of capitalist society.

If that overthrow is necessary for women's liberation, it is not going to happen automatically. It needs organisation. This won't occur within the Labour Party, and it won't be done by an autonomous women's movement. The struggle for liberation needs to be based on the only power to change society—the working class, organised through a revolutionary party of women and men.

We have already seen that when the working-class struggle does rise, women come to the fore. In the Chartist movement of the 1840s, the New Unions of the 1880s, the Great Unrest of 1910–14, up to the struggles of the late 1960s and early 1970s, women played often a crucial role. Even under Thatcher, the nurses and the miners' wives stand out as some of the best class fighters.

When the struggle rises again, we can have every confidence that the nine million women workers will once more begin to organise and to fight, and in the process to change themselves and the world in which they live. Then we will see the real potential for liberation among women workers: a potential for revolutionary change which can also help liberate the whole of humanity, by ending the confines of class society for good.

References

Abbott, Pamela and Roger Sapsford, *Women and Social Class*, (London 1987)

Alexander, Sally, "Women's Work in the Nineteenth Century", in Mitchell and Oakley

Alexander, Sally and Sue O'Sullivan, "Sisterhood under Stress", in *Red Rag*, 8 February 1975

Alexander, Sally and Barbara Taylor, "In defence of 'patriarchy'", in *New Statesman*, 1 February 1980

Amsden, Alice (ed.), *The Economics of Women and Work* (Harmondsworth 1980)

Anderson, Michael, *Family Structure in 19th Century Lancashire* (Cambridge 1971)

Aries, Philippe, *Centuries of Childhood: A Social History of Family Life* (London 1965)

Barrett, Michele, *Women's Oppression Today* (London 1980)

Barrett, Michele and Mary McIntosh, "The family wage", in Whitelegg

Barrett, Michele and Mary McIntosh, *The Anti-Social Family* (London 1982)

Barrios de Chúngara, Domitila (with Moema Viezzer), *Let Me Speak* (New York and London 1978)

Beechey, Veronica and Elizabeth Whitelegg (eds), *Women in Britain Today* (Milton Keynes 1986)

Black, Clementina (ed.), *Married Women's Work* (London 1983)

Boston, Sarah, *Women Workers and the Trade Unions* (London 1980)

Bradshaw, Jonathan and Jane Morgan, "Budgeting on a Benefit", in *New Society* (London), 6 March 1987

Bradshaw, Jonathan and Jane Morgan, "Budgeting on benefit: the consumption of families on social security" (Family Policy Studies Centre 1987)

Braverman, Harry, *Labor and Monopoly Capital* (New York and London 1974)

Brayshaw, AJ, *Public Policy and Family Life* (London 1980)

Brenner, Johanna, "Women's self-organization: a Marxist justification", in *Against the Current* (New York), Fall 1980

Brenner, Johanna and Maria Ramas, "Rethinking Women's Oppression", in *New Left Review* (London), 144, March/April 1984

Brownmiller, Susan, *Against Our Will* (Harmondsworth 1976)

Bruegel, Irene, "What keeps the family going?", in *International Socialism*, 2:1, Summer 1978

Burr Litchfield, R, "The Family and the Mill", in Anthony Wohl (ed.) *The Victorian Family* (London 1978)

Campbell, Beatrix, "Sweets from a Stranger", in *Red Rag*, 13, 1978

Campbell, Beatrix and Valerie Charlton, "Work to Rule", in *Red Rag*, 14 (November 1978)

Campbell, Beatrix, "United we fall", in *Red Rag*, August 1980

Campbell Beatrix, *Wigan Pier Revisited* (London 1984)

Campbell, Beatrix and Anna Coote, *Sweet Freedom* (London 1982)

Chafe, William, *The American Woman: Her Changing Social, Economic and Political Role 1920–1970* (New York 1972)

Cliff, Tony, *Class Struggle and Women's Liberation* (Bookmarks: London 1985)

Cole, GDH, *A history of the Labour Party from 1914* (New York 1969)

DallaCosta, Mariarosa and Selma James, *The Power of Women and the Subversion of the Community* (Bristol 1975)

Daly, Mary, *Gyn/Ecology* (London 1979)

Dangerfield, George, *The strange death of Liberal England* (London 1983)

Deckard, Barbara Sinclair, *The Women's Movement* (New York 1979)

Delphy, Christine, "The main enemy", in *Close to Home* (London 1984)

Dex, Shirley, *The Sexual Division of Work* (Brighton 1985)

Drake, Barbara, *Women in Trade Unions* (Virago: London 1984)

Eisenstein, Zillah (ed.) *Capitalist Patriarchy and the Case for Socialist Feminism* (Monthly Review Press: New York 1978)

Engels, Friedrich, *The Condition of the Working Class in England* (Moscow 1973)

Engels, Friedrich, *The Origin of the Family, Private Property and the State* (Peking 1978)

Ennis, Kath, "Women's Consciousness", in *International Socialism* (London), 1:68, April 1974

Evans, Richard, *The Feminists* (London 1977)

Evans, Sara, *Personal Politics* (New York 1979)

Feminist Anthology Collective, *No Turning Back: Writings from the Women's Liberation Movement 1975–1980* (London 1981)

Firestone, Shulamith, *The Dialectic of Sex* (London 1971)

Foster, John, *Class Struggle in the Industrial Revolution* (London 1974)

Friedan, Betty, *The Feminine Mystique* (London 1971)

German, Lindsey, "Child Abuse", in *Socialist Worker Review* (London), 112, September 1988

Gittins, Diana, *The Fair Sex* (London 1982)

Gittins, Diana, *The Family in Question* (London 1985)

Glucksmann, Miriam, "In a class of their own? women workers in the new industries in inter-war Britain", in *Feminist Review*, 24, November 1986, pp.7–37.

Goodsell, William, *A History of the Family as a Social and Educational Institution* (USA 1915)

Gregory Jeanne, "Equal Pay and Sex Discrimination: why women are giving up the fight", in *Feminist Review*, 10, 1982, pp.75–89

Griffin, Jean and David Thomas, *Caring and Sharing: The Centenary History of the Cooperative Women's Guild* (Manchester 1983)

Hakim, Catherine, "Sexual Divisions within the Labour Force: Occupational Segregation", in *Department of Employment Gazette*, November 1978, pp.1264–79

Hall, Catherine, "The home turned upside down", in Whitelegg

Harrison, John, "The Political Economy of Housework", in *Bulletin of the Conference of Socialist Economists* (London), volume 4, Spring 1974

Harman, Chris, *Explaining the Crisis* (London 1984)

Harman, Chris, "Base and Superstructure", in *International Socialism*, 2:32, Summer 1986

Hartmann, Heidi, "The Unhappy Marriage of Marxism and Feminism", in *Capital and Class* (London), 8, Summer 1979

Hartmann, Heidi, "Summary and response: Continuing the Discussion", in Sargent

Hewitt, Margaret, *Wives and Mothers in Victorian Industry* (London 1958)

Hewlett, Sylvia Ann, *A lesser life* (New York 1986)

Hinton, James, *The First Shop Stewards' Movement* (London 1973)

Holborow, Marnie, "Women in Italy", in *Socialist Review*, 13, July/August 1979

Howell, David, *British Workers and the Independent Labour Party 1888–1906* (Manchester 1983)

Humphries, Jane, "The Working-Class Family, Women's Liberation and Class Struggle: The Case of Nineteenth Century British History", in *Review of Radical Political Economics* (New York), 9:3 (1977)

Humphries, Jane, "Class struggle and the persistence of the working class family" in *Cambridge Journal of Economics*, volume 1 (September 1977); reprinted in Amsden (1980)

Humphries, Jane, "Protective Legislation, the Capitalist State and Working-Class Men: The Case of the 1842 Mines Regulation Act", in *Feminist Review* (London), 7, Spring 1981

Hurford, Mandy and Diane Watts, "Report on North London Women's Voice group", in *Women's Voice*, 30, June 1976

Iglehart, Alfreda, *Married Women and Work* (Massachusetts and Toronto 1979)

Jones, Lynne (ed.) *Keeping the Peace* (London 1983)

Kapp, Yvonne, *Eleanor Marx*, volume 2 (New York 1976)

Kappel, Sybille and Erika Leuteritz, "Battered Women Need Refuges" (Women's Aid Federation 1975), reprinted in Feminist Anthology Collective

King, Ynestra, "All is connectedness: Scenes from the Women's Pentagon Action, USA", in Jones

Klein, Viola, *Britain's Married Women Workers* (London 1965)

Knight, Patricia, "Women and Abortion in Victorian and Edwardian England", in *History Workshop*, 4, Autumn 1977

Kolko, Gabriel, "Working Wives: their effects on the structure of the working class", in *Science and Society*, 3, 1978

Kuhn, Annette, "Structures of patriarchy and capital in the family", in Kuhn and Wolpe

Kuhn, Annette and Ann-Marie Wolpe (eds), *Feminism and Materialism* (London 1978)

Lasch, Christopher, *Haven in a Heartless World* (New York 1977)

Leacock, Eleanor Burke, *Myths of Male Dominance* (New York and London 1981)

Leacock, Eleanor Burke, Helen Safa et al, *Women's Work* (Massachusetts 1986)

Lenin, VI, *Left-wing Communism: an infantile disorder*, in *Selected Works* (Moscow 1977)

Lewenhak, Sheila, *Women and Trade Unions* (London 1977)

Lewenhak, Sheila, *Women and Work* (London 1980)

Lewis, Jane, *Women in England 1870–1950* (Brighton 1984)

Lewis, Jane (ed.) *Labour and Love* (Oxford 1986)

Liddington, Jill, *The life and times of a respectable rebel* (London 1984)

Liddington, Jill and A Jill Norris, *One Hand Tied Behind Us* (London 1978)

Lovenduski, Joni, *Women and European Politics* (Brighton 1986)

Lovenduski, Joni and Jill Hills, *The politics of the Second Electorate* (London 1981)

Mansbridge, Jane, *Why we lost the ERA* (Chicago 1986)

Martin, Jean and Ceridwen Roberts, *Women and Employment: A lifetime perspective* (Office of Populations, Censuses and Surveys: London 1984)

Marx, Karl, "Wage Labour and Capital", in *Selected Works* (Moscow 1968)

Marx, Karl, preface to *A contribution to the critique of political economy* (London 1971)

Marx, Karl, *Capital*, volume 1 (Harmondsworth 1976)

Marx, Karl and Friedrich Engels, *The German Ideology* (Moscow 1964)

Marx, Karl and Friedrich Engels, *The Communist Manifesto*, in *Selected Works* (Moscow 1968)

McAllister, Pam (ed.), *Reweaving the web of Life: Feminism and non-violence* (Philadelphia 1982)

McDonough, Roisin and Rachel Harrison, "Patriarchy and Relations of Production", in Kuhn and Wolpe

Meepham, GJ, *Problems of Equal Pay* (Institute of Personnel Managers 1969)

Milkman, Ruth, "Women, Work and Economic Crisis: Some lessons of the Great Depression", in *Review of Radical Political Economics* (New York) 8:1, Spring 1976, pp.73–97.

Milkman, Ruth, *Gender at Work* (Chicago 1987)

Millett, Kate, *Sexual Politics* (London 1971)

Milne, Kirsty, "Why women are still paid less", in *New Society*, 3 April 1987

Minge, Wanda, "The Industrial Revolution and the European Family: 'Childhood' as a Market for Family Labor", in Leacock, Safa et al

Mitchell, Juliet, *Psychoanalysis and Feminism* (London 1975)

Mitchell, Juliet and Ann Oakley (eds), *The Rights and Wrongs of Women* (Harmondsworth 1976)

Mitchell, Juliet and Anne de Winter, "The [London] N7 women's liberation workshop", in *Shrew*, 3:9, December 1971

Molyneux, John, "Do working-class men benefit from women's oppression?", in *International Socialism*, 2:25, Autumn 1984

Morgan, Robin (ed.) *Sisterhood is Powerful* (New York 1971)

Mount, Ferdinand, *The Subversive Family* (London 1982)

Nield Chew, Doris, *Ada Nield Chew: The Life and Writings of a Working Woman* (London 1982)

Oakley, Ann, *Housewife* (Harmondsworth 1976)

Osterud, Nancy Grey, "Gender Divisions and the Organization of Work the Leicester Hosiery Industry", in Angela John (ed.) *Unequal Opportunities: Women's Employment in England 1800–1918* (Oxford 1986)

O'Sullivan, Sue, "Passionate Beginnings: Ideological Politics 1969–72", in *Feminist Review*, 11, 1982

Pankhurst, Sylvia, *The Suffragette Movement* (London 1977)

Phillips, Anne, *Hidden Hands* (London 1983)

Phillips, Anne, *Divided Loyalties* (London 1987)

Pinchbeck Ivy, *Women Workers and the Industrial Revolution 1750–1850* (London 1981)

Political Economy of Women Group, *On the political economy of women*, Conference of Socialist Economists (CSE) pamphlet (London 1977)

Ramelson, Marian, *The Petticoat Rebellion* (London 1967)

Reid, Catherine, "Reweaving the web of life", in McAllister

Reiter, Rayna (ed.), *Towards an Anthropology of Women* (New York 1975)

Renvoize, Jean, *Web of Violence* (London 1978)

Reskin, Barbara and Heidi Hartmann (eds) *Women's Work, Men's Work: Sex Segregation on the Job* (Washington 1986)

Rimmer, Lesley and Jennie Popay, "The family at work", in *Employment Gazette*, June 1982

Rix, Sarah E (ed.), *The American Woman 1987–88* (New York 1987)

Rogers Ann, "The forgotten majority: women at work", in *International Socialism*, 2:32, Summer 1986

Rosen, Andrew, *Rise Up, Women* (London 1974)

Ross, Ellen, "Labour and Love: Rediscovering London's Working-Class Mothers, 1870–1918", in Lewis (1986)

Rover, Constance, *Women's Suffrage and Party Politics in Britain* (London 1967)

Rowbotham, Sheila, "The beginnings of women's liberation in Britain", in *The Body Politic* (Stage 1: London 1972)

Rowbotham, Sheila, *Woman's Consciousness, Man's World* (Harmondsworth 1973)

Rowbotham, Sheila, *Women, Resistance and Revolution* (Harmondsworth 1974)

Rowbotham, Sheila, *A new world for women* (London 1977)

Rowbotham, Sheila, "The trouble with 'patriarchy'", in *New Statesman* (London), 28 December 1979

Rowbotham, Sheila, *The past is before us* (London 1989)

Rowbotham, Sheila, Lynne Segal and Hilary Wainwright, *Beyond the Fragments* (London 1979)

Rubery, Jill (ed.) *Women and Recession* (London 1988)

Rubin, Lillian, *Worlds of Pain* (New York 1976)

Rule, JG, *The Labouring Classes in Early Industrial England 1750–1850* (London 1986)

Sargent, Lydia (ed.) *The Unhappy Marriage of Marxism and Feminism* (London 1981)

Seccombe, Wally, "The housewife and her labour under capitalism", in *New Left Review*, 83, 1974

Segal, Lynne, *Is the future female?* (London 1987)

Seyd, Patrick, "Bennism without Benn", in *New Socialist* (London), 27, May 1985

Sennett, Richard, *Families Against the City: Middle Class Homes in Industrial Chicago 1872–1890* (Cambridge, Mass. 1979)

Shorter Edward, *The Making of the Modern Family* (London 1975)

Smelser, Neil, *Social Change in the Industrial Revolution* (London and Chicago 1959)

Smith, Joan, "Women and the Family", part 1, in *International Socialism*, 1:100, July 1977

Smith, Paul, "Domestic labour and Marx's theory of value", in Kuhn and Wolpe

Snell, Mandy, "The Equal Pay and Sex Discrimination Acts: Their impact in the workplace", in *Feminist Review*, 1, 1979, pp.39–43

Social Trends (Central Statistical Office: London)

Soldon, Norbert, *Women in British Trade Unions 1874–1976* (London 1978)

Spender, Dale, *Women of Ideas* (London 1982)

Stanley Holton, Sandra, *Feminism and democracy: Women's Suffrage and reform politics in Britain 1900–1918*, (Cambridge 1986)

Stone, Lawrence, *The Family, Sex and Marriage in England 1500–1800* (London 1977)

Taylor, Barbara, *Eve and the New Jerusalem* (London 1983)

Tilly, Louise and Joan Scott, *Women, Work and Family* (Holt Rinehart Winston: New York and London 1978)

Tilly Louise, "Paths of Proletarianization: Organization of Production, Sexual Division of Labour, and Women's Collective Action", in Leacock, Safa et al

Thompson, Dorothy, "Women, and Nineteenth Century Radical Politics", in Mitchell and Oakley

Trotsky, Leon, *The Revolution Betrayed* (London 1972)

Trotsky, Leon, *Women and the Family* (London 1974)

Ware, Celestine, *Women Power* (New York 1970)

Waterson, Julie, "Equal Jobs and Rights", in *Socialist Worker Review*, 74, March 1985

Weir, Angela and Elizabeth Wilson, "The British Women's Movement", in *New Left Review*, 148, November/December 1984

Whitelegg, Elizabeth (ed.), *The changing experience of women* (Oxford 1982)

Women Against Rape, *Women at WAR* (Bristol 1978)

Further reading

The following articles are based on the same theoretical understanding of women's oppression as Lindsey German's book. Some are more recent and others are more relevant for an Australian audience. They are all available at the *Marxist Left Review* website: https://marxistleftreview.org/.

Sandra Bloodworth, "The poverty of patriarchy theory", *Socialist Review*, 2, Winter 1990.

Tess Lee Ack, "The Marxist tradition and women's liberation", *Socialist Review*, 4, Winter 1991.

Sandra Bloodworth, "Rape, sexual violence and capitalism", *Socialist Review*, 5, Autumn 1992.

Sandra Bloodworth, "Marx and Engels on women's and sexual oppression and their legacy", *Marxist Left Review*, 1, Spring 2010.

Diane Fieldes, "The impact of women's changing role in the workforce", *Marxist Left Review*, 6, Winter 2013.

Louise O'Shea, "Marxism and women's liberation", *Marxist Left Review*, 7, Summer 2014.

Sandra Bloodworth, "The roots of sexual violence", *Marxist Left Review*, 10, Winter 2015.

Katie Wood, "Australian unions and the fight for equal pay for women", *Marxist Left Review*, 10, Winter 2015.

Sandra Bloodworth, "Russia 1917: Gender, class and the Bolsheviks", *Marxist Left Review*, 14, Winter 2017.

Sandra Bloodworth, "The origins of women's oppression—a defence of Engels and a new departure", *Marxist Left Review*, 16, Winter 2018.

Sarah Garnham, "Against reductionism: Marxism and oppression", *Marxist Left Review*, 16, Winter 2018.

April Holcombe, "The freedom to be: Marxism, gender oppression and the struggle for trans liberation", *Marxist Left Review*, 20, Winter 2020.

Sarah Garnham, "The failure of identity politics: A Marxist analysis", *Marxist Left Review*, 22, Winter 2021.

This work was published by Red Flag Books, an Imprint of the revolutionary socialist organisation Socialist Alternative.

Red Flag Books offers hundreds of other titles covering Marxist politics, revolutionary history, and much more.

Browse our store at shop.redflag.org.au

www.ingramcontent.com/pod-product-compliance
Lightning Source LLC
Chambersburg PA
CBHW070109030426
42335CB00016B/2071